D1283208

JUSTICE, LAW, AND ARGUMENT

SYNTHESE LIBRARY

STUDIES IN EPISTEMOLOGY,

LOGIC, METHODOLOGY, AND PHILOSOPHY OF SCIENCE

Managing Editor:

JAAKKO HINTIKKA, *Florida State University*

Editors:

DONALD DAVIDSON, *University of Chicago*

GABRIËL NUCHELMANS, *University of Leyden*

WESLEY C. SALMON, *University of Arizona*

VOLUME 142

CH. PERELMAN

Université Libre de Bruxelles, Centre de Philosophie du Droit

JUSTICE, LAW, AND ARGUMENT

Essays on Moral and Legal Reasoning

with an introduction by

HAROLD J. BERMAN
Ames Professor of Law, Harvard University

D. REIDEL PUBLISHING COMPANY

DORDRECHT : HOLLAND / BOSTON : U.S.A.
LONDON : ENGLAND

Library of Congress Cataloging in Publication Data

Perelman, Chaïm.
    Justice, law, and argument.

    (Synthese library ; v. 142)
    Chapters translated into English by various persons.
    Includes bibliographical references and index.
    1. Justice—Addresses, essays, lectures.   2. Law—
Methodology—Addresses, essays, lectures.   3. Law-Philosophy—
Addresses, essays, lectures.   4. Law and ethics—Addresses, essays,
lectures.   I.   Title.
K239.P47   340'.1   80–16892
ISBN 90–277–1089–9
ISBN 90–277–1090–2 (pbk.)

*Chapter 1 translated into English by John Petrie; Chapter 2–6 and 17 by Susan Rubin;
Chapter 8 by Graham Bird; Chapter 9 by Melvin T. Dalgarno; Chapter 10 by Heather
Relihan; Chapters 11–16 by William Kluback*

Published by D. Reidel Publishing Company,
P.O. Box 17, 3300 AA Dordrecht, Holland

Sold and distributed in the U.S.A. and Canada
by Kluwer Boston Inc., Lincoln Building
160 Old Derby Street, Hingham, MA 02043, U.S.A.

In all other countries, sold and distributed
by Kluwer Academic Publishers Group,
P.O. Box 322, 3300 AH Dordrecht, Holland

D. Reidel Publishing Company is a member of the Kluwer Group

Printed in The Netherlands

TABLE OF CONTENTS

PREFACE

This collection contains studies on justice, juridical reasoning and argumentation which contributed to my ideas on the new rhetoric.

My reflections on justice, from 1944 to the present day, have given rise to various studies. The first of these was published in English as *The Idea of Justice and the Problem of Argument* (Routledge & Kegan Paul, London, 1963). The others, of which several are out of print or have never previously been published, are reunited in the present volume.

As justice is, for me, the prime example of a "confused notion", of a notion which, like many philosophical concepts, cannot be reduced to clarity without being distorted, one cannot treat it without recourse to the methods of reasoning analyzed by the new rhetoric. In actuality, these methods have long been put into practice by jurists. Legal reasoning is fertile ground for the study of argumentation: it is to the new rhetoric what mathematics is to formal logic and to the theory of demonstrative proof.

It is important, then, that philosophers should not limit their methodological studies to mathematics and the natural sciences. They must not neglect law in the search for practical reason.

I hope that these essays lead to be a better understanding of how law can enrich philosophical thought.

CH. P.

INTRODUCTION

Ever since Descartes, Western philosophy has been dominated by the view that what we cannot prove by formal logic, what we cannot know with mathematical certainty, is necessarily arbitrary, irrational, subjective. For more than three decades Chaim Perelman has been fighting the premises upon which this view is based. He has attacked the Cartesian — and contemporary — dichotomies of object and subject, reality and value, reason and passions. He has contended that there is a logic of ends, and not only a logic of means, but that it is a dialectical logic, not a formal logic. It is the logic of rhetoric in the ancient sense: the logic of reasoned discourse, of argumentation, of justification of choices. And it finds its most important manifestation in law. Indeed, it is no accident that law in the West was once studied as a branch of rhetoric.

As Professor Perelman says in the Preface to this book, "Legal reasoning is to rhetoric what mathematics is to formal logic."

The essays contained in this book reveal many ways in which philosophical inquiry can be enriched by the analysis of legal experience. For example, philosophers such as Kant and Bentham, who have laid down broad universal principles of behavior, should be required, Professor Perelman states, to "examine the repercussions of the controversies which would arise from [the] application and interpretation [of those universal principles] in situations [of] conflict." Similarly, moral philosophers who are concerned with more specific norms, such as whether euthanasia is justified, would do well to consider, for example, the legal fiction implied in the frequent practice of jury acquittal of persons charged with euthanasia. Professor Perelman states that, in his view, this legal result is to be preferred to a general rule, although it is "inconceivable in [conventional] morality."

More broadly, law can teach the philosopher ways of reasoning about values — e.g., how to balance values against each other, and how to bring about a synthesis of values. The philosopher will then see better that "reasons in the plural are at least as important as reason in the singular." "Reasons in the plural" have a historical dimension; they vary, depending upon circumstances. "There is a reality here that can entirely modify our perspective on reasoning in general."

Underlying Professor Perelman's plea for an understanding of legal reasoning is his concern that modern philosophy encourages a relativism and a skepticism that ultimately destroys rationality itself. He writes: "If the application of means to ends is the sole object of rational investigation and the ends themselves are the results of irrational choices, which reasoning does not allow us to decide, then our highly qualitative technological civilization will be put in the service of irrationally uncontrollable passions, desires, and aspirations."

Although Professor Perelman takes the position of a philosopher writing about law for philosophers, he also has much to say to lawyers about law as well as about philosophy. In fact, his philosophic position depends upon his theory of law. It is a theory that by no means all, or possibly even most, contemporary lawyers would share. For the fact is that lawyers, too, especially American lawyers, have been strongly influenced by modern skepticism concerning the possibility of reasoning about ends, and they, too, despite the truths implicit in their own discipline, have been infected by the dualistic analysis that sharply separates subject and object, emotion and reason, ends and means.

Not long ago skepticism concerning the integrity of legal argumentation, and even concerning the validity of language all together, had reached such a point in the United States that leading jurists were building schools of legal thought on essentially irrationalist premises. Legal argumentation was thought to be purely manipulative: judges, it was said, decide cases on the basis of their prejudices and then make up reasons — which are not real reasons but mere rationalizations. Any case can be decided any way, it is always possible to find a justification, etc., etc. Today these "realistic" views of law have more or less subsided, but it is not by any means sure that they have been replaced by a belief that legal reasoning is, in Professor Perelman's sense, reasoning about ends and not only about means, or, to put it somewhat differently, that legal reasoning about ends is ever genuinely persuasive.

Professor Perelman has much to say about law itself that will be helpful to lawyers who start from such skeptical premises. He defines justice in terms that most English and American lawyers, at least, whether or not they are skeptics, will find congenial: "the basic rule of justice," he states, "is that essentially similar situations be passed on in a uniform way." In the language of the English common law, like case should be decided alike. The purpose of rational legal argumentation, he then states, is to determine the similarities. The standard of judgment is that of the audience. However, each speaker postulates a "universal audience"; this seems to mean that he appeals to standards held by the actual audience (for example, a particular legal rule as interpreted by the particular tribunal) but seeks to identify those standards with ones which (in the view of the actual audience) all persons similarly situated would share. In other words, Professor Perelman's "universal audience" is not the same audience in all times and places but rather the principle of universality conceived in rhetorical terms. It is "common sense" in the seventeenth-century English meaning of that phrase.

Lawyers may have some difficulties understanding Professor Perelman's discussion of justice, partly because his style is terse and even cryptic, and partly because his analysis presupposes some familiarity with the philosophical literature on the subject. Within his definition of justice as equality of treatment ("to each the same thing"), he lists five alternative criteria of deserts: the same according to merits, according to works, according to needs, according to rank, and according to legal entitlement. The last, which is legal justice, differs from the other four in that the judge, Professor Perelman states, is not free to ask further what is justice. Yet that very question is often posed by the law itself, which may say expressly that the defendant is legally entitled to "justice" ("due process of law," "equal protection of the laws," etc.). The judge *must* then ask whether "justice" means "according to merits," "according to works," "according to needs," etc.

Also Professor Perelman does not in this book offer extensive justifications of his identification of justice with the principle of consistency of treatment of similar situations. He does indicate that this principle is acceptable to a universal audience. Yet there are other principles that are equally acceptable, and some of them conflict with the principle of consistency as well as with each other. This may only bear out the author's point, however, that justice is a "confused notion," that is, it cannot be reduced to clarity without being distorted.

Finally, it will help the reader to keep in mind that much of what Professor Perelman writes about law and justice derives primarily from his study of the legal system and legal thought that prevails in his native Belgium as well as in some other countries of Europe. Thus his attack on "mechanical jurisprudence" and his criticism of the myth that judges only apply pre-existing legislative enactments refer, as he indicates, to the European legal ideology that grew out of the French Revolution. On the other hand, his criticism of legal positivism is applicable both to "Anglo American" and to "Continental" legal thought, and his occasional comparisons of the style of Belgian and French law with that of English and American law are suggestive and deserve to be expanded.

Those readers for whom this small book of essays is their first introduction to the writings of Chaim Perelman on rhetoric and law will naturally want to turn to his many other works to supplement it. Those for whom this book is a supplement to his other writings will be grateful for its additional insights.

National Humanities Center   HAROLD J. BERMAN
North Carolina
January 3, 1980.

ACKNOWLEDGEMENTS

I am grateful to Routledge & Kegan Paul (London) for the permission to reprint Chapter 1; to Graham Hughes and the New York University Press for Chapter 7; to the Brussels Center for the Philosophy of Law and E. Bruylant, for Chapter 8; to the Archiv für Rechts- und Sozialphilosophie and Steiner Verlag (Wiesbaden) for Chapters 9 and 14; to Logique et Analyse (Leuven) for Chapter 10; to Nijhoff (The Hague) for Chapter 11; to Herder (Wien) for Chapter 12; to J. Vrin (Paris) for Chapter 15 and to Prof. H. J. van Eikema Hommes and the Dutch Society for Legal Philosophy for Chapter 16.

CH. P.

CHAPTER ONE

CONCERNING JUSTICE *

I. SETTING OF THE PROBLEM

A logical analysis of the idea of justice would seem to be a very hazardous business. Indeed, among all evocative ideas, that of justice appears to be one of the most eminent and the most hopelessly confused.

Justice is considered by many people as the principal virtue, the source of all the others.

'Thought and terminology,' says Professor Dupréel,[1] 'have always incited men to confuse with the value of justice that of morality as a whole. Ethical and religious literature recognise in the just man the man who is utterly and entirely honourable and given to well-doing. Justice is the common name of all forms of merit, and the classics might be said to express their fundamental idea in saying that moral science has no other object than to teach that which it is just to do and that which it is just to forbear. Moral science might also be said to assert that reason ought to teach us the distinction between the just and the unjust, a distinction in which the whole science of good and evil consists. Thus justice, which on the one hand is one virtue among the others, on the other embraces the whole of morality.'

It is when taken in this latter sense that justice outweighs all other values. *Pereat mundus, fiat justitia.*

For Proudhon 'justice, under various names, governs the world — nature and humanity, science and conscience, logic and morals, political economy, politics, history, literature and art. Justice is that which is most primitive in the human soul, most fundamental in society, most sacred among ideas, and what the masses demand today with most ardour. It is the essence of religions and at the same time the form of reason, the secret object of faith, and the beginning, middle and end of knowledge. What can be imagined more universal, more strong, more complete than Justice?'[2]

It is always useful and important to be able to qualify as just the social conceptions which one advocates. Every revolution, every war, every overthrow has always been effected in the name of Justice. And the extraordinary thing is that it should be just as much the partisans of a new order as the defenders of the old who invoke with their prayers the reign of Justice. And

1

when a neutral voice proclaims the necessity of a just peace, all the belligerents agree, and affirm that this just peace will come about only when the enemy has been annihilated.

Let us note that there need be no bad faith in these contradictory affirmations. Each of the antagonists can be sincere and believe that his cause alone is just. And no one is wrong, for each is speaking of a different justice.

'An ethical idea,' writes Professor Dupréel,[3] 'corresponds neither to a thing which has only to be seen in order for one's assertion to be verified, nor to a demonstration to which one cannot but yield, but rather to a *convention* which is designed to define the idea in a certain manner. Accordingly, when an opponent has taken the offensive and, in doing so, has ranged the appearance of Justice on his side, then the other party will tend to give such a definition of justice as is admittedly agreeable to his cause.'

Each will defend a conception of justice that puts him in the right and his opponent in the wrong.

One has only to remind oneself that for thousands of years every antagonist, in public and private conflicts, in wars, in revolutions, in lawsuits, in clashes of interest, has always declared, and has done his best to prove, that justice is on his side; that justice is invoked every time recourse is had to an arbiter — and at once one realises the unbelievable multiplicity of meanings attached to the idea, and the extraordinary confusion provoked by its use.

It is vain to try to enumerate all the possible meanings of the idea of justice. Let us, however, give a few examples which constitute the most current conceptions of justice, and whose irreconcilable character is at once obvious:

1.   To each the same thing.
2.   To each according to his merits.
3.   To each according to his works.
4.   To each according to his needs.
5.   To each according to his rank.
6.   To each according to his legal entitlement.

Let us take a closer and more precise look at each of these conceptions.

1. To each the same thing

According to this conception, all the people taken into account must be treated in the same way, without regard to any of their distinguishing particularities. Young or old, well or sick, rich or poor, virtuous or criminal, aristocrat or boor, white or black, guilty or innocent – it is just that all should be treated in the same way, without any discrimination or differentiation. In popular imagery the perfectly just being is death, which touches every man on the shoulder regardless of any of his privileges.

2. *To each according to his merits*

Here we have a conception of justice that no longer demands universal equality, but treatment proportional to an intrinsic quality – the merit of the human person. How are we to define this merit? What common measure are we to find between the merits or demerits of different beings? Is there, generally speaking, such a common measure? What are the criteria we must have regard to in establishing this merit? Should we have regard to the result of the action, to the intention behind it, to the sacrifice made, and, if so, how far? Ordinarily we do not answer all these questions: indeed, we do not even put them to ourselves. If we are driven into a corner we tell ourselves that it is after death that all beings will be treated in accordance with their merits; that their 'weight' of merit and demerit will be established by means of a balance; and that the result of this 'weighing' will indicate automatically, so to speak, the fate in store for them. Life beyond the grave, heaven and hell, constitute the just recompense or the just punishment for life one earth. The intrinsic moral worth of the individual will be the sole criterion of the judge, who will be blind to all other considerations.

3. *To each according to his works*

This conception of justice also does not call for equal treatment, but for proportional treatment. Only the criterion is no longer ethical, for regard is no longer had either to intention or to sacrifice made, but solely to the result of action.

This criterion, in that it ceases to make demands relative to the agent, we find less satisfying from the ethical point of view. But it becomes infinitely easier to apply in practice, and, instead of constituting an ideal practically impossible of realisation, this formula of justice makes it possible to take account, for the most part, only of elements which can be reckoned up, weighed and measured. It is this conception – of which incidentally several variants are possible – that underlies the payment of workers' wages, whether at time-rates or at piece-rates, and which also underlies examinations and competitions in which, regardless of the effort exerted, account is taken only of the result — the candidates' answers and the work he has shown up.

4. To each according to his needs

This formula of justice, instead of having regard to the merits of the man or of his output, seeks above all to lessen the sufferings which result from the impossibility in which he finds himself of satisfying his essential needs. It is in that respect that this formula of justice comes nearest to our conception of charity.

It goes without saying that this formula, if it is to be socially applicable, must be based on formal criteria of the needs of each person, the divergence between these criteria giving rise to the differing variants of the formula. Thus regard will be had to a basic minimum of which each man must be assured, to his family responsibilities, to the more or less precarious state of his health, to the care and attention required in his youth or his old age, etc., etc. It is this formula of justice which, making itself felt more and more in contemporary social legislation, has reversed the liberal economy in which labour, treated as though it were an article of sale, was subject to the fluctuations resulting from the law of supply and demand. Protection of labour and the worker, all the laws on the minimum wage, the limitation of hours of work, insurance against unemployment, sickness and old age, family allowances and so on — all these spring from the desire to assure to each human being the satisfaction of his most essential needs.

5. To each according to his rank

Here we have an aristocratic formula of justice. It consists in treating human beings, not in accordance with criteria intrinsic to the individual, but according as they belong to such or such a determined category of beings. *Quod licet Jovi non licet bovi,* says an old Latin saw. The same rules of justice do not apply to beings springing from categories which are too widely separated. Thus it is that the formula 'to each according to his rank' differs from the other formulas in that, instead of being universalist, it divides men into various categories which will be treated differently.

In antiquity different treatment was reserved for the native and the foreigner, for the free man and the slave. At the beginning of the Middle Ages the Frankish masters were treated differently from the native Gallo-Romans.

Later, distinction was made between the nobles, the bourgeoisie, the clergy and the serfs bound to the soil.

At the present day white and black are treated differently in the colonies. In the army there are different rules for officers, non-commissioned officers and private soldiers. There are well-known distinctions based on criteria of race, religion, wealth, etc., etc. The characteristic which acts as a criterion is of a social nature and, for the most part, hereditary, and so independent of the will of the individual.

If we regard this formula of justice as aristocratic it is because it is always maintained and bitterly defended by its beneficiaries, who demand or enforce favourable treatment for the categories of beings whom they put forward as being superior. And this claim is normally sustained by force, whether by force of arms, or by the fact of being a majority as against a defenceless minority.

6. *To each according to his legal entitlement*

This formula is the paraphrase of the celebrated *cuique suum* of the Romans. If to be just means to attribute to each what is his own, then, if a vicious circle is to be avoided, it is necessary to be able to determine what each man's own is. If we allow a juridical meaning to the phrase 'that which is each man's own' we arrive at the conclusion that to be just means to accord to each person what the law entitles him to.

This conception enables us to say that a judge is just, that is, impartial and uncorrupt, when he applies the same laws to the same situations (*in paribus causis paria jura*). To be just is to apply the laws of the country. This conception of justice, unlike all the previous ones, does not set itself up as a judge of positive law, but limits itself to applying it.

This formula in practice naturally admits of as many variants as there are different codes of law. Each system of law assumes a justice relative to that law. What may be just under one code may not be so under another. In effect, to be just is to apply the rules of a given juridical system, and to be unjust is to misapply them.

Professor Dupréel contrasts this conception with all the others.[4] He characterises it as 'static justice', because it is based on the maintenance of the established order; and he contrasts with it all the others which are considered as forms of 'dynamic justice' because they are capable of modifying that order and the rules which define it. 'Dynamic justice is a factor of change, and appears as an instrument of the reforming or, to take its self-given name, the *progressivist* spirit. Static justice, essentially conservative, is a factor of rigidity.'⁵

This summary analysis of the most prevalent conceptions of the idea of justice has demonstrated to us the existence of at least six formulas of justice, most of them admitting numerous variants, and all of them normally irreconcilable. True, by recourse to more or less forced interpretations and to more or less arbitrary assertions one can attempt to bring one of these different formulas into line with another. Nevertheless, they present aspects of justice which are quite distinct and are for the most part mutually opposed.

Given this state of affairs, there are three possible standpoints.

The first would consist in declaring that these differing conceptions of justice have absolutely nothing in common; that characterising them in one and the same manner is improper and creates hopeless confusion; and that the only possible analysis would consist in distinguishing the different meanings, it being accepted that these meanings are not united by any conceptual link.

If this is the case we shall, if all misunderstanding is to be avoided, be driven to characterise in different fashion each one of these six conceptions. Either we shall deny the name of justice to any of them or we shall regard one of them as alone capable of being characterised as just.

This latter mode of action would lead indirectly to the second standpoint. This consists in choosing from among the various formulas of justice only one, and in trying to convince us that that is the only admissible, the only true, the only really and thoroughly just formula.

Now it is precisely this way of reasoning that we would wish to avoid at any cost; it is the one against which we have warned the reader. Whatever our reasons for choosing one formula, antagonists would advance equally valid reasons for choosing another. The debate, far from bringing about agreement, would serve only to provoke a conflict, which would be the more violent in so far as each party was more bitter in defence of his own conception. And anyway the analysis of the idea of justice would be little forwarded thereby.

That is why we give our preference to the third standpoint. This would shoulder the extremely delicate task of seeking out what there is in common between the various conceptions of justice that could be formulated. Or at least — to avoid the impossible requirement of seeking out the element which is common to an indefinite multitude of different conceptions — there would be an attempt to find what there is in common between the conceptions of justice most currently accepted, those, namely, that we have distinguished in the preceding pages.

II. FORMAL JUSTICE

For a logical analysis of the idea of justice to constitute an irrefutable step forward in the clarification of this confused notion, that analysis must succeed in giving a precise description of what there is in common between the various formulas of justice and in showing the points in which they differ. This preliminary discrimination will enable us to consider it a formula of justice on which unanimous agreement will be possible − a formula which will retain all that there is in common between the contrasting conceptions of justice.

This does not mean in the least that the disagreement prevailing between the champions of the various conceptions of justice will be reduced to nothing. The logician is not a conjurer, and it is not his job to spirit away that which exists. On the contrary, it is his duty to fix the point at which disagreement arises, bring it out into the light of day and demonstrate the reasons why, setting out from a certain common idea of justice, men nevertheless arrive at formulas that are not merely different but in fact irreconcilable.

To everyone the idea of justice inevitably suggests the notion of a certain equality. From Plato and Aristotle, through St. Thomas Aquinas, down to the jurists, moralists and philosophers of our own day runs a thread of universal agreement on this point. The notion of justice consists in a certain application of the notion of equality. The whole problem is to define this application in such fashion that, while constituting the element common to the various conceptions of justice, it leaves scope for their divergencies. This is possible only if the definition of the idea of justice contains an indeterminate element, a variable, whose various specific applications will produce the most contrasting formulas of justice.

In his treatise on 'The Three Kinds of Justice'[6] de Tourtoulon endeavours to establish a link between the differing conceptions of justice by having recourse to the notion of limit.

For him, perfect justice would consist in the complete equality of all mankind. The ideal of justice would correspond to the first of our six formulas. But this perfect equality, as everyone at once realises, cannot be achieved in practice. It can, therefore, only constitute an ideal towards which we may strive, a mathematical limit which we can seek to approach only within the bounds of the possible. On this theory, all other conceptions of justice are no more than imperfect attempts to bring about this

equality. Men try at least to bring about a partial equality, which is the easier
to attain as it is further removed from the stated ideal of complete equality.

'Logically,' says de Tourtoulon,[7] 'the various conceptions of justice
equality, far from being contradictory, are essentially the same. They differ
only in their potentialities. Perfect equality being a limit-idea, its potentiality
for being realised in practice is nil. The potentialities increase in proportion as
the other egalitarian conceptions depart from the point which is set at in-
finity.'

'One might,' he says,[8] 'call justice charity, or equality charity, when it
tries to come to the help of those who are naturally unfortunate and to
secure for them the largest possible share of the satisfaction others can enjoy.

'Distributive justice has for object another kind of equality which takes
account of individual capacities and efforts in conferring benefits. Its motto is
— to each according to his merits. Removed as it is from equality as a
mathematical limit, it comes nearer to being something that could be realised
in practice.

'Commutative justice, however, is not concerned with individual life taken
as a whole. It seeks to establish equality in each and every juridical act, with
a view to ensuring that a contract shall not ruin one party while enriching the
other. With it we may associate compensatory justice, by means of which an
equality prejudiced by the fault of others is redressed . . . .

'The fact that the equality contained in the idea of justice appears under
so many and so different guises is often employed as a weapon in order to
reject all these conceptions *en bloc* as having no logical validity. But this is far
too superficial an argument. Between these differing notions of equality there
is no contradiction whatever. On the contrary, they are so many points that,
taken on an abscissa whose limit is "perfect equality", come nearer and
nearer to the ordinate constituted by the "potentiality of being realised".'

This conception undeniably represents a worthy attempt at the understanding of the idea of justice. Two objections may be advanced against it.

The first objection is this. The conception, faced with the various formulas
of justice, makes the arbitrary choice of a single one; and this seems, with
good reason, quite unacceptable to very many, if not most, consciences. Are
all men to be treated in the same fashion without regard to their merits, their
deeds, their origin, their needs, their talents or their vices? A great many
moralists would be entitled to rise up against this pseudo-justice, of which the
most that could be said is that from no point of view does it make itself felt
as necessary.

The second objection is decisive from the point of view of logic. It is that the link which de Tourtoulon would like to establish between the different conceptions of justice is quite illusory. In effect, if it were the function of the different formulas of justice to promote partial equalities, then either they ought to have flowed one from another by syllogism, like a part contained in the whole; or else they should have been capable of complementing one another, like two different parts of one and the same whole. Now, whatever de Tourtoulon may say, the different formulas of justice frequently contradict one another. It is usually impossible to reconcile the formulas 'to each according to his merits' and 'to each according to his needs', not to mention the other formulas which ought, taken as a whole, to form a coherent system. In any case, the best proof of the impossibility of resuming all the formulas of justice in the one which advocates the perfect equality of all mankind is this: the champions of the other conceptions of justice rebel against it, regarding it not only as arbitrary but also as utterly opposed to our innate sense of justice.

In contrast to de Tourtoulon's idea (which regards the differing conceptions of justice as resulting from a different interpretation of the expression 'the same thing' in the formula 'to each the same thing') one might try to reduce the divergencies to a differing interpretation of the notion of 'each' in the same formula.

Aristotle observed long since that it was necessary that there should exist a certain likeness between the beings to whom justice is administered. Historically, indeed, it can be stated plausibly enough that justice began by being administered to the members of one and the same family, to be extended later to the members of the tribe, the inhabitants of the city, then of a territory, with, as the final outcome, the notion of a justice for all mankind.

In an interesting article[9] Tisset says, 'There must exist between individuals something in common whereby a partial identity may be established, if there is to be any attempt to realise justice as between them. Where there is no common measure, and therefore no identity, the question of realising justice does not even arise. And it may be noted that to this day the principle, in the human intellect, remains unchanged. There can, for instance, be no question of justice in the relations between men and plants. If today the idea of justice has been more widely extended and applies to all mankind, the reason is that man has come to recognise all his fellows as his fellows: the idea of humanity has little by little emerged . . .'

A priori, the field in which justice can and should be applied is not laid down. It is therefore susceptible of variation. Every time we speak of 'each' in a formula of justice we may be thinking of a different group of beings. This variation in the field of application of the idea of 'each' to variable groups will produce variants not only of the formula 'to each the same thing' but also of all the other formulas. But this is not the way in which it will be possible to solve the problem we have set ourselves. Indeed, far from demonstrating the existence of an element common to the different formulas of justice, the foregoing reflections prove, on the contrary, that each one of the formulas can in turn be interpreted in different ways and give rise to a very large number of variants.

Let us, then, after these unfruitful attempts, take up our problem again from the very beginning. The question is to find a formula of justice which is common to the different conceptions we have analysed. This formula must contain an indeterminate element – what in mathematics is called a variable – the determination of which will give now one, now another, conception of justice. The common idea will constitute a definition of *formal* or *abstract* justice. Each particular or *concrete* formula of justice will constitute one of the innumerable values of formal justice.

Is it possible to define formal justice? Is there a conceptual element common to all the formulas of justice? Apparently, yes. In effect, we all agree on the fact that to be just is to treat in equal fashion. Unfortunately, difficulties and controversies arise as soon as precision is called for. Must everyone be treated in the same way, or must we draw distinctions? And if distinctions must be drawn, which ones must we take into account in administering justice? Each man puts forward a different answer to these questions. Each man advocates a different system. No system is capable of securing the adherence of all. Some say that regard must be had to the individual's merits. Others that the individual's needs must be taken into consideration. Yet others say it is impossible to disregard origin, rank, etc.

But despite all their differences, they all have something in common in their attitude. He who requires merit to be taken into account wants the same treatment for persons having equal merits. A second wants equal treatment to be provided for persons having the same needs. A third will demand just, that is, equal, treatment for persons of the same social rank and so on. Whatever, then, their disagreement on other points, they are all agreed that to be just is to give the same treatment to those who are equal from some particular point of view, who possess one characteristic, the same, *and the only one to which regard must be had in the administration of justice*. Let us qualify this characteristic as *essential*. If the possession of any characteristic whatever always makes it possible to group people in a class or category defined by the fact that its members possess the characteristic in question, people having an essential characteristic in common will form part of one and the same category, the same essential category.

We can, then, define formal or abstract justice as *a principle of action in accordance with which beings of one and the same essential category must be treated in the same way*.

Be it noted at once that the definition we have just offered is of a purely formal idea, leaving untouched and entire all the differences that arise in respect of concrete justice. Our definition tells us neither when two beings participate in an essential category nor how they ought to be treated. We know that beings must be treated not in such or such a manner, but equally, so that it is impossible to say that one has been placed at a disadvantage by reference to another. We know, too, that equal treatment must be provided only for beings forming part of the same essential category.

The six formulas of concrete justice, among which we have been seeking as it were a common denominator, differ in as much as each one of them regards a different characteristic as the only one to be taken account of in administering justice. In other words, they determine membership of the same essential category in different ways. Equally, however, they indicate, with more or less precision, how the members of the same essential category ought to be treated.

Our definition of justice is formal for the reason that it does not lay down the categories that are essential for the administration of justice. It makes it possible for the differences to come into play at the point of transition from a common formula of formal justice to differing formulas of concrete justice. Disagreement arises as soon as it comes to settling the criteria essential for the administration of justice.

Let us take up again one by one our different formulas of concrete justice and show how they are all differing resolutions of the same conception of formal justice.

1. To each the same thing

The conception of justice advanced by this formula is the only purely egalitarian one, in contrast to all the others, which call for a certain degree of proportionality. In effect, all the beings to whom it is desired to administer justice form part of one single and unique essential category. Whether we are concerned with all mankind or merely with a few kinsmen taking part in the sharing of an inheritance, all those brought into consideration when we speak of 'each' have no other distinguishing characteristic. The view is taken that no characteristics other than those that have served to determine the totality of persons to whom the formula 'to each the same thing' must be applied can be taken into account; that the differences between these persons are not, from this point of view, essential.

This leads us, in considering the qualities that differentiate one person from another, to distinguish those qualities that are essential from the secondary qualities which are irrelevant for the administration of justice. Admittedly, the debate on distinguishing essential from secondary qualities could not be settled to everyone's satisfaction. Its solution would bring with it the solution of all other problems concerning values.

The formula 'to each the same thing' may establish an egalitarian conception of justice. It does not necessarily coincide with an egalitarian humanitarianism. Indeed, to make that true, it would be necessary that the class of beings to whom it was desired to apply the formula should consist of all mankind. It is, however, possible for this application to be limited to a much smaller category. Sparta applied this egalitarian formula to none but the 'homoioi', the aristocrats, the superior class of the population. It would never have occurred to the 'homoioi' of Sparta to try to apply this conception of justice to the other strata of the population, with which they felt they had nothing in common.

The same phenomenon is to be found in an analogous institution, notwithstanding that it arose in quite different circumstances of time and space — that of the peers of France and of England. The uppermost stratum of the aristocracy, recognising nothing higher than itself, expects the same treatment for all its members, as being equal one with another and superior to everyone else.

We see, then, that the egalitarian formula of justice, so far from manifesting an attachment to a humanitarian ideal, may constitute nothing better than a means of strengthening the links of solidarity within a class regarding itself as incomparably superior to the other inhabitants of the country.

In so far as we can arbitrarily determine the category of beings to whom egalitarian justice is applicable, we are enabled to show the points in which this formula, rather than the others, appears to give real effect to the ideal of perfect justice.

Indeed, on the basis of the formula we can succeed in framing a second definition of formal justice. All that is necessary is to specify that by 'each one' is meant the members of the same essential category. Thus we get the formula 'to each member of the same essential category, the same thing', which is equivalent in every point to the definition of formal justice we offered earlier. It was, perhaps, this possibility that was unconsciously glimpsed by de Tourtoulon when he thought to make of the egalitarian formula the unattainable ideal of perfect justice.

2. *To each according to his merits*

This formula of justice requires beings to be treated in proportion with their merits. That is, beings forming part of the same category so far as concerns their merit — and the degrees of merit will serve as criteria for settling the essential categories — are to be treated in the same way.

Let us observe that the application of justice in proportion with the degree of intensity of a quality susceptible of variation, such as merit, raises problems of logic which are elucidated in a striking work by Messrs. Hempel and Oppenheim.[10]

To form part of the same essential category is not merely a matter of possessing one identical given characteristic. It must be possessed in the same *degree*. If two people are to be treated in the same way it is not enough that each should have merit. They must further have that merit to the same degree.

We must, then, have available for the application of this formula a criterion which will enable us either to measure the degree of merit — if we wish the rewards to be numerically comparable — or else to range beings according to the size of their merit, if we want higher merit to receive a higher reward. Naturally, the reward must be capable of varying to the same extent as the merit, if, that is, strict proportionality is desired.

If, in the administration of justice, we are not content with giving rewards but also wish to be able to punish, the idea of merit must be widened so as to take in demerit also.

In order that two people should have the same conception of concrete justice, it is not enough that they should both wish to apply the formula 'to each according to his merits'. They must also accord the same degree of merit to the same acts, and their system of rewards or penalties must be equivalent.

For two people to judge in the same way when applying the formula 'to each according to his merits', they must not only have the desire to apply the same formula of concrete justice. They must further have the same statement of the facts submitted to their consideration.

A judgment could be characterised as unjust —

1.   Because it applied a formula of concrete justice which is not accepted.
2.   Because its conception of the same formula of justice was a different one.
3.   Because it was founded on an inadequate statement of the facts.
4.   Because it infringed the specifications of formal justice requiring the same treatment for beings forming part of one and the same essential category.

Let us at once observe that the two first reasons are very often based on an equivocation. In effect, they are valid only in so far as the judge is bound to observe certain rules of justice, which is what happens in law, but never in ethics. In principle, a person cannot be considered unjust simply because he applies a different formula of concrete justice. For example, a man cannot be required to make an equal distribution when, according to him, the distribution ought to be made in proportion with the needs of each of the beneficaries. Since injustice consists in violating the rules of concrete justice in accordance with which one is supposed to be judging, an act cannot be regarded as unjust if the formula of justice employed to criticise the judgment is not that of the judge.

If the judge violates the rules of concrete justice he has himself accepted, then he is unjust. He is so involuntarily if his judgment proceeds from an inadequate presentation of the facts. He is so voluntarily only when he infringes the specifications of formal justice.

3. To each according to his works

The formula of concrete justice 'to each according to his works' is arrived at by considering as forming part of the same essential category those whose production or knowledge have equal value in the eyes of the judge. If, from a certain standpoint, certain works or certain pieces of knowledge are regarded as equivalent, the same treatment must be accorded to those who have performed the work or whose knowledge is under examination.

This formula of justice is usually employed when it comes to remunerating workmen or marking candidates in an examination or competition.

Society has invented a tool for the common measure of labour and its products — namely, money. The ideas of 'just wage' and 'just price' are merely applications of the formula 'to each according to his works'. But it is very difficult to determine the just wage and the just price, seeing how disturbing are the effects of the law of supply and demand.

If it is desired to fix wages proportionally to the work carried out, account can be taken of the duration of the work, its output and its quality, this last usually varying with the length of the period of apprenticeship. But acceptable results can be obtained by proceeding in this way only so long as the work in question is such that its performance does not call for special capacity. For, as soon as there is need for a certain degree of talent, not to mention genius, to bring a task to completion, the common measure breaks down. That is why in such a case we usually prefer to judge the task on its own merits, with the help of its intrinsic qualities — to take stock of the result of the work rather than use as a basis the time necessary to carry out the task in question. The same applies to examinations and to competitions, where, instead of trying to measure the industry of the candidate, one is content to test his knowledge in the light of his answers or the work which he submits.

In all such cases we give up the attempt to establish a common measure for all tasks and remain content with comparing those for which a like criterion is accepted — tasks of the same kind. We will not attempt to compare pictures with works of literature, or symphonies with works of architecture. It may be true that at first sight the price of these works may seem to offer such a common measure, but that can be the case only when we are assured that this price is the just price, that is to say that it corresponds to their value. Now, if the price constitutes the sole element of comparison between works it is impossible to see how to determine their value in order to be able to know whether the price is just or not.

On the other hand, when it comes to comparing not works but knowledge, as in the case of an examination, recourse to money as a standard of measurement is not merely insufficient but quite impossible. The examiner can then judge the candidates only by reference to a purely internal criterion, the requirements which he himself formulates in the matter. The examination will make it possible to establish a relation between these requirements and the candidate's answers.

The examination postulates a kind of convention between the parties. In order to be able to submit to it, the candidate must be in a position to know the requirements of the judge. That is why the judge is accused of injustice every time he fails to observe the rules of the convention and sets a question 'which is not in the syllabus'.

In order to be able to compare candidates judged by different examiners on the basis of different syllabuses, we must be able to establish a relation between those syllabuses and also to assume that the judges evaluate the candidates' failings in the same way. As these comparisons are normally made only on practical and purely formal grounds – equivalence of diplomas, for example – the rival syllabuses ordinarily have reference to knowledge of the same kind, while, in the absence of special reasons, the differences between the examiners are disregarded.

Whereas the formula 'to each according to his merits' has its claims to universality in that it asserts its ability to constitute a common measure applicable to all men, the application of the formula 'to each according to his works' usually makes claims that are more modest and more immediately useful. When it comes to comparing work or knowledge, this latter formula of justice, which is one of the most common in social life, is limited, in the absence of a universal criterion and for purely practical reasons, to the comparison of work and of knowledge of the same kind.

4. To each according to his needs

The application of this formula calls for like treatment of those who form part of the same essential category from the point of view of their needs.

In social life it is only quite exceptionally that the application of this formula will be preceded by a psychological study of the needs of the men under consideration. In effect, we do not wish to take account of the individual's every whim, but only of his most essential needs, those alone that are to be retained in putting the formula into practical effect. The formula ought rather to be enunciated as 'to each according to his essential needs'. This limitation will at once give rise to argument about what is to be understood by 'essential needs', the differing conceptions producing variants of this formula of justice.

Often enough indeed, for the sake of facilitating the application of this formula, there will be a tendency to disregard needs that are considered important but whose existence is difficult either to discover or to check. Usually the attempt will be to determine these needs with the help of purely formal criteria, taking as a basis the requirements of the human organism in general. Only in so far as the application of this formula is restricted to a limited number of persons can the particular needs of each one be brought progressively into account. One of the most delicate problems of statistics in social affairs is to settle the details the inquiry is to concern itself with, given the number of persons to whom it extends. In its application to large numbers, such an inquiry will for preference take account only of numerically measurable elements, such as, for example, the number and ages of the persons in a family, the amount of money available to them, the number of calories in their diet, the cubic footage of air in their dwelling, the number of hours allotted to work, rest, leisure, etc.

Only rarely do we try to apply the formula 'to each according to his needs' to more refined and more individual needs. Indeed − and this is the difference between charity and this formula of justice which comes closest to charity − justice can be applied only to beings considered as elements of a whole, of the essential category. Whereas charity has regard to beings as individuals and takes account of the characteristics proper to them, justice, on the other hand, tends to discount the elements that are not common to a number of beings − their individual peculiarities, in fact. He who seeks out of charity to satisfy the desire of his neighbour will go to more trouble to take into account the individual and psychological factor than will the man moved by his conception of justice.

The man who desires to apply the formula 'to each according to his needs' will have not only to establish a distinction between essential needs and other needs but also to range the essential needs in an order of importance. Thus it will be known which needs call for priority in satisfaction, and the price of that satisfaction will be determined. This operation will lead on to the definition of the idea of the basic minimum.

Everyone knows what bitter controversies have been roused by this notion and all the ideas associated with it. Almost all the differences arising in this connection result from a different conception of the essential needs of man, that is to say, of the needs that ought to be taken into account by a social justice based on the principle 'to each according to his needs' − a justice that works towards settling the obligations of society towards each of its members.

5. To each according to his rank

The application of this formula assumes that the beings in respect of whom one would wish to be just are divided into classes, generally, though not necessarily, ranged in a hierarchical order. This formula regards it as just to adopt a different attitude towards the members of the various classes, provided that the same measurement is given to those who form part of the same class, that is to say, of the same essential category.

This division into classes, in the broad sense, can be effected in various ways. It can be based on the colour of the skin, on language, on religion or on the fact of belonging to a social class, to a caste or to an ethnic group. The subdivision of human beings can also be effected in accordance with their functions, their responsibilities and so on.

It is possible for the classes so distinguished not to be ranged in order. To treat the members of one class in a different way from those of another might not be favourable in all respects to a given category. Most often, however, the various classes are ranged in order. The upper classes, the privileged classes, enjoy more rights than the others. But ordered societies, according as they are in full flower or decadent, will impose greater burdens of duty on their élites or else will establish no correspondence between the rights accorded and the duties or responsibilities. The saying *noblesse oblige* is the expression of an aristocracy conscious of its specific duties and realising that it is only by paying that price that it will succeed in justifying its privileged situation.

Generally speaking, a régime is workable only if each member of its upper class is made to face his responsibilities, and if the rights accorded to him flow from the burdens laid on him. Where specific rights do not coincide with special responsibilities, the régime, thanks to the generalising of the factor of the arbitrary, will soon degenerate into a system of calculated favouritism — an 'old boy network'.

These reflections are applicable not only to régimes in which superior status goes by birth but also to quite different régimes, such as the democratic. In effect, in every régime there exists a superior class, the class which has at its disposal power and force in the state. A régime will be workable in the long run only if the demands laid on this class are quite specific and if the severity exercised in calling each individual's management to account is proportional to the responsibilities he has undertaken.

6. *To each according to his legal entitlement*

This formula of justice is to be distinguished from all the others in that the judge, the person made responsible for applying it, is not now free to choose the conception of justice he prefers: he is bound to observe the established rules. Classification, division into essential categories — these are laid down for him, and he must, as a matter of obligation, take account of them. Here we have the fundamental distinction between the ethical and the juridical conceptions of justice.

In ethics, there is freedom to choose the formula of justice that one intends to apply and the interpretation that one desires to give it. In law, the formula of justice is laid down, and its interpretation is made subject to the control of the highest court of the state. In ethics, the rule adopted is the result of the free adherence of the conscience. In law, it is necessary to consult the established order. In ethics, he who judges has first to settle the categories in accordance with which he will judge, then to see which are the categories applicable to the facts. In law, the sole problem to be entertained is that of knowing how the facts under consideration fit into the established juridical system, and how they are to be characterised. In modern law the two authorities — the one which settles the categories and the one which applies them — are rigorously kept apart. In ethics, they are united in the same conscience.

In law, how far has the judge, in the exercise of his functions, the means of bringing to bear his own particular conception of justice? How far is the law influenced by ethical conceptions?

The answer to the first question will be different according as by judge is meant any individual official whatever having the responsibility of administering justice, or jurisprudence as a whole. This in the case of a judge who rests content with following the beaten tracks of jurisprudence and has no desire for innovation, his role is not entirely passive. Indeed, since every vision of reality is to some extent subjective — the more so in that it is a question of a reconstruction rather than of a direct vision — the upright judge will, even involuntarily, be led, in his evaluation of the facts, to make the law and his own inner feeling for justice coincide. By making his stand on certain evidence or by denying its importance, by having regard to certain facts or by so interpreting them as to deprive them of all meaning, the judge is able to produce a different picture of reality and to deduce from it a different application of the rules of justice.

As for jurisprudence, in so far as it interprets the laws, it can even go farther. On it depends the definition of all the confused ideas, all the equivocal expressions, of the law. It will be for it an easy matter to define those ideas and to interpret those expressions in such fashion that the judge's feeling of justice and the exigencies of the law shall not clash too violently. In some case, when laws were in question whose meaning was difficult to distort, jurisprudence has even been content quite simply to forget their existence, and by dint of not administering them has caused them to fall into desuetude. In Roman law the *praetor* could allow himself to take advantage of fictions so as to modify the application of the categories established by the law, whereas now the determination of those categories is the work of the legislator. He will make it his business to give legal force to the conception of justice of those who hold power in the state.

A priori, nothing can be said of the ethical character of the law, of the way in which the categories established by the legislator coincide with those of the mass of the population. Everything depends on the relation between that mass and those who hold power. According as these latter are or are not the true reflection of the majority of the nation, the juridical categories laid down will coincide more or less with popular feeling. In any democratic régime the law, albeit with some delay, follows the evolution undergone by the conception of justice in the minds of the majority of the citizens. During the period for which there is failure to correspond, jurisprudence makes it its business, as best it may, to reduce to a minimum the disadvantages due to the inevitable slowness of the legislative power.

Can justice conflict with law? Is there an unjust law? The question can be put in this way only if no account is taken of the distinction we have established between formal justice and concrete justice. Indeed, an attempt to judge law in the name of justice is possible only by means of a confusion. Law will be judged by means, not of formal justice, but of concrete justice, that is of a particular conception of justice which assumes a settled scale of values. In effect, we shall not condemn or reform in the name of justice, but in the name of a vision of the universe — sublime perhaps, but in any case regarded arbitrarily as the only just one. Whereas one conception of the world is condemned by means of another, we must not say that law is condemned in the name of justice, unless, that is, we want to create confusions advantageous only to the sophists. Indeed, positive law can never enter into conflict with formal justice, seeing that all it does is to establish the categories of which formal justice speaks, and without whose establishment the administration of justice is quite impossible.

We have now reviewed the principal conceptions of concrete justice and have seen how all of them can be regarded as determinations of formal justice. We can, then, affirm the existence of an element common to the more usual formulas of justice — an element making it possible to define the formal part of any conception of justice.

The application of formal justice calls for the prior establishment of the categories regarded as essential. Now, we cannot say which are the essential characteristics — those, that is, which must be taken into account for the application of justice — without positing a certain scale of values, a determination of what is important and what is not, of what is essential and what is secondary. It is our view of the world, the way we distinguish what has value from what has none, that will bring us to a given conception of concrete justice.

Any moral, social or political evolution leading to a modification in the scale of values will at the same time modify the characteristics regarded as essential for the application of justice. By the same token, it brings about a reclassification of mankind into fresh essential categories.

For the distinction between fellow-countryman and barbarian, free man and slave, Christianity substitutes the distinction between believer and unbeliever, and this alone counts in the last resort for divine justice. The French revolution regrouped the members of the nation into one single essential category and recognised only citizens equal before the law, whereas the *ancien régime* had recognised nobles, clergy, bourgeoisie and serfs, each subject to a different juridical system.

The humanitarian conception of the nineteenth century sought to reduce national and religious distinctions to the minimum, and to extend to the maximum the civil rights accorded to all the inhabitants of a state, even to make of these rights attributes flowing, by virtue of natural law, from the simple quality of being man.

Whereas the liberal conception of the state determined the status of citizenship by means of purely formal criteria, the national-socialist conception sought to envisage the state under the guise of a people's community (*Volksstaat*) to which only the members of one and the same race, one and the same ethnic group, could belong. The administration of justice had to take this distinction as its essential basis, and had to treat in radically different ways those who, by virtue of their origin, were subjects in law and those who could be treated only as within the jurisdiction, no more than objects at law.

It is clear from these different examples how modifications in the scale of values bring about modifications in the administration of justice. But, whatever the differences between the conceptions of concrete justice, all assume the same definition of formal justice, which requires beings forming part of the same essential category to be treated in the same way.

If the idea of justice is confused it is because each of us, in speaking of justice, feels obliged to define concrete justice. The result is that the definition of justice carries with it also the determination of the categories regarded as essential. Now this, as we have seen, implies a given scale of values. In seeking to define concrete justice, we include in the same formula the definition of formal justice and a particular view of the world. Hence flow such divergencies, misunderstandings and confusions that, in fastening on the differences that set the various formulas apart, we do not even notice that they have an element in common – the same conception of formal justice. Yet we have shown that there is no reason why disagreement on the application of justice – the result of the various conceptions of concrete justice – should stand in the way of agreement on the definition of the formal part of justice.

Be it noted that the confusion between formal justice and concrete justice is the reason why every conception of justice has seemed to comprise a conception of the world: in effect, every definition of concrete justice implies a particular view of the universe. Hence the attraction of the idea of justice and the importance attached to its definition. But from the very fact that the definition of formal justice does not in the least prejudge our judgments of value, we shall find all the less difficulty in reaching agreement on this definition, since, when it is presented in this way, the idea of justice loses at once much of its attraction and nearly the whole of its emotive meaning.

The idea of formal justice is clear and precise, and its purely rational character stands out sharply. The problem of justice is thus partially clarified. Indeed, the difficulties raised by concrete justice cease to exist when we are preoccupied with formal justice alone.

We see how formal justice can be reconciled with the most varied philosophies and codes of law, how we can be just in attributing the same rights to all men, and just in attributing different rights to different categories of men, just in accordance with Roman law and just in accordance with Germanic law.

True, all the difficulties raised by the idea of justice are still far from being smoothed out, and formal justice cannot burden itself with all the contradictory usages of the idea of justice. On the contrary, every time we speak of justice we must put to ourselves the question – are we concerned with formal justice or with one of the innumerable conceptions of concrete justice? Not but what the introduction of this latter distinction offers a double advantage. First, there is the advantage of not importing into the examination of formal justice the difficulties inherent in employing a formula of concrete justice. Secondly, there is the advantage of being enabled to elucidate the difficulties proper to the employment of formal justice, in particular those that derive from the relations between formal justice and concrete justice.

NOTES

* The English translation of my study 'De la justice' (1945) under the title 'Concerning Justice' originally appeared in *The Idea of Justice and the Problem of Argument*, Routledge and Kegan Paul, London, 1963, pp. 1–60. This excerpt is from pp. 5–29.

[1] E. Dupréel, *Traité de Morale,* Brussels, 1932, Vol. II, p. 483.

[2] Proudhon, *De la Justice dans la Révolution et dans l'Eglise,* new edition, Brussels, 1868, p. 44.

[3] *Traité de Morale*, Vol. II, p. 484.

[4] *Ibid.*, Vol. II, pp. 485–496.

[5] *Ibid.*, Vol. II, p. 489.

[6] P. de Tourtoulon, *Les Trois Justices,* Paris, 1932.

[7] *Ibid.*, p. 47.

[8] *Ibid.*, *Les Trois Justices*, pp. 48–49.

[9] P. Tisset, 'Les notions de droit et de justice', *Revue de Métaphysique et de Morale*, 1930, p. 66.

[10] C. Hempel and P. Oppenheim, *Der Typusbegriff im Lichte der Neuen Logik*, The Hague, 1937.

FORWARD TO CHAPTERS 2–6 (*Five Lectures on Justice*)*. It is exactly twenty years since I completed my first essay on justice. But instead of considering my task finished, I have not ceased to reflect on this notion, which, although apparently rational, has paradoxically given rise to discussions and divergent points of view very much opposed to the traditional idea of reason and the rational.

Are the values and norms presupposed in the establishment of justice expressions of reason, or are they no more than the expressions of our passions and our interests? How does one reason about values and norms? What is practical reason? These questions have engaged my philosophical thinking during the past twenty years and have given rise to investigations whose results I have published in various studies.

In April 1964, Professor Sciacca, who is chairman of the Department of Philosophy at the University of Genoa, invited me to give a series of five lectures in which I was to present a synthetic view of my ideas on justice and to show how these ideas had developed since my first essay on the subject. I eagerly accepted this opportunity to sum up my conceptions on the matter and am happy to be able to present to the public the text of these lectures, slightly modified for publication.

CHAPTER TWO

JUSTICE AND ITS PROBLEMS

Justice is one of the most highly respected notions in our spiritual universe. All men — religious believers and nonbelievers, traditionalists and revolutionaries — invoke justice, and none dare disavow it. The search for justice inspires both the objurgations of the Hebrew prophets and the reflections of the Greek philosophers. It is invoked to protect the established order as well as to justify its overthrow. And so, justice is a universal value.

A striving for justice leads men to envision ideal cities and to revolt against inequities of actions, situations, and institutions. It provides sufficient motivation for the most sublime sacrifices as well as for the worst misdeeds. The same zealous urge that propels men to the pursuit of a better world can also mercilessly sweep away whatever is an obstacle to it: *Pereat mundus, fiat justitia.*

But justice is far from being an exclusively revolutionary value. The courts of justice are shields that protect the established order; its guardians are the judges, whose role is to apply the law and to punish those who violate it. For the traditionalists, not violating the law is the accepted way of implementing justice.

Whether in the law court or on the battlefield, both sides always call for the victory of the just cause. If a neutral voice pleads for the establishment of a just peace, no one will accuse him of partiality, for each side is convinced that through the victory of its own cause, justice will triumph.

This paradoxical situation does not mean that at least one of the adversaries must be acting in bad faith. Another explanation is not only possible, but more plausible: The opposing camps simply do not have the same conception of justice. Having noted that justice is a universal value — that is to say, one that is universally acknowledged — we must now add that the notion is also confused.

In his *Traité de Morale* (Treatise on Ethics) Eugène Dupréel has dwelt at length on this aspect of the question:

Since an ethical notion corresponds neither to something that one need only observe in order to verify what is said about it, nor to a demonstration to which one can do nothing but yield, but rather to an agreement to define it in a certain way — then, if one of the adversaries has taken the offensive in claiming to be on the side of justice, the other will tend to define justice in such a way that his own cause is in conformity with it.[1]

In opposition to Plato's realism of ideas, Dupréel denies the existence of any one true justice and thus adopts a conventionalist point of view in accord with his nominalism. In his view, everyone is free to define justice as he likes, and as it suits his own interests. Hence the irremediable confusion of the notion.

Must we conclude that conceptions of justice are purely arbitrary? Was Pascal right in affirming that, in the absence of an objective criterion, power can always assume the appearance of justice without fear of contradiction, since 'it is power that makes opinion?'[2]

But must we always, on the question of justice, as on so many other questions, oscillate between a realistic, objective, dogmatic conception and a nominalist, subjective, arbitrary one? Is there no way to escape from this dilemma, both of whose horns appear equally disastrous to me?

Whatever the answer to the last question will be, it is an undeniable fact that justice has many facets, depending on the theses of the contending parties. For thousands of years, in public conflicts and in private ones, in wars and in revolutions, in lawsuits and in clashes of interest, antagonists have declared and attempted to prove that justice was on their side. And so the notion seems inextricably confused.

Our first task must thus be to analyze scientifically the concept of justice. This, like a prism which breaks down white light into its elements, will permit us to distinguish the variety of its meanings and uses.

The beginning of an analysis were presented by Aristotle in the fifth book of his *Nicomachean Ethics*. Aristotle observed that the idea of justice, like that of injustice, is an ambiguous one; for, according to the accepted definition:

... the term 'unjust' is held to apply both to the man who breaks the law and the man who takes more than his due, the unfair man. Hence it is clear that the law-abiding man and the fair man will both be just. "The just" therefore means that which is lawful, and that which is equal and fair, and the "unjust" means that which is illegal and that which is unequal or unfair.[3]

If we continue our examination of Aristotle's text, we shall see to how great an extent the two meanings he juxtaposes differ.

'Now all the various pronouncements of the law,' says Aristotle, 'aim . . . at the common interest of all . . .'[4] Thus, in accordance with the sense in which 'just' is synonymous with 'legal,' we describe just as '. . . anything that produces or preserves happiness or its components for the political community.'[5] It follows from this that one will be just by accomplishing the good prescribed by law and avoiding the evil that the law prohibits — in a word, by being courageous, temperate, and calm. 'Justice in this sense,' Aristotle adds, 'is not a part of Virtue, but the whole of Virtue . . .'[6] Thus justice is but virtue itself as directed toward others.

Aristotle's main purpose, however, is to examine justice not as virtue in general, but as a specific virtue distinct from all others. As such, this virtue encompasses a sense of equality. It embodies a striving for rationality in action. If the notion of justice is interpreted in its wider sense, one might say it is just to be charitable and unjust to be cruel; but if the notion is taken in its narrow sense, it becomes conceivable for justice to coincide with cruelty, and charity with injustice, since the just action is one that provides equal treatment for all those who are equals, and the unjust action one that favors or disfavors some people over others. Then the school principal who treats all his students with equal harshness will be just but cruel, while the judge who through pity acquits a guilty man will, in a formal sense, be unjust even though charitable.

This same contrast seen by Aristotle between justice as virtue in general and justice as a specific virtue can be found in present-day debates about the justice of political institutions. Some theorists equate the just society and the ideal society. Iredell Jenkins, for example, in the volume of *Nomos* devoted to the concept of justice, writes that every society must formulate its aims and program, and that it matters little whether those aims and that program are presented in the name of justice, of the general interest, of progress, of democracy, or of communism; justice is only the name given to the common good.[7] By contrast, in another article of the same volume, John Rawls insists on the fact that 'justice is only one of the many virtues of political and social institutions, for an institution may be, among other things, outdated, inefficient and degrading without being unjust.'[8] This is also the view of William K. Frankena who, in his article on the concept of social justice, sees in justice one of the many features of an ideal society: 'Societies can be loving, efficient, prosperous, or good as well as just, but they may be just without being notably benevolent, efficient, prosperous, or good.'[9]

For Rawls and Frankena, the justice of social institutions is like Aristotle's just action, in that it can be defined by purely rational criteria. They thus consider justice as a specific virtue, not as the global attribute of an ideal society *per se*, however differently conceived.

As a virtue specific to certain actions, rules, and institutions, justice does indeed seem more easily definable in terms of rational criteria. But rationality does not have to fail us when we conceive of justice as conformity to the law as Aristotle did, or even as the all-encompassing virtue of an ideal society, as Jenkins does today.

Taking justice as conformity to the law, we may wonder if any arbitrary decision on the part of the legislator creates a norm of just conduct, or if it is necessary for the law itself to aim at the common interest, at the production and preservation of the happiness of the political community, as formulated by Aristotle. Does every decree whatsoever of the legislator merit obedience and respect? Why must laws be obeyed? Whence comes their authority? This problem, which is central to all political philosophy, calls for examination.

According to a great many writers, the law draws its authority from the source whence it emanates. The least contested source of moral and juridical norms is custom. When a given social arrangement has been accepted — either explicitly or, as is more frequent, implicitly — and when people have conformed to it long enough to have made it customary or traditional, then it is regarded as normal and just to adhere to this arrangement and unjust to deviate from it. A mode of behavior that has been adopted without protest creates a precedent, and no one will object to actions that conform to precedents. The principle of inertia transforms every habitual way of doing things into a norm. This is a natural way of thinking even for small children, and it is the basis for the rules that develop spontaneously in any given

society. A customary form of behavior, one which conforms to the expecta-
tions of the members of the group, needs no justification; it will be accepted
spontaneously as just, because it is as it should be.

Since Hume many have pointed out that one cannot logically deduce a
right from a fact, nor what ought to be from what is. But no logical
deduction is made when one is dealing with behavior that is customary, or
with a situation that is traditional. It is only when someone maintains that
what ought to be is different from what is that proof has to be supplied.
Proof is incumbent upon the man who asserts that the customary action is
unjust, not upon him who acts in accordance with custom. It is presumed
that what is, is what ought to be: Only in upsetting a presumption must proof
be given. The principle of inertia thus plays an indispensable stabilizing role
in social life. This does not mean that what is must remain forever, but rather
that there should be no change without reason. *Change only must be
justified.*

A frequent justification for change is that someone, or some group, with
the authority to decide, wants this change. God may have willed it, or some
private individual, or the nation.

Divine commandments — whether they sanctify and thus reinforce custom
or whether they modify it — must be followed. In theocratic societies all
norms are reputed to be, directly or indirectly, of divine origin. God is the
incarnation of supreme justice, and the just man is the one who obeys God.
When God orders him, it is just for Abraham to sacrifice his beloved son
Isaac. It is just for believers to observe the commandments of the Decalogue.
'Ye shall diligently keep,' says Moses, 'the commandments of the Lord your
God, and his testimonies, and his statutes, which he hath commanded thee.
And thou shalt do that which is right and good in the sight of the Lord . . .'
(Deuteronomy 6:17—18). A rule that emanates from a sacred source contains
a sufficient guarantee of its justice. Religion and the authorities that it has
sanctified formulate divine commandments which are not to be violated —
prescriptions considered mandatory by the faithful.

Individuals may, within the limits of their recognized autonomy and insofar as they respect the rules of the group, take on commitments that they will
then have to honor: *Pacta sunt servanda.* The man who accepts a change de-
trimental to himself cannot, except in a case of fraud or error, complain of
having been treated unjustly: *Volenti non fit injuria.*

Agreements, too, must be respected. Thus the covenant made by Abraham
with his God, a pact sealed in blood and which has to be ratified through
circumcision of every male descendant of Abraham, is an example of a social

contract by which the tribe commits itself to accept Yahweh as sole God and legislator. In all theories in which a social contract is seen as the origin of a constituted society, the authority of the law is derived from the individual's prior autonomy – that is, from his capacity to take on commitments and from the correlative obligation to honor them.

We know how Rousseau presented the social contract as the basis for a power that is sovereign, absolute, sacred, and inviolable. Laws express the general will and must be obeyed; they cannot be unjust, since they reflect the will of every member of the society. For Rousseau (as later for Hegel, who justified the sovereignty of the State as the expression of the national will), laws that emanate from the State, and therefore from the general will, must by virtue of that very fact be just.

Custom, divine will, the will of individuals, and the will of the nation represented by the State – these constitute, historically, the four sources for the legitimacy of norms and commandments. But are there any objective criteria for the justice of a law, other than its source? Are there any rational criteria that transcend historical contingencies? If so, they would have to stem from concepts such as equality, proportionality, efficacy, or conformity to the nature of things. It is to the elaboration of such criteria that the various theories of natural or rational law have addressed themselves.

The search for rules of law based on something other than custom or a sovereign will was at one time imposed on the *praetor peregrinus*, the Roman magistrate in charge of settling conflicts in which foreigners were involved. Formally speaking, Roman law was not applicable to them. Nevertheless, when the praetor thought that the presceiptions of the *jus civile* – the code of laws in force for Roman citizens – were applicable to foreigners as well, he integrated them into the *jus gentium*, or code of laws applicable to all. To achieve this, he applied the fiction that foreigners were Roman citizens.

On the other hand, when Roman law was not applicable, because the case to be settled had not been foreseen, the praetor had to discover rules that would be equitable. He looked for reasonable rules in accordance with the nature of things – that is, with what was normal in the relationships between men; the just law would be one leading to consequences that both parties, acting in good faith, ought normally to expect even if they had not foreseen the turn of events. To find such a law, it was quite often sufficient to explicate, to extend, and to enforce the customary rules worked out by the merchants of the Roman Empire. The role of the praetor was not to invent a new law, but to apply a supposedly pre-existing one, even if the latter had not yet been officially enacted.

The pretense that such a law applicable to all exists, conformed to the world view of the Stoics.[10] An eloquent rendition is this well-known passage from Cicero:

True law is right reason in agreement with nature; it is of universal application, unchanging and everlasting; it summons to duty by its commands, and averts from wrongdoing by its prohibitions. And it does not lay its commands or prohibitions upon good men in vain, though neither have any effect on the wicked. It is a sin to try to alter this law, nor is it allowable to attempt to repeal any part of it, and it is impossible to abolish it entirely. We cannot be freed from its obligations by senate or people, and we need not look outside ourselves for an expounder or interpreter of it. And there will not be different laws at Rome and at Athens, or different laws now and in the future, but one eternal and unchangeable law will be valid for all nations and all times, and there will be one master and ruler, that is God, over us all, for he is the author of this law, its promulgator, and its enforcing judge. Whoever is disobedient is fleeing from himself and denying human nature, and by reason of this very fact he will suffer the worst penalties, even if he escapes what is commonly considered punishment.[11]

For natural law to be recognized as such, it must have more than divine origin. It must in fact impose itself not on a single people — like the Mosaic law, which binds only the descendants of Abraham by virtue of the covenant — but on all men, whatever the historical contingencies. The will of God can be the origin of a natural law only if there is one God ruling the universal community of men, and if the laws that he prescribes are acknowledged by all reasonable beings. What the laws command or prohibit should follow from the nature of things, as God created them. Added to the natural laws that regulate the course of natural phenomena, there would thus exist a set of rational prescriptions ordering men to act in accordance with the nature of things. These prescriptions would be just and mandatory.

Christian thought, as formulated in the *Decretum* of Gratian (circa 1140), identified the natural law described by Cicero as the prescriptions of the Old and New Testaments (*Jus naturale est quod in lege et Evangelio continetur* . . .); and from there the scholastic theory of natural law developed. Gratian affirmed that natural law has absolute priority over customs and laws. Whatever has been accepted by tradition or set down in writing, if it is incompatible with natural law, must be considered null and void.[12] Here natural law is used not only to extend an already existing body of law, as in Rome, but also to judge the existing law and, if there is reason to do so, to condemn it.

In this perspective, natural law for St. Thomas from Aquino is nothing but the participation of rational creatures in the eternal law imposed by God on the universe. God enlightens our reason and allows us to distinguish good from evil. Man, fallen by his original sin, is unable to behave justly without the aid of divine grace; but he is not prevented from telling good from evil, using reason alone.

One more step in the acknowledgment of human reason, and we reach the secular theories of natural law.

These were developed in the seventeenth and eighteenth centuries, notably in the writings of Grotius, Pufendorf, and Montesquieu. Grotius affirmed in the prolegomena of his *De jure belli ac pacis* that natural law is founded on rational evidence. Its principles are clear and evident, like the principles of mathematics. Even God could not modify them: 'Just as God could not make two plus two equal to something other than four, so he cannot make what is intrinsically evil become something that is not an evil.'[13] This analogy was taken up again by Montesquieu: 'To say that there is nothing just or unjust but what is commanded or forbidden by positive laws, is the same as saying that before the describing of a circle, all the radii were not equal. We must therefore acknowledge relations of justice antecedent to the positive law by which they are established ...'[14] Since these relationships do not depend upon divine will, they would stay the same whether God existed or not. This is the logical conclusion that Montesquieu drew from these premises in his famous letter on justice:

If there is a God, my dear Rhédi, he must necessarily be just, for if he were not, he would be the most wicked and imperfect of all beings.

Justice is a true relation between two things: this relation is always the same, no matter who examines it, whether it be God, or an angel, or lastly, man himself. It is true that men do not always perceive these relations; often, even when they do perceive them, they turn away from them, and their self-interest is what they perceive most clearly ...

Men can commit unjust acts because it is to their advantage to do so ... But God cannot possibly commit an unjust act ... Thus, even if there were no God, we should still be obliged to venerate justice; that is, we should do everything possible to resemble that being of whom we have such an exalted notion and who, if he exists, would necessarily be just.[15]

For the rationalists, justice is an objective relationship, independent of divine will. Yet God, if he exists, can only be just; and men should take him as the model for their conduct: They ought to obey God's voice in themselves, for it is the voice of conscience. If reason enables us to recognize just laws, it is conscience that teaches us, in every circumstance, how to act morally. We should take as our model, says Kant, 'the conduct of this divine man within us, with which we compare and judge ourselves, and so reform ourselves, although we can never attain to the perfection thereby prescribed.'[16]

According to the advocates of natural law, reason is thus a faculty that enables us to recognize not only what is objectively true or false, but also what is just or unjust. Is that really the case? Do there exist norms for actions that are just because they are in conformity with reason? Another two-century-old tradition, which runs from Hume to Kelsen, opposes the idea of practical reason. It denies the existence of a natural law accessible to all through the sole use of reason, a law that would provide us with norms of just conduct to guide our will.

Must we side either with the advocates or with the adversaries of natural law? Is practical reason anything more than a delusion? If we recognize that it plays a role in our actions, how are we to understand that role when men do not agree on what is just? Is the traditional ideal of Philosophy as Wisdom's mistress and the community's guide a simple illusion, a myth like the myth of Paradise Lost? If philosophy is not a purely theoretical and critical activity, but one that can fulfill a constructive function in the behavior of individuals and societies by rationally determining norms and values, then we must present the relation between justice and reason with greater precision. That is what I shall attempt to do in the subsequent chapters of this study.

NOTES

* This Foreword and the Five Lectures were published under the title *Justice*, Random House, New York, 1967 (out of print).

[1] Eugène Dupréel, *Traité de Morale*, Editions de la Revue de l'Université de Bruxelles, Brussels, 1932, Vol. II, p. 484.

[2] Pascal, *Pensées, Oeuvres complètes*, Bibliothèque de la Pléiade, Paris, 1950, nos. 235–42.

[3] Cf. Aristotle, *Nicomachean Ethics*, trans. H. Rackham, Harvard University Press, Cambridge, Mass. 1912, 1129a, 32–34.

[4] *Ibid.*, 1129b, 13.

[5] *Ibid.*, 1129b, 17.

[6] *Ibid.*, 1130a, 8.

[7] Iredell Jenkins, 'Justice as ideal and ideology,' in Carl J. Friedrich and John Chapman (eds.), *Justice, Nomos VI*, Atherton Press, New York, 1963, pp. 202–3.

[8] *Ibid.*, p.98.

[9] William K. Frankena, in Richard B. Brandt (ed.), *Social Justice*, Prentice-Hall, Englewood Cliffs, N.J., 1962, p.3.

[10] Cf. the very stimulating book by A. P. d'Entrèves, *Natural Law*, Hutchinson's University Library, London, 1951, p. 21.

[11] Cicero, *De re publica*, trans. C. Walker Keyes, Putnam, New York, 1928, III, xxii, 33.
[12] *Decree of Gratian*, I, i; I, viii, 2.
[13] Grotius, *De jure belli ac pacis*, I, I, X, 5.
[14] Montesquieu, *L'Esprit des lois*, trans. Thomas Nugent, Hafner, New York, 1949, Vol. I, p. 1.
[15] Montesquieu, *Les Lettres persanes*, no. 83, in Norman L. Torrey, trans., *Les Philosophes*, Capricorn, New York, 1960.
[16] Immanuel Kant, *Critique of Pure Reason*, trans. Norman Kemp Smith, St. Martin's Press, New York, 1929, p. 486.

CHAPTER THREE

EQUITY AND THE RULE OF JUSTICE

Of all the virtues that should guide our conduct, two have always been considered rational: prudence and justice.[1]

Prudence is the virtue that makes us choose the surest and least onerous means of arriving at our ends. If self-interest were our only concern, prudence would advise us to act in such a way that our acts would be the most useful and offer us the most advantages and the fewest inconveniences.

But to what extent should we be concerned only with our own interests? Or with those of others? What are our rights and our obligations? How are we to act so that our behavior may be not only effective but also just? These things we cannot learn from prudence alone. If we want to submit to the criterion of reason the whole of an action and not just its instrumental and purely technical aspects, we are forced to resort to the concept of justice; for it is justice that is the characteristic virtue of the reasonable man.

Justice, says Leibniz, is the charity of the wise; and it includes, according to him, 'besides the inclination to do good by relieving suffering, the Rule of Reason as well.'[2] The just action must show evidence of a rationality that would be missing in an action that was merely charitable. Leibniz adds that the Rule of Reason requires that we adjust the good we wish to procure for all to the needs and merits of each man.[3] But is there no criterion other than needs and merits? Is not the principle of *cuique suum* − to each man what is his, the rights and obligations of each being determined by law − the most often cited definition of justice? It is regarded as just to accord to men exactly what the law ascribes to them. Is it not also sometimes just to treat everyone in the same fashion, and at other times just to make one's treatment proportionate to accomplishment and rank? None of these points of view is entirely negligible, but in practice they often lead to different, even incompatible consequences. What then?

We shall proceed step by step in our analysis.

A form of behavior or a human judgment can be termed just only if it can be subjected to rules or criteria. Thus, esteem can be just if it is in proportion to the merits of the person esteemed, but the idea of a just love would seem ridiculous to us. Indeed, love is directed toward an object that is regarded as being unique and incomparable, whether that object be a person or a personified entity such as the fatherland. Such love cannot result simply from a just evaluation of the qualities and faults of the object, nor of the advantages and disadvantages to which it gives rise. Nothing is more alien to love than such reasoning. If we say that love is blind, it is precisely because love does not see things as they are, and *a fortiori* does not weigh the faults of the beloved object. For justice, it is the weighing alone that matters. The blindfold that traditionally covers the eyes of statues of justice attests to the fact that for justice nothing matters but the results of the weighing; it will not let itself be influenced by any other considerations. Love extends favors; justice concerns itself with being impartial. Love is strictly personal; justice knows no acceptance of individuals.

Just behavior is regular. It conforms to rules, to standards. Can reason help us to determine them? Ever since the ancient Greeks, this has been the essential problem for those who see in reason, as expressed in philosophy, a guide capable of enlightening our judgment and directing our action.

We have seen that in Aristotle the concept of justice was already linked with that of equality. An analysis of the concept of equality will doubtless throw some light on the idea of justice. Two objects, A and B, are said to be identical if they are interchangeable, that is, if every property of one is also a property of the other. It is therefore just that two identical beings be treated in the same fashion, since nothing justifies their being treated unequally. Consequently, what is said of one should also be said of the other; this is the pragmatic formulation of the principle of identity. Thus, at a first approximation, the rule of justice posits the requirement of equal treatment for identical beings.

This rule is indisputable — but what is its scope? Its field of application seems in fact to be extremely limited. Indeed, it will turn out to be nonexistent if we admit Leibniz's principle of indiscernibles, according to which no two identical beings — that is, two beings all of whose properties are the same — exist. If that is so, then the affirmation that A and B are identical would be a contradiction in terms.[4] If no identical beings exist, the Rule of Justice loses all interest for us unless it can tell us how to treat beings who are not identical. In fact, that is the only question that matters.

When we hear people complaining of injustice because they have not received the same treatment as their neighbors or their rivals, none of us thinks of these people as being identical to those with whom they compare themselves nor that any difference would be sufficient, in their eyes, to justify unequal treatment. On the contrary, these people insist expressly on the differences: They say that the other man is richer or more influential, that he is the friend or relative of such and such an official, that he is a member of a clan or of a political or religious group close to the sources of power. They complain all the more because of these differences, which, they are persuaded, should not have influenced the final decision. Other people complain of equal treatment and in the name of justice lay claim to pre-ferential treatment. To justify their contentions, they enumerate the essential differences that have been overlooked, and which should have been taken into consideration.

The man who believes himself to be unjustly treated claims that only certain elements relevant to the situation should have influenced the decision: It is unjust to overlook these elements, as well as it is unjust to consider other elements which are foreign to the situation. Injustice, as it is thus conceived, is never a result of the unequal treatment of identical beings. In the first case, one complains of the unequal treatment of different beings. In actual fact, if the differences do not involve essential characteristics, all the parties should have been treated equally, as if they had been alike. Conversely, in the second case it is an equal or undifferentiated treatment that is found to be unjust, since it was accorded to people who, by accepted standards, are essentially different and therefore belong to different categories.

But which are the differences that matter and which are the ones that do not, in any given situation? Here the disagreements arise.

Let us suppose that a system of food rationing is instituted during a period of scarcity. Should all the inhabitants of the country be treated alike? Or, on the contrary, should the treatment of every individual be adapted to his particular situation so that the needs of the old and the sick, of children and pregnant women be especially taken into account? Should supplementary rations be distributed to those who do physical labor and to the most useful members of the community? Should men and women, citizens and foreigners, be treated in the same way? What about differences of race, class, religion, or political affiliation — should these be ignored or not? Justice, for the officials in charge of applying the final set of rules, consists in following them — that is, in giving to everyone the rations that the law assigns to him.

Of all the possible apportionments, are some more in accord with the Rule of Reason than others? It is not easy to answer this question. But let us note from the start that whatever ruling is finally adopted, it will always be an example of the application of the Rule of Justice. This rule, to the extent that it is meant to apply to beings who are not identical, does not require the equal treatment of identical beings but rather the equal treatment of beings who are essentially alike. By beings who are essentially alike we mean those between whom there exist no essential differences — that is, differences that matter and must be taken into account in the situation.

The Rule of Justice thus defined is a formal rule, because it does not specify *when* two beings are essentially alike, nor *how* they must be treated if one wants to be just.[5] In concrete situations, it is indispensable to specify these two elements. When the law itself furnishes the criteria of its application, the Rule of Justice becomes, explicitly, the Rule of Law, requiring that all those who are alike in the eyes of the law be treated in a fashion determined by law. The Rule of Law is the Rule of Justice purveyed with modalities determined by the will of the legislator. An act that conforms to the Rule of Law is just, because it is a correct application of the law.

What is the importance of the Rule of Justice when it is conceived as a purely formal rule? It is limited to the requirement that people be faithful in their actions to a regular line of conduct. This requirement defines what Dupréel calls *static justice*,[6] because it is characterized by conformity to established rules or to recognized precedents, whatever these might be. When an authorized decision has settled a case, it is just to treat an essentially similar case in the same way (*stare decisis*). We transform into a precedent — that is, into an example of the application of an implicit rule — any previous decision that has emanated from a recognized authority.[7] In the domain of thought, as in that of action, the Rule of Justice accepts as normal the repetition of a given mode of action. It lends juridical certainty and is embodied in the judicial syllogism that directs a judge to treat each member of a given category as every other member of that category is to be treated.

The impartial judge is just because he deals in the same way with all those to whom the same ruling applies, whatever the consequences may be. Thus he may be compared to a pair of scales or to a machine to which all passion is foreign: They can be neither intimidated, nor corrupted, nor moved to pity. *Dura lex, sed lex.* The rule is equality before the law, or to put it another way, it is the interchangeability of justiciables.

According to this conception of justice, the judge in his role as judge is not supposed to question the law. This conception, while morally unacceptable, is founded on the principle of the separation of powers, which assigns to the legislature the exclusive right to legislate and to the highest court the limited role of controlling the judiciary and of seeing to it that the judges do not violate the law in their judgments and decrees. It goes without saying, as we shall see later, that one cannot thus limit the function of the judge if one permits him an active role in the elaboration of the law, and above all not if, as in the case of common law, he is supposed to judge in equity.

All the great ethical and religious traditions contain among their precepts the Golden Rule, which calls upon us to treat others as ourselves. The following are some of the better known formulations of this rule:

> Thou shalt love thy neighbor as thyself.
> Do not do unto others as you would not have them do unto you.
> Do unto others as you would have them do unto you.
> Act as you would have others like yourself act.

This last formulation brings us close to Kant's categorical imperative ('Act so that the maxim of your will can always at the same time hold good as a principle of universal legislation.') and to Singer's principle of generalization ('What is right or wrong for one person must be right or wrong for any similar person in similar circumstances.').[8]

We can see in the various formulations of the Golden Rule some examples of the application of the Rule of Justice, with certain of its elements specified. The Rule of Justice does not say when two creatures are to be regarded as being essentially alike; the Golden Rule specifies that we must understand by 'alike' our neighbors or all those who are men like ourselves. The Rule of Justice does not say how they should be treated; the Golden Rule takes as its model the kind of conduct that we should like to see practiced with regard to ourselves or our fellowmen. Thanks to the Rule of Justice, a subjective judgment can become transformed into an ethical norm, a Golden Rule.

The Rule of Justice, with its requirement of uniformity, leads to predictability and security. It permits the coherent and stable functioning of a juridical order. But that is not enough to satisfy our need for justice. It is necessary that the order, thus realized, be in itself just.

Besides, is it not true that equity is sometimes opposed to the uniform and mechanical application of a given rule, with no concern for the consequences? And is it not possible for the application of a rule – which works satisfactorily in settling the most ordinary cases – to produce ethically unacceptable results when applied to exceptional cases? Aristotle foresaw this objection, and did not hesitate to make room for equity:

Equity, though just, is not legal justice, but a rectification of legal justice. The reason for this is that law is always a general statement, yet there are cases which it is not possible to cover in a general statement. In matters, therefore, where, while it is necessary to speak in general terms, it is not possible to do so correctly, the law takes into consideration the majority of cases, although it is not unaware of the error this involves. And this does not make it a wrong law; for the error is not in the law or the lawgiver, but in the nature of the case: the material of conduct is essentially irregular. When therefore the law lays down a general rule, and thereafter an exception arises which is an exception to the rule, it is then right, where the lawgiver's pronouncement, because of its absoluteness, is defective and erroneous, to rectify the defect by deciding as the lawgiver would himself decide if he were present on the occasion, and would have enacted, if he had been cognizant of the case in question.[9]

This is how Aristotle justifies the recourse to equity, which I have elsewhere qualified as 'the crutch of justice,'[10] since it is only to be utilized when the law appears to be lame. Now this fact is not to be taken for granted; on the contrary, any departure from the law needs to be justified.

The recourse to equity is thus a recourse to the judge as against the law: We appeal to the judge's sense of equity whenever a precedent followed to the letter, or a law rigorously applied in conformity with the rule of justice, leads to unjust consequences. We can cite three reasons for this: First, as alluded to by Aristotle, there is the obligation to apply the law to an unusual case not foreseen by the legislator; the second comes into play when external conditions, such as a devaluation of currency or a war or a catastrophe, so modify the conditions of a contract that its strict execution would gravely injure one of the parties; thirdly, the evolution of moral sentiment may result in the fact that certain distinctions, neglected by legislators or judges, become essential in the present evaluation of the facts.

When the legislator himself realizes that the situations that he wants to set in order are so varied and so mobile that he cannot make exact rules about them, he will sometimes be content with a few general indications, leaving to the equity of the judge their application in each particular case (as was the case in many laws limiting rents in some European countries after World War I). Ordinarily the law does not allow the judge so much freedom of evaluation; nevertheless, the judge will try to interpret the law in such a way as to avoid unjust consequences. This is true of the judge in the United States who must interpret the terms of the American Constitution, as well as of the British common-law judge who is supposed to abide by precedents.[11]

Neither laws nor precedents are applied mechanically. Obliged to sit in judgment on all cases that come under his jurisdiction, the judge has at his command powers of interpretation, so that he can fulfill his task. Indeed, under Article 4 of the Napoleonic Code a judge may not refuse a case by using the silence, the obscurity, or the inadequacy of the law as an excuse. Similar prescriptions can be found in all systems of national law, exceptions being known only in international public law. The judge must decide what is right, even if he cannot justify his decision by pointing to a law that is indisputable and clear in all its terms. We notice that the judge's power of interpretation is in inverse proportion to the clarity and precision of the law.

Here are some examples that will show more clearly how the judge is not content merely to apply the Rule of Justice, but uses his powers of interpretation and evaluation in order to make his decisions conform to his sense of equity: Article 11 of the French (and Belgian) Civil Code states that 'a foreigner in France (or Belgium) shall enjoy the same civil rights as those that are or will be accorded to Frenchmen (or Belgians) by the treaties of the nation to which that foreigner belongs.' But what about the stateless – those who do not belong to any nation? Should civil rights be refused altogether to those foreigners whose countries have not concluded any treaty of reciprocity with Belgium? The problem was posed with special urgency in 1880, at a time when the Civil Code had been in use in Belgium for almost half a century. Since the normal application of Article 11 would have led to morally unacceptable consequences, the Belgian Highest Court decided, by its decree of October 1, 1880,[12] to interpret the text of the law in such a way as to eliminate its unjust effects. The Court decided that the term 'civil rights' as used in Article II designates only civil rights over and above the natural rights of individuals (as, for example, the right to public assistance in case of need) but that it did not include such natural rights as the right to marry, the right to bring an action in a court of law, or the rights of property and succession. These would be accorded to foreigners in all events.

Another outstanding example of creative jurisprudence is furnished by the successive interpretations of Article 1382 of the Napoleonic Code, which merely states that 'Any act whatsoever that is carried out by one man and causes damage to another obliges the one through whose fault the damage occurred to make reparation for it.' Through successive interpretations, French and Belgian jurisprudence has been able to extend and even to transform the meaning of the terms 'cause' and 'fault' in such a way as to impute the responsibility for damage not only to the man who committed the offense, but also to the man who was at the source of the danger. This extension has consequently led to obligatory insurance for the risks involved in the use of an automobile or in the management of an industry.

Similarly, the common-law judge, who seems to be bound by precedents (*stare decisis*), has nevertheless been able to escape from the excessive rigidity that generates injustice by limiting the scope of precedents to the *ratio decidendi*, which he then defines in his own way, introducing distinctions whenever they are deemed necessary.[13]

Instead of adapting the law by interpreting its terms, one can modify it by means of qualifying the facts and thereby acting upon the field of application of its terms.[14] By deciding either to include or to exclude a particular case from the field of application of a law, a judge can modify the effects of that law. That was the technique employed by the Roman praetor in order to extend to foreigners the application of a law that concerned Roman citizens only. It is to such fictions that a judge, especially an appeals judge, may have recourse when, for example, he denies, against all evidence, that punishable actions actually took place.

A few years ago, a Belgian jury tried a case in which a mother was accused of having killed her newborn baby with the aid of her doctor, because the baby had been born deformed, as a result of her having taken a dangerous tranquilizing drug (Softenon). Now the jury did not even consider extenuating circumstances. In order to obtain the acquittal that was desired by public opinion, it simply denied the facts of which the mother was accused.

The role of equity in the application of the law does not permit us to affirm that in order for a decision to be just, it is necessary and sufficient for the decision to conform to the Rule of Justice. The Rule of Justice tells us only that an act is *formally* just if it treats one member of a fixed category in the same way that all members of that category are to be treated. Such an act is formally just because it is in conformity with the conclusion of a judicial syllogism. But equity may take precedence over security, and the desire to avoid unjust consequences may lead a judge to reinterpret the law, to modify the conditions of its application. Even if we deny the judge the right to legislate, we are obliged under our system to leave to him his power to interpret. Thanks to the use that he will make of it, the judge will be able, in certain cases, to go beyond the traditional interpretation and to correct the application of the law from mere conformity to the Rule of Justice. But in order to avoid arbitrariness, he will have to justify and give special reasons for those decisions that deviate from the precedents.

If the Rule of Justice is not always adequate for a just application of the law, it is altogether powerless when it comes to judging the law itself — that is, to determining whether the law is just or unjust. In effect, the Rule of Justice tells us nothing about the content of rules.

He who can modify the rules will be able to escape accusations of formal injustice, even though he acts in the most arbitrary fashion. All he has to do, in effect, is to introduce into the rules certain distinctions that serve his aims. If he does not wish to apply the rule as it stands to someone who fits into a category determined by the law, all he need do is introduce a supplementary condition that will distinguish two different subclasses within the given category. If the law prescribes that 'All M's must be P,' he can simply decide that from now on 'All M's born in Europe must be P,' or, in general, that 'All M's possessing the quality Q must be P.' As soon as he has done that, the law no longer applies to M's born after 1900, to those who were not born in Europe, or to those who do not possess the quality Q; and if these M's are not required to be P, he can not be accused of violating the law and breaking the Rule of Justice.

An example may serve to show how it is possible, by the creation of new rules, to contradict the spirit of justice, even while remaining true to the letter and conforming to the Rule of Justice. Let us suppose that, as the result of a trade agreement with government G, Denmark is the beneficiary of a 'most-favored nation' clause, according to which G must grant to Denmark the same reduction in import duties that it grants to any other country for any product whatever. Now G is prepared to grant to Switzerland a reduction of duties on Swiss butter, but it does not wish to allow Denmark to profit from this concession. Nor does it wish, however, to make itself guilty of a flagrant violation of its treaty with Denmark. To reconcile these incompatible desires, G decides to specify that the reduction of duties will apply only to butter that comes from cows whose pastures are located at altitudes of a thousand meters or higher. Obviously, Danish butter does not fulfill these conditions. The ploy is made, and the letter of the agreement with Denmark respected. But could anyone claim that G's action is really in accord with the obligations it pledged to Denmark?

This example shows that the Rule of Justice, while undeniably important when it comes to judging the correct — and therefore formally just — application of existing rules to particular situations, by no means exhausts the content of the idea of justice. We want the just act to be defined, not simply by the correct application of a rule, whatever that rule may be, but rather by the correct application of a just rule.

Are there any rational criteria that permit us to distinguish just rules from unjust ones? Is reason capable of going beyond the purely formal exigencies of the Rule of Justice in order to guide us in our search for just rules?

The theorists of natural law tried to provide an affirmative reply to this question, but they have not convinced the majority of those philosophers of law who are endowed with critical minds. Is it possible to discover principles of justice as indisputable as the principles of mathematics? If that is not the case, must we consider all such principles as rationally arbitrary? Can we, by turning away from both extremes, agree on some reasonable criteria for a just rule? The rest of my analysis will attempt to answer these fundamental questions.

NOTES

[1] For the beginning of this chapter, see 'The rule of justice' in Ch. Perelman, *The Idea of Justice and the Problem of Argument,* The Humanities Press, New York, 1963, pp. 79–87.

[2] Cf. G. Grua, *Jurisprudence universelle et théodicée selon Leibniz,* Presses Universitaires de France, Paris, 1953, p. 212.

[3] *Ibid.,* p. 507.

[4] A famous analysis by the German logician Gottlob Frege has shown that one can without contradiction affirm the identity of *A* and *B*; that would mean that *A* and *B* are two names for a single object that is designated in different ways, as for example in the affirmation that the Morning Star is identical to the Evening Star. Cf. G. Frege, 'Uber Sinn and Bedeutung,' *Zeitschrift fur Philosophie und philosophische Kritik,* C (1892), 25–50.

[5] Cf. my essay 'The rule of justice,' *op. cit.,* p. 82.

[6] Eugène Dupréel, *Traité de Morale,* Editions de la Revue de l'Université de Bruxelles, Brussels, 1932, Vol. II, p. 485.

[7] 'The rule of justice,' *op. cit.,* p. 82.

[8] Cf. Marcus George Singer, *Generalization in Ethics,* Knopf, New York, 1961, p. 5.

[9] Aristotle, *Nicomachean Ethics,* trans. H. Rackham, Harvard University Press, Cambridge, Mass., 1912, 1137b.

[10] 'Concerning justice,' in *The Idea of Justice and the Problem of Argument, op. cit.,* p. 36.

[11] Cf. Edward H. Levi, *An Introduction to Legal Reasoning,* University of Chicago Press, Chicago, 1961.

[12] Belgian Pasicrisie, 1880, I, 292.

[13] Cf. Levi, *op. cit.* See also Rupert Cross, *Precedent in English Law,* Oxford University Press, New York, 1961.

[14] Cf. Centre Belge de recherches de logique, *Le Fait et le Droit,* Bruylant, Brussels, 1961.

CHAPTER FOUR

ON THE JUSTICE OF RULES

Observance of the Rule of Justice assures regularity, security, and impartiality in the administration of justice. But it is incapable of judging the rules themselves. Are there any rational criteria to guide us in this matter, any criteria that will permit us to qualify, as either just or unjust, laws and rules of all kinds? It is, in fact, against the arbitrariness and injustice of the laws that those who want to modify or revise the established order protest. Often it is to counteract the abuse of power on the part of the rulers, especially on the part of the legislators, that the theorists of natural law have recourse to just reason and to the nature of things. But are their theories based on anything other than incommunicable intuitions and controversial points of view?

We have seen that the Rule of Justice does not indicate which distinctions should or should not be taken into account in the setting up of categories of essentially similar beings, nor how such beings are to be treated. Now, in fact, it is toward one or the other of these two points that any criticism of a law that is decried as unjust will be directed. The critic will say that the distinctions established by the law, or else the treatments that it sets down, are arbitrary and unjustified.

Let us suppose that the total number of people with whom a given law is concerned are divided into three categories, *A, B, C,* and that the law prescribes the following: 'All *A*'s must be *P*,' 'All *B*'s must be *R*,' and 'All *C*'s must be *S*.' The critic who is attacking either the principle of classification or the kind of treatment that is prescribed for the members of each category will try to modify one or the other, and sometimes both, of the elements of the law.

A law that brings into effect a system of family allowances is presented, for example, as the expression of a desire to satisfy the fundamental needs of the workers. A critic could then attack the very principle of this legislation, as well as the classifications that it sets up, by finding it to be a matter of injustice that, in the determination of the wages of workers, any considerations other than the amount of work supplied or accomplished is taken into account. If one endorses the formula of 'equal work, equal pay,' then one will find irrelevant, nonessential, and arbitrary all distinctions and classifications that are based on the sex, age, race, or family status of the workers. It might appear to some to be profoundly unjust not to overlook these differences, and to base a graduated salary scale upon them. Others, while supporting the basic principle of the legislation, might criticize it for different reasons. While admitting, for example, that family obligations must be taken into account in determining workers' wages, they might protest that it is altogether unjust to allocate three times as much money for a fourth child in the family as for a first child, since it is the first child that causes the greatest increase in family expenditures.

The two criticisms strike at different aspects of the legislation. The first one objects to mixing social or political considerations with what it considers to be a purely economic problem; accordingly, only considerations of the quality, duration, and output of the work can furnish the relevant elements for an acceptable system of classification. The second criticism, by contrast, accepts the basic point of view adopted by the legislation but criticizes its practical implementation.

As another example, we may consider Proudhon's impassioned criticism of the French penal code:

> The poor devil whose children are crying for food breaks into the back room of a bakery and steals a loaf worth four pounds. The baker has him condemned to eight years of forced labor, according to the law . . . But if the same baker is caught putting plaster in his bread instead of flour, and sulfuric acid instead of yeast, he is charged with a five-pound fine – according to the law. Now our conscience cries out that the cheater is a monster, and the law itself absurd and hateful.[1]

Proudhon is violently attacking the injustice of a penal code that doles out disproportionate punishments for the two types of crime. For him, the baker's crime is infinitely more odious than that of the thief, whereas the punishment for it is much less severe. Proudhon demands that the punishment fit the crime. For him, this means that the punishment should be proportionate to the amount of damage done to society; otherwise, it is unjust or arbitrary.

Again, if one is asked whether it is just that a doctor should earn twenty times more than a laborer, one could sidestep the issue by arguing that, in a liberal economy, prices and wages are functions of the law of supply and demand, and for that reason cannot be considered under the heading of justice. But a reply cannot be avoided if both the doctor and the worker are employees of the State. In that case, we have to justify the difference in earnings by showing that it is not arbitrary, but rather proportionate to some measurable factor – for example, the service rendered by each of the two men to the community at large.

These few examples illustrate the concept of injustice, as applied to a rule or to a piece of legislation.

In dealing with the problem of formal justice or injustice — that is, with the correct or incorrect application of the Rule of Justice — we compare the various treatments accorded to members of the same basic category; but we have no means of comparing members of different categories, nor of judging the treatments accorded to them. Yet it is precisely this problem with which we are dealing when we declare that a rule is unjust on the grounds that its criteria of classification are irrelevant and the treatments it prescribes, arbitrary. To refute the first part of our criticism, one would have to show that the system of classification established by the legislation in question is indeed relevant, as well as superior to the system with which one might want to replace it. To refute the second criticism, one would have to show that the treatments prescribed, whether they be rewards or punishments, are not arbitrary but rather conform to certain general principles that permit their rational systematization.

An absolutely just system of rules, that would be recognized as such by all reasonable men, would have to establish categories and prescribe treatments with which no one could disagree, because those categories and treatments would be the only ones that wholly conform to reason. Is not the quest for such a system illusory? Given the great variety of human societies — the variety of religious, philosophical, and political conceptions to be found in them — is it possible to elaborate a set of rationally grounded principles that could serve as a basis for institutions that all reasonable men would consider just? Before answering this question, in all its generality, let us examine a recent attempt by Professor John Rawls of Harvard University to provide an affirmative reply to the question.[2]

Rawls defines justice as a specific virtue, which, when applied to an institution or to a practice, requires the elimination of arbitrary distinctions and the establishment within their structure of an appropriate equilibrium between opposing claims.[3] The principles of justice ought to specify under what conditions the apportionment, or the share of every individual, can be considered appropriate and just, and what distinctions justify differences in treatment that would not be arbitrary. In examining the role of justice in the community, Rawls is concerned only with the justice of the rules that, by defining offices and positions, rights and duties, privileges and penalties, give social activity its shape and structure.[4]

Rawls' conception of justice as a function of the idea of 'fairness' is clearly inspired by the model of 'fair play.' According to him, it is the idea of fairness that underlies the application of justice to practices defined by rules. The conception of justice, whose consequences he goes on to develop, is founded on the following two principles, which seem to him to be rational:

1. Each person participating in an institution or affected by it has an equal right to the most extensive liberty compatible with like liberty for all.

2. Inequalities as defined by the institutional structure or fostered by it are arbitrary unless it is reasonable to expect that they will work out to everyone's advantage and provided that the positions and offices to which they attach or from which they may be gained are open to all.[5]

Thus it is considered just that all the participants in an institution or in a practice should possess the same amount of freedom, as is usually the case with players at the beginning of any game. Inequalities are considered arbitrary and unjust, unless they can be justified by showing that they are advantageous to all and that no one is excluded *a priori* from an advantageous function. It goes without saying that the Rule of Justice that requires equal treatment in all essentially similar cases will be observed in the appraisal of institutions and practices. But as soon as one has established, through the rules of a system, a distinction that is advantageous or disadvantageous to some, that distinction will be considered unjust as long as one has not proved that it is not arbitrary according to the second principle. Even an equal limitation on the rights of everyone will be permitted only if it is proved to be indispensable for the good of all. The situation that does not require any justification − because it appears to conform to reason and justice − is the one that provides the greatest freedom for each individual, which is consistent with the same freedom for everyone.

Rawls postulates no need to justify all the differences that the system establishes. Only those distinctions in the assignment of functions and of situations that produce, either directly or indirectly, inequalities in the apportionment of advantages or disadvantages need to be justified.[6] But inequalities and limitations on freedom will not be considered justifiable solely on the grounds that they produce advantages for the whole of society: They must in addition be advantageous to each one of its members. On this point Rawls is more demanding than the utilitarians.

On the other hand, he does not present his principles as the foundations for a new social contract; he is perfectly aware that in our society, with its already functioning set of institutions and laws, starting everything from scratch is out of the question. His suggestions aim only at providing certain principles that are capable of rendering the functioning of society more just than it is at present. Toward that end he presents rules of procedure that should permit the realization of the aim he proposes.

One preliminary condition — and it is an indispensable one — is that we deal with reasonable people who are able to recognize their own interests, to foresee the probable consequences that would result from the adoption of a given set of rules, to abide by the rules once they are adopted, and to resist the temptations that would lead to their violation. They would also have to be able to resist the envy they might feel at seeing the superiority of some other person. It is to be further supposed that these people have similar and complementary interests, so that their collaboration would prove advantageous; and also, that they are sufficiently equal in power and ability so that no member of the group would, under normal circumstances, be capable of dominating the others.[7]

To better their institutions and laws by rendering them more just, the members of society come together in open discussion, with everyone registering his complaints and presenting his claims. Everyone should be free to make the most of his own point of view, but the decisions made should conform to the following rules:

1. If the criteria for decision proposed by any one member are accepted, the claims of the others shall be judged according to the same criteria.

2. No complaint shall be heard until everyone has agreed, in general, on the principles according to which complaints shall be judged.

3. The principles proposed and recognized on any given occasion shall be considered obligatory, except for special circumstances, for all subsequent occasions.

Rules thus instituted would, according to Rawls, form a just system, for they would be the rules of a system conceived by someone who knew that anyone who is hostile to him could have the right to assign him his place within the system.[8]

To what extent can these principles and rules of procedure be considered rational, effective, and sufficient to enable us to render with certainty the functioning of human institutions more just? First, let us note that every organized society possesses laws and regulations that have to do not only with its foundation, but also with the recognized procedures by which existing laws are applied or modified. Since Rawls does not wish to make a clean sweep of the past, but desires only to improve existing institutions, his three proposed rules of procedure – to the extent that they are not already accepted in the society that he wishes to change – must prove to be in conformity with the laws and regulations then in force. Almost all modern systems of law accept the value of precedents in settling conflicts, even though the status of precedents may vary from one system to another. We should note, however, that judges are indispensable for deciding whether a new case is or is not essentially similar to a case previously judged.

If, therefore, the first rule of procedure is generally accepted, the second demands clarification. In effect, Rawls requires that everyone be in agreement with the procedures adopted. When taken literally, this principle is inapplicable, for we obviously cannot ask for the agreement of newborn infants or of madmen who are incapable of sane reasoning. In any case, the requirements of Professor Rawls' system are such that it can function only with the collaboration of eminently reasonable beings. But then, does it not become necessary, even in a relatively egalitarian society, to limit the right to vote and, in general, the right to participate actively in public affairs? Are we to deny the exercise of their political rights only to children below a certain age and to all those adults who have not successfully passed examinations of their intelligence and knowledge? Should we grant political rights to foreigners, residing in the country? What shall we do when, under the pretext that only reasonable persons are able to exercise their political rights, whole classes of a society are denied the right to vote? This is, as we know, the slogan of every paternalistic political organization. Must we conform to the procedures in force in a society, even if they seem to us to be profoundly unjust; or can a just revolution try to modify the existing state of things?

It should also be noted that the requirement of unanimity, even among those who exercise their political rights, leads to the *liberum veto* and hence to anarchy. If everyone's support cannot be mustered, it then becomes indispensable for certain techniques to be elaborated that permit a decision to be reached; on the basis either of a simple majority or of a qualified one, the decision will be deemed representative of the general will. Can one, in that case, assume that all majority decisions will be just? Is it not necessary to provide for guarantees against abuses of majority rule, in order to protect defenseless minorities? Can we, without fear of error, rest assured that the functioning of a democracy, even of a democracy that is based on equal and universal suffrage, will never lead to an injustice in the application of the two fundamental rules that Rawls considers to be necessary and sufficient for the elaboration of just institutions?

But let us suppose that all these preliminary difficulties have been resolved, and that an agreement exists on the rules of procedure that will allow everyone to present his claims and grievances. Are we sure, now, that the institutions will be progressively improved, to become as just as possible? How do we know that we will not, in fact, rapidly wind up with a society like the one that the theorists of classical liberalism wanted to set up? In their society the functioning of the economic laws, while capable of being perfectly correct – or, to use Rawls' terminology, perfectly 'fair' – would nevertheless result in a very unequal distribution of wealth.[9]

In elaborating his system, Rawls assumes that reasonable men, being capable of foreseeing the consequences of their acts, will establish rules that, egalitarian from the beginning, will maintain this equality indefinitely. But what if that hope is not realized? If the members of a society have accepted certain rules of content and procedure, are their children and grandchildren bound forever by the conventions of their ancestors? This is what seems to be implied by Rawls' third rule for the settling of conflicts. Must every generation, on the contrary, be urged at regular intervals to conclude a new social contract, or at least to feel free to agree on new procedures for the adoption and modification of rules, with no concern for existing procedures? Must each generation establish anew an egalitarian point of departure, in conformity with Rawls' second rule – for example, by suppressing the right of inheritance? But once that path is taken, would it not also be necessary to limit the individual's right to dispose of private property even while he is alive, in order to eliminate the arbitrary inequalities that exist in the midst of society?

Experience teaches us, in fact, that procedures which were originally meant to be egalitarian may lead to consequences that, in the long run, turn out to be unjust. We know that the French Revolution, by abolishing all the privileges of the Old Régime, was supposed to establish a new regime founded on liberty and equality, even though it maintained the rights of property and inheritance. The flagrant inequalities that resulted from it provoked the opposition of the socialists, and provided substance for their attacks on the private ownership of the means of production. This well-known story teaches us that the very idea of privilege, defined as unjustified inequality, is susceptible to different interpretations. Something that to the liberal bourgeoisie has not seemed to be related to the principle of equality can be interpreted by others as the basis of all inequalities and the root of all injustices.

The questions just raised, and the difficulties they reveal, show us the inadequacy of a system that is modeled on the idea of a well-played game, when it comes to satisfying all the demands of those who aspire to greater social justice.

Rules of fair play are easy to establish when one is dealing with a game in which everyone starts out under conditions of relative equality, in which all the moves that are permitted and forbidden are known in advance, in which it is easy to foresee all possible developments, as well as all the situations that determine whether one wins or loses. Every player, before beginning, is familiar with the rules of the game and accepts them; the presence of a referee or judge guarantees, if need be, that they will be observed to the letter. No one is obliged to participate in a game whose rules he does not accept, and no one would ever try, in the name of the rules, to force anyone to do something that runs counter to his most profound convictions. But when we are dealing with the workings of social and political institutions and with the rules that regulate them, the problem of justice appears in an entirely different context.

The rules of a constituted society – the rights and obligations, as well as the respective situations, of those who possess political rights in that society – are for the most part products of a historic past. Must we, in the name of abstract principles of justice, thumb our noses at that past and decide, at regular intervals, to wipe out everything and start again from scratch? That is the sort of objective we find in rationalist thinkers like Descartes, who, after making a clean sweep of the prejudices, traditions, and customs of their environment, propose to construct a new knowledge *ab ovo*. But such thinkers have at their disposal, or at least so they think, a new method which, being based on rational evidence, will allow them to construct, on a firm foundation, a science worthy of that name. To succeed in constructing a perfectly just society along the same lines, its members would have to accept the evidence that it is just to give up the advantages thus far obtained for them by their historical situation. They would have to succeed in finding self-evident rules to justify the socially accepted inequalities and others that people would have to accept in order to find just solutions to their conflicts.

But if it is just and reasonable to give up historically acquired positions, why should we seek to improve the institutions of a politically organized society which is itself a product of history? Why not try from the start to establish equal justice among the inhabitants of the earth, by suppressing as far as possible the inequalities in wealth and ability that now exist among the various regions of the world, some of which are in a state of permanent poverty?

It is true, no doubt, that just laws and regulations cannot be arbitrary. But must we accept as evident, and without any need for justification, the principle of the complete equality of all those who take part in the workings of an institution, while on the other hand we regard as arbitrary any inequality that is not justified by the advantages that it secures for everyone?

Should the ideal equality recognized at the start be negative or positive? Should it consist in everyone's equal right to live, to worship, to speak and publish, to assemble, and to work, in the sense that the State will not, without sufficient cause, limit any one of these freedoms, but will on the contrary protect the exercise of them? Or must the requisite equality be defined positively – for example, by saying that the State will make it possible for each one to exercise the rights guaranteed to him, by setting up institutions of all kinds – such as hospitals, schools, factories, and churches?

Rawls seems to favor the liberal – that is, the negative – conception of equality, for he would limit individual freedom only to the extent that such limitations secure advantages for each one, rather than for the greatest number. The principle that he presents as self-evident, and so rational that it would persuade all men who aspire to a just society, suffers from the ambiguities of the notion of equality, which is given diametrically opposed interpretations by liberal and socialist ideologies. Indeed, in almost every field there exists an opposition between those who call for a minimum of government intervention in what they consider to be their private affairs, and those who call for increased intervention by the collectivity, hoping thereby to satisfy, at the expense of the community, a growing number of individual needs. A minimum of political experience will reveal to us that it is vain to hope for a spontaneous accord among all the members of society on these essentially controversial questions. Indeed, that is why political institutions, far from being rooted in self-evident principles, have been organized in such a way as to function even in the absence of an agreement that is guaranteed by self-evidence.

In a democratic and pluralistic society, everyone is free to adopt his own ethic, elaborate his own rules for living, choose his own ideal, and live his own life – provided he does not transgress the rules of public order. But it is different when it comes to making juridical rules which determine the rights and obligations of each individual in accordance with the desires and aspirations of the politically organized collectivity, at least as these latter are conceived and interpreted by the representatives and officials of the collectivity. Since it is useless to hope that the expression of these desires and the formulation of these aspirations will always be unanimously agreed upon, even by the elected representatives of the nation, the law in each State has to see to it that controversial questions are not settled by recourse to violence. It will therefore have to provide for rules of procedure concerning the elaboration and modification of the laws, as well as for rules of jurisdiction for the settlement of conflicts that arise as a result of the application of those laws. Political and social justice presupposes, in effect, legislators and judges.

Moral and juridical rules regulate, in complementary fashion, the relations among members of a society. They often affect each other, in fact: Moral sentiments can play a considerable role in the adoption and interpretation of laws, while the promulgation of laws can in turn modify moral sentiments. But in certain respects, law and ethics differ greatly from each other. Ethical ideals depend on the individual conscience; every man is, in this area, his own judge and the judge of his fellows. But when rules have become public in character, and are therefore sanctioned by legal constraints, only the judicial or the administrative power is qualified to promulgate the law. In effect, the legal norms that determine public law must comprise rules of procedure and of proof in order to limit juridical uncertainty and to compensate, through the appointment of competent judges and administrators, for the absence of objective and impersonal criteria in the resolution of possible conflicts.

If the principles proposed by Rawls for the elimination of what is arbitrary in social and political institutions had been so rational as to be able to enforce themselves on everyone, morality and law would coincide in matters of justice. There would be no need then to set up a legislative or a judiciary branch of government; no constraints would be necessary to make all reasonable members of society conform to what is just. Revolutionaries and conservatives alike would acknowledge the evidence of the same rules. Is this not the aspiration – and the illusion – of every utopia?[10]

In fact, there are very few laws on which all men would agree, and to which they would give the same interpretation. Nothing is more controversial than the justice or injustice of laws. In the face of such divergences, which seem to be inherent in the very nature of things, can we still believe in the practical use of reason? Our two last chapters will be devoted to an examination of this question.

NOTES

[1] Proudhon, *De la Justice dans la Révolution et dans l'Eglise,* new edition, Brussels, 1868, Vol. III, p. 169.
[2] See, for example: 'Two concepts of rules,' *Philosophical Review* LXIV (1955), 3–32;

'Justice as fairness,' *Journal of Philosophy* **LIV** (1957), 653–62; 'Justice as fairness,'
Philosophical Review **LXVII** (1958), 164–94 [reprinted in *Justice and Social Policy*, ed.
F. A. Olafson, Prentice-Hall, Englewood Cliffs, N.J., 1961, pp. 80–107] ; 'Constitutional
liberty and the concept of justice,' in Carl J. Friedrich and John Chapman (eds), *Justice,
Nomos VI*, Atherton Press, New York, 1963, pp. 98–125. Since this was written Robert
Paul Wolff published a paper 'A refutation of Rawls' *Theorem on Justice'* in the *Journal
of Philosophy* **LXIII** (1966), 179–90.

3 'Constitutional liberty and the concept of justice,' *op. cit.*, p. 99.

4 *Ibid.*

5 *Ibid.*, p. 100.

6 *Ibid.*, pp. 101–2.

7 *Ibid.*, pp. 103–4.

8 *Ibid.*, pp. 104–5.

9 The foregoing constitutes the fundamental objection formulated by Professor Chapman against the concept of justice as fairness. In comparing the system invented by
Professor Rawls with utilitarianism, Chapman shows the advantage of the latter: For, in
taking into account the consequences of acts, rather than their conformity to certain
procedures that are considered to be just simply because they are 'correct,' utilitarianism
seeks a more equitable distribution of wealth. This would in turn allow for the establishment of more justice in the possibilities of satisfying the fundamental needs of all
members of society. This is also the underlying inspiration of modern liberalism, as it is
expounded by Lord Beveridge. Cf. John W. Chapman, 'Justice and Fairness,' *Justice,
Nomos VI*, pp. 147–69.

10 Cf. the chapter, 'Ce qu'une réflexion sur le droit peut apporter au philosophe,' in my
Justice et Raison, Presses Universitaires de Bruxelles, Brussels, 1963, pp. 244–255. See
also Chapter 17 of the present volume.

CHAPTER FIVE

JUSTICE AND JUSTIFICATION

Twenty years ago I published a study on the notion of justice, in which I tried to delimit the rational aspects of this notion.[1] I found then that an act may be qualified as just insofar as it is an application of a rule in conformity with the Rule of Justice, and that a rule is just insofar as it is not arbitrary, for example, insofar as it can be justified by means of general principles. Thus, a criminal law will be just if the punishments it prescribes are proportional to the seriousness of the crimes. A regulation fixing the salaries of public officials will be just if it makes the salaries proportional to rank and to the services rendered to society. But what are the criteria that will permit us to evaluate the seriousness of a crime or the utility of a service rendered? The point I was trying to make in that study was this: That no matter how hard one might try to deduce such criteria from other norms, in the end one will always come up against a certain irreducible vision of the world expressing nonrational values and aspirations.[2]

It seemed to me that the various ideals we might have of a perfect society are all arbitrary, since they could be founded neither on experience nor on logic. In effect, neither rigorous deduction nor any induction based on experience can guarantee the passage from what is objectively given and true, to the ideal we seek to realize and to the values it promotes and to the rules that it justifies. I therefore concluded that we could only go so far in our effort to justify rules by eliminating what is arbitrary in them; in the end we would inevitably rest on unjustified and not self-evident principles, on positions we ourselves chose, on values which could be controverted. It seemed utopian to expect all men to agree on the same ideal of a just society. To different human aspirations, arranged in different hierarchies, there correspond different conceptions of the ideal community. If someone found a rule unjust, because it divided people into different categories from those he would have chosen — and this because his particular vision of the world made him judge differently of what was or was not important or relevant — then no rational argument seemed to me capable of resolving the contradiction; there was nothing to do but record it. Given the plurality of often incompatible and always arbitrary values, it seemed to me that reason was incapable of reconciling antagonists. A rigorous analysis had to limit itself to pointing out the different values that underlie different social systems. This is the kind of work done by Enrico di Robilant in his *Sui principi di Giustizia*, where by comparing the Prussian (*Landrecht*) Code of 1794 and the present Italian Constitution, he shows convincingly the different values that inspired them. But was it possible to find objective criteria that would allow one to demonstrate the undeniable superiority of one of these value systems over the other? This seemed to me absolutely impossible. My analysis twenty years ago led to the following skeptical conclusion:

Let us take the example of a normative system which has the peculiarity of attaching the highest merit to the stature of individuals. From this system will flow rules imposing the obligation to treat men in a fashion more or less proportional to their height. From this system one can try to eliminate every arbitrary rule, all unequal treatment, all favoritism, all injustice. From the inside of the system, so long as the fundamental principle that serves as its basis is not called in question, justice will have a well-defined meaning — that of avoiding anything arbitrary in the rules, any irregularity in action.

We are thus led to distinguish three elements in justice — the value that is its foundation, the rule that sets it forth, the act that gives it effect.

Only the latter two elements — the less important, incidentally — can be subjected to the requirements of reasoning. We can require of the act that it should be in accordance with the rules, that it should extend the same treatment to persons who belong to the same essential category. We can require that the rule be justified, that it flow logically from the normative system adopted. As for the value that is the foundation of the normative system, we cannot subject it to any rational criterion: It is utterly arbitrary and logically indeterminate.[3]

By qualifying any value that founds a normative system as arbitrary and logically indeterminate, I was expressing my conviction that such a value could be neither the result of experience nor the logical consequence of incontestable principles. I continue to believe this today. Yet is this a reason for drawing the much more general conclusion that all the fundamental values and norms that guide our actions are devoid of rationality? that they can be neither criticized nor justified? and that all discussion of them is but the expression of our interests and passions? This conclusion is enough to reduce a rationalist to despair. Yet it must be adopted by those who say that proof must be founded on either logic or experience, since deduction and induction are the only forms of convincing reasoning. If we adopt this point of view, we must indeed subscribe to a conclusion that jars common sense — namely, that all values are equally arbitrary, since none can be demonstrated rationally. Is it really necessary to subscribe to the view of reason and of reasoning to which we have become accustomed by modern logic? Is it really true that deduction and generalization based on experience are the only acceptable bases for proof, and that it is impossible to reason on values?

In 1927 the French logician Edmond Goblot published a book on the logic of value judgments. In this interesting work Goblot analyzed only instrumental values, values that constitute either means or obstacles to desired ends. The ends themselves were treated as given – namely, founded on intuitions that eluded all rational control. Numerous works have also been published over the last thirty years on the logic of norms or deontic logic. These have been concerned only with general rules of transformation for propositions containing expressions like 'it is obligatory,' 'it is forbidden,' 'it is necessary,' 'it is allowed.' They have made no attempt whatsoever to guide us in the choice of particular rules or values.

Must we then conclude that the determination of non-instrumental values – as well as of norms that would determine our rights and obligations – escape all logic and all rationality? Must we abandon all philosophical use of practical reason and limit ourselves to the technical use of reason in the domain of action? Must we use our reason only to adjust our means to totally irrational ends? Affirmative answers to these questions form the position of all positivist philosophers, from Hume to Ayer. Must we then resign ourselves, and consider the whole classical tradition of Western philosophy as nothing more than the expression of a millenarian dream? Are the search for a rational foundation for our individual and collective actions and the desire to elaborate an ethic, a philosophy of law, and a political philosophy nourished only on illusion and illogic?[4]

It seemed to me that before accepting the theses of positivism concerning values, someone should make a renewed effort to elaborate a logic of value judgments based not on the reasoning techniques of modern logic but rather on a detailed examination of how men actually reason about values. I undertook to do this work with the collaboration of Madame L. Olbrechts-Tyteca. Ten years after the beginning of our project, we had not found the logic of value judgments that we were looking for. We did, however, rediscover a long-neglected logic which had been completely forgotten by contemporary logicians, although it had been treated at length in the ancient treatises on rhetoric and in the *Topics* of Aristotle. This was the study of what Aristotle called dialectical proofs in contrast to the analytical proofs that interest modern logicians exclusively. In an extended empirical and analytical study called *Traité de l'argumentation*[5] Mme. Olbrechts-Tyteca and I were able to put forward this nonformal logic as a theory of argumentation, complementary to the theory of demonstration that is the object of formal logic.

58 CHAPTER FIVE

Our research convinced us that there exists no specific logic concerning values; rather, the same techniques of reasoning which we use to criticize and to justify opinions, choices, claims, and decisions, are also used when it comes to criticizing and justifying statements that are usually qualified as value judgments. That is why the practical use of reason cannot be understood without first integrating it into a general theory of argumentation. Losing sight of argumentation as the technique of reasoning that is indispensable for practical judgment, and by overlooking discursive means of convincing not founded on formal logic or experience, modern thinkers were inevitably led to the conclusion that values were logically arbitrary and therefore devoid of rational justification. In the absence of a theory of argumentation one could not even imagine what was specific to the process of justification, much less specify its relationship to the idea of justice.

The object itself of any justification is very different from the object of a demonstration. The latter is developed from statements or propositions of which we can ask whether they are true or false, whereas the former is of an entirely practical nature: We justify an action, a kind of behavior, a disposition to act, a claim, a choice, a decision.[6] We can speak only indirectly of the justification of a person acting or of a proposition. The justification of an agent consists in justifying his conduct, or sometimes in dissociating him either wholly or in part from an act or a decision that is imputed to him. But in the latter instance it is more a question of excusing than of justifying: One simply wants to prevent the judgment of an act from being transferred to the person performing it.

The justification of a proposition or of a rule, on the other hand, consists in justifying one's adherence to it or one's statements in favor of it. It is, then, a justification of behavior. Since we consider it reasonable to adhere to a true statement, the proof of the truth of a statement can certainly constitute the greatest part of our justification. But no demonstration or verification will allow one to justify his adherence to an axiom or to a norm; it is precisely here that the particularities of justificatory reasoning come into play. This kind of reasoning constitutes what Professor Feigl calls *vindicatio actionis*, the justification of an action, rather than *validatio cognitionis* or proof of the validity of knowledge.[7] But even in this last instance we are dealing with the justification of a belief, of a kind of behavior.

For centuries logicians have been able to neglect the problem of the justification of one's choice of axioms, by considering the latter either as self-evident or as arbitrary. In the first case, since we must bow to the evidence, we have no choice and therefore no need to justify our acceptance. In the second case, since all choices are considered equally arbitrary, it is impossible to justify any one by showing it to be preferable to any other. When we reject both of these extremes, so reminiscent of realism and nominalism, when we admit that a choice of axioms is possible and that it is not entirely arbitrary, then the justification of choice ceases to be a negligible problem.

If we transpose the same reasoning to the first principles of philosophy, which are conceived of as being neither self-evident nor arbitrary, the very center of philosophical thinking becomes transferred from the realm of theory to that of practice; we are heading toward the justification of our philosophical choices and decisions. But a philosophical justification cannot refer to the interests and passions of a particular group: If it is not presented as being universally valid, it does not constitute an admissible philosophical justification. A philosophical justification must be rational, or at least reasonable.

To admit the possibility of a rational or reasonable justification is at the same time to recognize the practical use of reason. It means that we are no longer limiting reason to a purely theoretical usage (for example, the discovery of truth or error), as Hume wished.[8] To reason is not merely to verify and to demonstrate, but also to deliberate, to criticize, and to justify, to give reasons for and against – in a word, to argue.

It would never occur to us to want to justify every one of our actions or beliefs. Methodical doubt as practiced by Descartes is conceivable only if a self-evident, indubitable intuition allows us to eliminate it. The problem of justification arises only in the practical realm, when it is a question of a decision, an action, or a choice that has no incontrovertible evidence to guarantee its validity. In this perspective, a desire to justify everything appears completely senseless, for it is unrealizable and would only lead to infinite regression. The enterprise of justification has meaning only if the acts one is seeking to justify are open to criticism; that is, if they possess some fault that makes them inferior to other acts which are uncriticized and therefore need no justification.

One often has the impression that justification is not the refutation of a criticism but rather the statement of positive reasons in favor of a choice or a decision. These reasons are meant to show that the choice or decision in question is above criticism, and especially above any criticism one might advance against possible alternatives. To allow for these various modalities, we may say that justification consists either in the refutation of specific criticism or in the indication that a proposition is entirely above criticism, or at least that it is less open to criticism than other alternatives.

The criticism of a proposed or already enacted measure, decision, or action is usually directed against its morality, its legality, its regularity (understood in its widest sense), its usefulness, or its opportuneness. In order to criticize, therefore, one must already have certain rules, values, or ends in mind, in whose name the criticism is advanced. Whenever a form of conduct or a project conforms indisputably to the accepted norms, or fully realizes some recognized end, it will thereby escape criticism as well as the correlative process of justification. The same is true of acts that do not have to conform to any norms and do not claim to pursue any determined end. The conduct of a God, for example, defined as an absolutely perfect will, is not subordinated to any norm; the same is true of a sovereign power considered to be *legibus solutus,* or superior to any law. Justification, therefore, can deal only with debatable things, and usually only with things that have been criticized for specific reasons.

An absolute value cannot be criticized, and it needs no justification: It is enough merely to show that by criticizing and justifying an absolute, one would transform it into a relative and subordinate value. But what is true of absolutes is also true of autonomous entities. Just as a sovereign power refuses to bend to laws imposed on it from the outside, so any discipline that claims to be autonomous — especially if its autonomy is claimed with regard to philosophy — refuses to submit its theses and presuppositions to philosophical criticism. Specialists in mathematics, history, or law would be stepping outside their disciplines if they had to concern themselves with philosophical principles and discuss seriously such matters as the existence of mathematical entities, the reality of the past, or the necessity of punishment. Their interest lies in modalities: how to construct mathematical entities, how to understand the past, how to elaborate a penal code.

This conception of philosophical problems as having nothing to do with a specific discipline — a conception well-nigh taken for granted in scientific and technological circles — seems incomprehensible to anyone who adopts the traditionally accepted point of view of Western philosophy. According to this point of view, whatever is not certain must be questioned; but since certainty is the same for all reasonable beings, everyone should arrive at the same certainties — that is to say, at the same principles. It would be inadmissible for science and philosophy to have different starting points; they should both accept the same criteria and the same norms of criticism and of justification. This consequence is a necessary one if all human beings endowed with reason are interchangeable, and if facts and truths announce themselves to all attentive listeners. It matters little what qualifications or special capacities a critic possesses if his objections are admitted by everyone, if the criteria and norms of their validity are universally admitted. But if the criteria and norms in whose name a criticism is made are not unanimously accepted and if their interpretation as well as their application to specific cases can give rise to divergent opinions, then the qualifications and the specific competence of the commentators become an essential element, and sometimes even a pre-requisite for debate.

It is true that the search for universally valid principles which would provide a common context for all criticisms and all justifications has been a millennial aspiration of all philosophy, and especially of all rationalist philosophy. But, in fact, criticism and justification are always found in a historically determined context. For all societies and for all intellects, there exist certain acts, certain agents, certain values and beliefs that at a given moment are approved without reservation and accepted without argument; hence, there is no need to justify them. These acts, these persons, these values, and these beliefs furnish precedents, models, convictions, and norms which in turn permit the elaboration of criteria by which to criticize and to justify attitudes, dispositions, and propositions. But one need not adopt an absolutist point of view at all in order to recognize this fact. Absolutism consists of the assertion that these acts, agents, convictions, and values will serve eternally and universally as models for the establishment of criteria for which they will have to furnish the basis. The classical idea of justification is based on an absolutist vision, since it looks for an absolute, irrefutable, and universally valid foundation.

If we reject the absolutist point of view, and if we accept the precedents and models, then the convictions and values (which indicate what is not subject to criticism or to justification, and when criticism and justification are admissible) are relative to a specific discipline and a specific environment and can vary in time and in space, and criticism and justification no longer appear non-temporal or universally valid. The problem of knowing who is qualified or competent to criticize and to judge, and the problem of determining the modalities of criticism and of justification, then become the essential problems. In this perspective, the juridical model takes on its full import-ance.[9]

The jurists whose role it is to maintain and to regulate a stable social order by reducing the number of conflicts and by searching for peaceful means of settling them, have devised institutions and rules of procedure, according to which, certain people have the power to legislate, others the power to govern, and still others the competence to judge and to elucidate the law. As H. L. A. Hart has convincingly shown, it is the existence of such rules that allows us to distinguish law from ethics.[10] Similarly, it is the presuppositions and the recognized methods of each discipline that allow us to distinguish it from philosophy.

Who has the authority to legislate? Who has the competence to judge? If we admit that every man is the reflection of a divine reason and that the same standards of good and evil are inscribed in the heart and conscience of all men, then the rules granting authority and competence turn out to be of no importance, for everyone will apply the same rules in the same way. This is the kind of optimism that justifies the anarchist doctrines advocating a society without government, legislators, or judges. Those, on the other hand, who insist that only an elite or even only a single individual can know the right rules and the art of applying them, will grant the authority and the competence to legislate and to judge only to an assembly of sages or priests, or else to a philosopher-king. But those who believe that anarchy leads to disorder, and that the utopia of a philosopher-king or of a government of wise men – whether they be priests, mandarins, or technocrats – leads to the despotism of one man or of a supposedly enlightened clique, will look elsewhere for the foundation of the authority of legislators and the competence of judges.

When objective and universally admitted criteria are lacking, we must fall back on personal criteria in order to avoid anarchy, and grant to certain people the authority to legislate and govern, and the competence to judge. These powers, whether they be possessed or conferred, must in turn be justified by the confidence that those who exercise the powers inspire and by the authority that is, in fact, recognized in them. This confidence manifests itself in various ways. It may become explicit at election time, when the people not only choose their representatives but also have a chance to control the manner in which they fulfill their duties. It may be implicit and taken for granted, as long as the people do not revolt against their rulers. Whenever it seems preferable to make certain posts permanent and certain judges irremovable, it is also necessary to allow for mechanisms of control and procedures for appeal.

The legislators, executives, and judges who are elected or appointed by those who possess the confidence of the people ought to exercise their mandates in conformity with the aspirations of the community they represent.

The role of the legislator, like that of the judge — insofar as the latter does not merely apply the law mechanically, but rather interprets and supplements it — does not consist in personal decisions as to what is just without taking into account the aspirations of the public which is the source of their power. These aspirations may be varied and often contradictory, ill-expressed, or even incoherent. That is precisely why the role of the legislator is a creative one.[11] Even while taking into account the wishes of the public, the legislator has to formulate rules and specify criteria that will synthesize those wishes. He will thus have to elaborate a juridical order that will be spontaneously accepted as just by the body of the people. Carl Friedrich rightly insists on this: 'The most just act is the one which is compatible with the greatest number — and the greatest intensity — of values and beliefs.'[12] It goes without saying that the values and the beliefs in question are those of the community in whose name political power is being exercised.

The laws, customs, and regulations of a community are assumed to be just by the mere fact of their existence, and there will be no need to justify them so long as no criticisms arise concerning them. If criticism does arise, the critics will have to show that a given law is unjust, either because it is ineffective, because it does not provide a good means for realizing its purported end, or again because it is incompatible with one of the accepted values of the community. Any criticism that is intended to reform a law must be submitted to the evaluation of the legitimate holders of legislative power, to those who possess the authority to vote and to modify the laws. In most cases their legitimacy is the consequences of their legality, power having been conferred on them in accordance with prevailing legal procedures. It is in their role as the holders of legitimate power that they have the authority to settle controversial problems. But in the long run the prestige of authority can be maintained only if it is exercised in such a way as not to deviate too much from what the people expect. If the authorities ignore too blatantly the aspirations of the people, they run the risk of increasing opposition, which will finally cause the overthrow of the government by elections, coup d'état, or revolution.

This analysis leads to the relativization of the notion of political justice. Politically just laws and regulations are those that are not arbitrary, because they correspond to the beliefs, aspirations, and values of the political community. If the restraints imposed by a legitimate power are in accordance with the wishes of the community, the decisions of that power are politically just, because it is the community's convictions and aspirations which furnish the criteria of political action. But if this reasoning is satisfactory from the

point of view of democratic ideology, is it equally satisfactory from the philosophic point of view?

If we were to equate what is politically just with what is philosophically
just, we would follow Rousseau in a deification of the general will and of
the absolutism that results from it. The adoption of the slogan *vox populi vox
Dei* would transform the general will into an absolute norm that nothing
would oppose, and no criticism could attack. At the same time, by bending to
the beliefs, aspirations, and values of the political community we would
abandon our search for a rational criterion of criticism for those beliefs,
aspirations, and values. Such a renunciation would have serious consequences.
It would mean not only that we considered some obviously imperfect and
variable human decisions as perfect and infallible, but also that we allowed
force and force alone to settle conflicts between political communities whose
aspirations and values turned out to be incompatible. By giving up the search
for criteria and norms which transcend those of politically organized
communities, we would give up the traditional role of ethics, of legal and
political philosophy. Incapable of fortifying justice, the practical philosopher
would by his skepticism limit himself to justifying force. Force would become the criterion and ultimate judge of values and of norms.

Our analysis leaves us floundering between Scylla and Charybdis. Wishing to
avoid the use of force in imposing values claimed as absolutes, we see that
only force seems capable of settling conflicts between relative values. Our
philosophical attempt to substitute reason for violence in practical affairs
seems to lead inevitably to failure.

But must we be cornered between these two equally disastrous solutions?
If we reject an absolutism that claims to be founded on self-evident intuitions, and reject also the anarchic disorder and despotic violence that result
from such claims, must we then cynically admit the ultimate arbitrariness of
all values and all norms? Must we inevitably admit that might is right, and
that force is the ultimate foundation of all systems of justice?

History has repeatedly taught us that it is dangerous to try to impose on
others by means of violence and inquisition the convictions and values
cherished by a philosopher or a prophet as absolutely true and just. Only a
step separates the philosopher-king and the armed prophet from the tyrant,
and a clear conscience makes a tyrant only more tyrannical. But if the philosopher must renounce the use of force in imposing his ideas, is it not his duty
to convince people, and by making them more reasonable make them more
just?

But in what sense can we affirm the reasonableness of values, criteria, and norms? Is it possible in the practical realm to transcend the aspirations of a political community? Do we possess philosophical criteria that will allow us to criticize and justify them? We will try to answer these questions in the last chapter.

NOTES

[1] Ch. Perelman, 'Concerning Justice,' in *The Idea of Justice and the Problem of Argument*, The Humanities Press, New York, 1963, pp. 1–60.

[2] *Ibid.*, pp. 52–53.

[3] *Ibid.*, p. 56.

[4] Cf. my 'L'Idéal de rationalité et la règle de justice,' *Bulletin de la Société Française de Philosophie* 55 (1961), 7–50.

[5] *Traité de l'argumentation* 2 vols., Presses Universitaires de France, Paris, 1958. English translation: *The New Rhetoric. A Treatise on Argumentation*, University of Notre Dame Press, 1969.

[6] Cf. my 'Jugements de valeur, justification et argumentation,' *Revue Internationale de Philosophie* 58 (1961). Reprinted in *Justice et Raison*, Presses Universitaires de Bruxelles, Brussels, 1963, pp. 234–43. English translation: 'Value judgments, justification and argumentation,' *Philosophy Today* 6 (1965), 45–50.

[7] Herbert Feigl, 'De Principiis non Disputandum,' in M. Black (ed.), *Philosophical Analysis*, Cornell University Press, Ithaca, New York, 1950.

[8] David Hume, *A Treatise of Human Nature*, III, pt. I, sec. 1.

[9] Cf. my 'Ce qu'une réflexion sur le droit peut apporter au philosophe, in *Justice et Raison*, pp. 244–55. See also in the present volume Chapter 17.

[10] H. L. A. Hart, *The Concept of Law*, The Clarendon Press, Oxford, 1961, Chap. 5.

[11] Cf. Clarence Morris, 'Law, Justice and the Public's Aspirations,' in Carl J. Friedrich and John Chapman (eds), *Justice, Nomos VI*, Atherton Press, New York, 1963, pp. 170–90.

[12] Carl J. Friedrich, 'Justice, the Political Act,' in *Justice, Nomos VI*, pp. 31ff. See also his *Man and His Government*, McGraw-Hill, New York, 1963, Chap. 17.

CHAPTER SIX

JUSTICE AND REASON

The legislators and judges who employ sanctions and constraints to assure respect for law and the execution of sentences, owe it to themselves to exercise their functions in the spirit in which those functions have been conferred on them. The legislators should elaborate laws that will be just because they are in harmony with the aspirations of the community they represent; the judges should apply the laws in a spirit of equity, in accordance with the traditions of the community whose magistrates they are. But the philosopher's role, unlike the judge's, does not consist of cultivating respect for the established order; nor does the philosopher, like the politician, have to conform to the wishes of an electorate in order to win their votes. If such a thing as a philosopher's mission exists, it is that he be the advocate of reason and the defender of universal values deemed to be valid for all men. In the words of Husserl, 'we philosophers are the civil servants of humanity.'[1]

In an absolutist perspective, be it that of a realist, an idealist, or a voluntarist, the notions of *reason* and of *universal value* present no difficulty. If there exists an absolute reality, an absolute mind, or an absolute will that enlightens our reason and commands our heart and conscience with a necessity and certainty that excludes both doubt and ambiguity, then the philosopher will have but to incorporate the inventory of those truths that impose themselves on all into a treatise of natural or rational law which no normal human being would think of contesting.

But, in reality, things are not so simple. True, we can all invoke certain universal values like truth, justice, and beauty; we all agree that they exist, and none of us would think of rejecting them. But our agreement lasts only so long as we remain on the level of generalities. As soon as we try to pass from this agreement *in abstracto* to some concrete applications, controversy begins. The fact that all admire and respect truth, justice, and beauty does not mean that all agree on what is to be qualified as being true, just, and beautiful.

Similarly, agreement could be reached on general norms presented as absolute and universally valid, such as 'One should do good and avoid evil,' 'No one should be made to suffer unnecessarily,' 'We should always aim for the greatest good of the greatest number,' and 'The principle of our conduct must always be valid as a rule of universal legislation.' Each one of these sentences expresses, in its own way, a universally valid norm. But is it not obvious that innumerable and ever-renewable discussions will arise each time we try to apply these rules to concrete situations? Does everyone always agree on what is good and what is evil, on the necessities that justify suffering, on what constitutes the greatest good for the greatest number, or on the valid rules of universal legislation? Practical reason, which is supposed to guide us in our actions, unfortunately does not lead all its spokesmen to the same decisions. Must we, then, in confronting these facts, unfortunately all too certain, draw the disenchanted conclusion that a general agreement on so-called universal values and norms is a matter only of vacant forms, rules that no one rejects because everyone is free to interpret them in his own fashion? This is, as we have seen, the conclusion of the positivists, who, by denying the use of practical reason, wind up in the position, in this area, of philosophical nihilism.

Lawmaking does not seem to seek universal norms. Yet to the extent that legal activity pretends to a certain rationality, it might be useful to examine the role of judges in applying the law, and that of legislators in formulating it. Such an examination can enlighten us concerning the role of reason in action.

How should one conceive the ideal of a just judge? What is his role in the administration of justice? A just judge is not an objective and disinterested spectator whose judgments are just because in describing faithfully what he sees they conform to some exterior reality. The judge cannot stop at letting the facts speak for themselves: He must take a position with respect to them. The just judge is impartial; having no tie with any of the litigants before him, he applies to all of them the juridical rules prescribed by the legal system. Yet the judge is not a simple spectator, for he has a mission, which is to state the law. Through his decisions he must make the norms of the community respected. The judge's mission may be clarified by considering the task of the arbiter.

When the litigants are not before a judge but before an arbiter freely chosen by them, they wish to be judged not according to norms imposed by law but according to norms shared by them and the arbiter. Who the arbiter will be is an essential consideration when litigants agree to submit to arbitration. It is not enough that the arbiter be impartial with regard to two parties indifferent to him — if that were the case, any unknown person could do the job. His decision must not be arbitrary, as if he were merely tossing a coin. The ideal arbiter will be he whose sense of equity is guided by the same values, the same principles, and the same procedures as the litigants before him. If that is the case, then the desired impartiality is not just an absence of prejudgment; it is an active commitment to common norms and values. Consequently, every time that the values, principles, and procedures of the litigants are different, they will have to have recourse to different arbiters.

To settle a conflict between management and labor, for example, someone will be called in who, while bound to neither of the parties, is nevertheless familiar with the principles according to which they wish him to act. Furthermore, he will also have to aim at contributing to the realization of an end that is common to both parties, such as the prosperity of the economy. If two people in the same branch of industry are in litigation, they will choose as their arbiter a respected member of their profession. The latter will have the confidence of both parties because he is familiar with the usages and customs of the profession and has regard for the honor of all its members. An arbiter chosen for a labor or commercial dispute would not necessarily be qualified to arbitrate a conflict between the United States and Cuba. In this instance a neutral would have to be found who, familiar with the principles of international law and devoted to the cause of peace and the maintenance of international order, would be guided by those ends and those principles in working out a just solution. In the same fashion, a just legislator looks for rules which, not favoring a particular side, seek to realize the values and the ends that correspond to the aspirations of the whole community.

Taking the judge, the arbiter, and the legislator as models, how should we define the role of the philosopher, who has to formulate just laws and judge in an impartial fashion according to those same laws, not for a given society or for a limited social or professional group, but for the whole of humanity? What distinguishes him as such is that he must look for criteria and principles and formulate values and norms that are capable of winning the adherence of all reasonable men.

If the philosopher succeeds in finding certain criteria and principles, certain values and norms which to his knowledge are not rejected by any reasonable being, he will gladly make these the point of departure for universal law-making. Such principles and values possess the advantage of not having to be justified — not because they are self-evident, but simply because they are not contested. Privileged principles of this sort will be most often ambiguous or equivocal and hence open to different interpretations. Then the philosopher's role will be to clarify and specify them, by discarding those formulations and interpretations that in his view could not be defended before a universal audience. He will act according to the same considerations in working out the techniques of proof and interpretation that are indis-

JUSTICE AND REASON   69

pensable for the establishment of facts and the application of laws. In his effort to formulate just rules, he will seek, like the common-law judge, precedents to guide his judgment, while accepting only those motivating principles of decision (*rationes decidendi*) that are capable of becoming the laws of a universal legislation.

The conclusion recalls Kant's categorical imperative. Let us examine Kant's ideas more closely. This will give a more exact idea of how my theses are similar to his, and how they differ from them.

At the beginning of Book I of the *Critique of Practical Reason,* Kant states the following definitions:

Practical principles are propositions which contain a general determination of the will, having under it several practical rules. They are subjective, or *maxims,* when the condition is regarded by the subject as valid only for his own will, but are objective, or practical *laws,* when the condition is recognized as objective, that is valid, for the will of every rational being.[2]

The categorical imperative, which is the fundamental law of pure practical reason, is formulated as follows: 'Act so that the maxim of your will can always at the same time hold good as a principle of universal legislation.'[3]

We may translate Kant's categorical imperative into judicial language as follows: 'You must conduct yourself as if you were a judge whose *ratio decidendi* was to furnish a principle valid for all men.' Apart from my emphasis on precedents, to which the *ratio decidendi* must be related, my formulation seems at first glance to differ very little from Kant's categorical imperative. Yet its actual meaning is different because of the clear distinction that Kant establishes between the subjective and the objective.

In opposing maxims to laws, Kant tells us that the maxim is subjective because the subject considers the condition that determines his will to be valid only for his will. The law, in contrast, is objective if the condition is recognized to be valid for the will of every reasonable man. This dichotomy, with its opposition between the individual and the universal, seems to me to be contradictory to the facts and altogether chimerical. As soon as we formulate principles of action, whatever they may be, those principles eliminate something of the arbitrary from our conduct. Our behavior, being regulated, is no longer entirely dependent on our subjective whims; that same regulation might even become the principle of action of a community, if its members were inclined to accept it. On the other hand, is any one of us the judge in the last instance of principles considered to be objectively valid –

that is, valid for the will of any reasonable man? Can any one of us declare, *a priori*, as a result of his own conviction, that any man who does not consider such principles to be objectively valid is not a reasonable man?

Experience of the relations between rules and the will shows us that there is rarely a purely subjective rule and that we can never be sure of dealing with an objective and universally valid rule. What we actually do find is a progressive universalization of our moral principles, which allows us gradually to elaborate reasonable principles of action for all mankind. The essential function of the philosopher is, perhaps, to formulate such practical principles, while the scholar exercises a similar function in the realms of science or theoretical reason. The specific role of philosophy is, in effect, to propose to humanity objective principles of action that will be valid for the will of all reasonable men. This objectivity will not consist either in conformity to some exterior object or in submission to the commands of any particular authority. It envisages an ideal of universality and constitutes an attempt to formulate norms and values such as could be proposed to every reasonable being. But to *propose* does not mean to *impose*. This distinction must be maintained at all cost. Otherwise we run the risk of a philosopher-king who would use the political authority and power of the State to ensure the supremacy of his convictions, his values, and his norms.

For Kant, a pure, practical law, established *a priori*, can only be formal — that is, its form alone makes it appropriate for universal legislation. My views go beyond that, for I do not believe that a philosopher should limit himself to the formulation of a purely formal law comparable to the Rule of Justice. It goes without saying, however, that the propositions the philosopher might present to all men cannot prevail with a necessity and an evidence which would put them beyond the test of any challenge.

We know that philosophers who invoke universal values such as truth, goodness, justice, and reality as opposed to appearance, are rarely in agreement as to the criteria and the content of those values. Does this mean that their efforts, and the conceptual constructs that result from them, are nothing but illusions, or that individual myths have merely replaced traditional and collective ones? This is what we would have to say, in effect, about metaphysical assertions, if we had to assimilate them to empirically verifiable scientific theories. But assertions that represent the systematic formulation of an ideal cannot be judged the way we judge factual judgments. Their role is not to conform to experience, but to furnish criteria for evaluating and judging experience and, if necessary, for disqualifying certain aspects of it. This is exactly what a philosopher does who opposes reality to appearance through the establishment of a hierarchy of values among the diverse manifestations of reality.

Philosophers who refuse to recognize this primacy of practical reason have often exposed themselves to the criticism of the positivist by presenting ontologies and theories of being as if they were on the same level as scientific theories of reality. But reality as conceived by philosophers is always normative, for it aims at the devaluation of those manifestations of reality that are qualified as appearance or illusion. This is true as well of the positivists, for their conception of reality validates that of the natural sciences and dismisses all other approaches to reality as mythical or illusory. The same normative approach can be seen in the philosophical use of the notion of 'nature,' whether it is a question of following nature or of opposing it. The term 'natural' will be applied to certain characteristics, and it will vary with those who use it. Nature for the Stoics coincides with reason, but for the romantics it coincides with passion and opposes social conventions which are considered to be artificial.

The activity of the philosopher, master of wisdom and guide for actions, consists in taking a stand correlative to his vision of the world; it is based on selection, on choice. The danger of choice is partiality — neglecting opposing points of view and closing one's mind to the ideas of others. The difficulty of the philosopher's task is that, like a just judge, he must arrive at decisions while remaining impartial. That is why the philosopher's rationality will be founded on a rule common to all tribunals worthy of that name: *Audiatur et altera pars*. In philosophy, opposing points of view must be heard, whatever their nature or their source. This is a fundamental principle for all philosophers who do not believe that they can found their conceptions on necessity and self-evidence; for it is only by this principle that they can justify their claim to universality.

Just as a judge, after he has heard the parties, must choose between them, so a philosopher cannot grant the same validity to all opinions. Many of the theses and values submitted to his scrutiny represent interests and aspirations of limited scope and conflict with views of universal import. To the extent that the philosopher bases his decisions on rules that ought to be valid for all mankind, he cannot subscribe to principles and values that cannot be universalized, and which could therefore not be accepted by the universal audience to which he addresses himself.

In questions of justification and of argumentation generally, where one is dealing with reasons for or against a given thesis, both the critics and the defenders of the thesis assume the existence of criteria, values, and norms recognized in advance by those who will have to judge the pertinence of the criticism or the soundness of the defense. A speaker who is trying to convince his audience, that is, the totality of those he is addressing, must, not to be guilty of *petitio principii,* base his argumentation only on principles that his audience admits at the start.

The notions of *discourse, speaker,* and *audience* are technical notions found in classical rhetoric. If we want to give them philosophical significance, we must generalize them. By discourse we mean any form of argumentation that is designed to win the support of others, regardless of length or manner of presentation. A speaker is the one who presents this argumentation. An audience is the totality of those whose adherence he wants to win. It is important to note that a speaker must adapt his discourse to his audience, whatever that audience may be — a crowd gathered in a marketplace, a learned society, a judge hearing a case, an individual deliberating, or finally the universal audience that incarnates what we traditionally call reason.

The appeal to reason has always been characteristic of philosophical discourse. Ever since Plato and Aristotle, but especially since Descartes, reason in philosophy has been defined as that faculty in every normal human being — whether or not it is a reflection of divine reason — that allows him to apprehend evidence, which by imposing itself on the reason of a single person, imposes itself on all beings endowed with reason. This faculty, characteristic of every man and common to all men, was supposed to grasp universally valid truths by means of intuition and is therefore supposed to be the same in every man, independent of his personality and environment, of his education and his past. It is against this supraindividual and antihistorical conception of reason that the romantics and existentialists rebelled.

Admitting the valid aspects of their criticism, I maintain nonetheless that all philosophy is an appeal to reason. But my conception of reason differs from the classical conception. I do not see it as a faculty in contrast to other faculties in man. I conceive of it as a privileged audience, the universal audience. The appeal to reason is but an attempt to convince the members of this audience — whom common sense would define as well-informed and reasonable men — by addressing them. It is to these men, or at least to the universal audience as he imagines it, that the philosopher speaks. It is this audience, with its convictions and its aspirations, that the philosopher wants to convince, starting from postulates and using arguments which he thinks will be acceptable to every one of its members. To achieve his end, the philosopher must use a rational argumentation conforming to Kant's categorical imperative: His postulates and his reasoning must be valid for the whole of the human community.[4]

In elaborating this argumentation, the philosopher is perforce obliged to imagine such an audience as he wants to convince — with the consequent danger that his imagination will not coincide with reality. That is why his theses must be tested by submitting them to the actual approval of the members of that audience. They may challenge the convictions and aspirations that the philosopher attributes to them, or resist the manner in which he selects, formulates, and specifies those convictions to fit the needs of his discourse, or object to the argumentation on which he bases his conclusions. Without this possibility of being always open to dialogue, without a readiness to listen to criticism and to take account of it if he cannot refute it, the philosopher cannot claim to transcend the beliefs, interests, and aspirations of the particular groups like those that make up the audiences addressed, for example, by theologians or politicians.

The characteristic of rational argumentation is the aim to universality — an aim whose realization is never assured. It is useless to try to define rational argumentation the way we define a demonstrative technique, namely, by its conformity to certain prescribed rules. Unlike demonstrative reasoning, arguments are never correct or incorrect; they are either strong or weak, relevant or irrelevant. The strength or weakness is judged according to the Rule of Justice, which requires that essentially similar situations be treated in the same manner. Relevance and irrelevance are to be examined according to the rules and criteria recognized by the various disciplines and their particular methodologies.

Unfortunately, there exists no methodology common to philosophy, which would allow one to decide the value of a philosophical argument. Philosophers usually borrow their postulates and their techniques of reasoning either from the history of philosophy by situating themselves in the continuation of a system, or else from one of the several disciplines from which they draw inspiration. Until he has constructed his own philosophy, a philosopher will possess no satisfying criteria for judging a philosophical argument in coherent fashion. His own philosophy is never complete, but as it moves toward completion it furnishes him with increasingly reliable and more fully elaborate criteria for judging the strength and relevance of his own arguments, as well as the arguments of those who oppose him. Because of the value he places on the coherence of his thought, he will find it more difficult to refute *ad hominem* arguments based on internal criticism of theses whose value he himself explicitly recognizes.[5]

However great the talents and the efforts of the philosopher, he will rarely succeed in convincing all his interlocutors. Often he will try to make up for it by disqualifying the man who doesn't agree with him. Are there men who do not believe in God? 'That is a great question,' says La Bruyère; and he continues: 'If there existed anyone like that, that would only prove the world is not devoid of monsters.'[6] La Bruyère here is using a technique of St Anselm, who treats the unbeliever as senseless.[7] This procedure of disqualification, which allows one simply to dismiss his adversaries, occurs more frequently than one might think. It is, however, not always possible, for sometimes the adversaries make up a considerable part of the universal audience. In that case, one might try to prove that the knowledge of true reality and true values is accessible only to an elite, only to those who through grace have special means of understanding not available to everyone. But to make such a claim consistent with philosophical thinking, the arguments on which it is based must be addressed to the universal audience, including those who will be subsequently disqualified by them.

Philosophical reasoning being what it is, we must resign ourselves to the fact that philosophical controversies are part of the very nature of philosophy. In effect, argumentation — even rational argumentation — is not by nature coercive. There exist no nonformal criteria transcending all philosophy to which rational argumentation has to conform. That is why, ultimately, philosophical reasoning implies the philosopher's freedom of judgment as well as his responsibility. The philosopher who judges commits himself; in judging a philosophy, we are also judging the man who is identified with it.

If this is true, the criteria, the values, and the norms of a philosophy do not constitute absolute and impersonal values and truths. They express the convictions and aspirations of a free but reasonable man, engaged in a creative, personal, and historically situated effort: that of proposing to the universal audience as he sees it, a number of acceptable theses. He will try to justify those theses, or else show that they do not require justification, taking into account any objections or criticisms that seem to him pertinent. Aware of his limitations, the philosopher knows that his efforts will not produce a definitive and complete work. Even if he has succeeded in surmounting difficulties and problems of which he is conscious, he foresees that the future will provide other difficulties and problems for mankind; and he is aware that the advancement of knowledge will shake and modify the convictions which today appear to him acceptable to the universal audience. It will be for others, who will come after him, to continue his efforts for more rationality and justice, and less violence, in the relations of men.

In short, these are our conclusions:

An unjust action is one which does not abide by the Rule of Justice, unless the irregularity is for reasons of equity.

An unjust rule is one that is arbitrary, that deviates from customs and precedents without due reason, or one that creates arbitrary discrimination.

An arbitrary deviation is one that is not justified rationally. The criteria and values invoked can never be deemed rational if they are partial to sectional interests, with no regard for values accepted by the universal audience.

As no criteria are absolute and self-evident, norms and values invoked in justification are never beyond criticism. If one aspires to more justice in human relations, one has to give consideration to every contention that one's reasoning is biased. For lack of impersonal criteria, the philosopher must ultimately rely on philosophical constructs to support his beliefs and ideals. For him such constructs are the last resort in matters of rationality and justice. But he remembers that for philosophy there is no *res judicata.*

NOTES

[1] E. Husserl, *Gesammelte Werke,* Vol. VI, Nijhoff, The Hague, 1954, p. 15.

[2] Immanuel Kant, *Critique of Practical Reason,* trans. Thomas K. Abbott, 6th ed., 1909, p. 105.

[3] *Ibid.,* p. 119.

[4] Cf. my 'Raison éternelle, raison historique,' in *Justice et Raison,* Presses Universitaires de Bruxelles, Brussels, 1963, p. 103.

[5] Cf. H. W. Johnstone, Jr., *Philosophy and Argument,* Pennsylvania State University Press, University Park, Penn., 1959.

[6] La Bruyère, 'Des esprits forts,' Number 15 in *Les Caractères, Oeuvres complètes,* Bibliothèque de la Pleiade, Paris, 1952, p. 473.

[7] St. Anselm, *Proslogium,* Chap. II.

CHAPTER SEVEN

JUSTICE AND REASONING*

I

If I decide to have dinner at the Waldorf Astoria or to go to Italy for a vacation or to ask a certain young lady to marry me and provided that my decision to do one of these things does not involve breaking some prior engagement or obligation, it would not occur to anyone to describe my behavior as unjust. Indeed, before we can say that any decision, choice or judgment is unjust or that any law or regulation is unjust, we must be ready to set out the reasons that would justify this characterization, and the reasons must be acceptable to the audience we are addressing.

It would not do to say that we base our judgment on some feeling or intuition or on some indefinable quality that arouses sympathy or antipathy as can happen when we are in love. The choice of the adjectives 'just' or 'unjust' presupposes that we are appealing to some established criterion, to some common standard, sometimes even to a communal standard, and that we are not simply expressing a prejudice.

Again, it would not be enough to show that the action we are characterizing as unjust caused injury to someone. We would have to go further and show that there was a culpable act, in the sense of a breach of some rule — whether explicit or implicit, whether moral or legal — and that there was a causal link between the culpable act and the injury sustained.

If a man says that he is the victim of an unjust fate, he is implicitly imputing to some divinity or to nature itself certain duties that he alleges have not been observed, such as the duty to treat beings of a certain kind in a more or less equal fashion. In the absence of at least such an implicit imputation, the victim is only expressing the feeling that he does not deserve what has befallen him and that such an outcome would have been unjust if it had been imposed on him by a responsible agent.

The feeling that one is the victim of injustice results initially from making a comparison with other people who, we believe, are in a situation essentially similar to our own and who have been treated more favorably than we have. We resent as unjust every breach of the *rule of justice*, which requires that people be treated equally and that essentially similar situations be passed

76

on in a uniform way.[1] A person who conforms to the requirements of the rule of justice, or who follows an appropriate precedent, *prima facie* escapes a charge of injustice and does not have to justify his conduct. By contrast, the person who is accused of breaking the rule of justice or of departing from an established precedent must come forward with a justification if he does not wish his behavior to be considered unjust. This justification will have to consist of reasons that take into account the existence of certain facts and their classification in terms of the rule that has been broken.

If the challenge is to the facts that are alleged, then we are concerned with truth and not with justice. Insofar as establishing the facts gives rise to problems of proof, then we have to distinguish between the realms of morality and law. In the realm of morality anyone is free to make use of all available modes of proof to establish the relevant facts or to challenge another version of them, but in law a variety of presumptions regulates the question of the burden of proof and in different ways limits the admissibility of different kinds of evidence. So, under the operation of the presumption of innocence, the facts in issue must be proven by the prosecutor or the plaintiff and the defendant can rest on a simple denial. In the same way, proof of facts with respect to which a period of limitation has run out is not permitted and evidence that would constitute a defamation is inadmissible. Certain legal transactions may only be proved by documentary evidence, while evidence that tends to deny paternity, for example, may only be given by certain persons and with certain time limits.

II

For the proved facts to constitute a violation of a moral or legal rule, they must be classified in such a way that they may be subsumed under a rule. What has been proved must be imputable to a person who is responsible for his conduct and who could have refrained from committing the act that is imputed to him. No one can be held accountable for doing something that was impossible to avoid. This special characterization of an act may be effected in two different ways: by treating the new set of facts as being essentially similar to a set of facts earlier passed upon (the technique of precedent) or by subsuming them under a general rule (the application of a general rule to a particular case). The classification thus demands an evaluation of the precedent that is cited or of the chosen rule. Such a judgment may be contested, for it could be argued that the precedent is inapplicable or that the rule that has been applied should have been applied in a way that would lead to an opposite result.

The judge who tries the case may also for a variety of reasons, especially if he is sitting in a court of final review, have recourse to a fiction. The device of a fiction, which is expressly a refusal to apply the rule in certain situations, can realistically be considered as a modification of the field of application of the rule by an official who does not have the legal power to modify it expressly. This, incidentally, explains why the notion of a fiction does not exist in moral judgment, for moral decision making does not incorporate a doctrine of separation of powers.

Another way of contesting a judgment occurs when the facts can be viewed in different lights. To some persons one aspect of the facts may seem to be the most significant, and this leads them to approximate the facts to some precedent other than that urged by their adversary or to adjudicate upon them on the basis of some rule other than the one he has applied. This situation – where two precedents or two rules can be applied to the facts with equal plausibility – can lead to antinomies in a legal system and to a conflict of duties in morality. In such a case it becomes necessary to choose which rule shall be accorded priority to settle the dispute in question. In every case, if the decision is not to appear arbitrary or unjust, the interpretation or application that is adopted must be justified by an argument that need not be closed to arguments to the contrary, but that must appear reasonable in the light of a variety of considerations. These considerations will usually be either teleological or pragmatic; that is to say, they will involve either appeals to the policy of the law or discussion of the practical consequences of deciding one way or the other.

A decision to view the facts of a case in a certain light amounts to fixing more precisely the field of application of a rule or the scope of a precedent. This may stem from certain general doctrines that express themselves in principles such as those relating to the abuse of a right[2] or to public international order[3] and that embody notions about public policy that are taken to limit the scope of a particular rule of law.

We should notice that these problems of interpretation and application arise in morality as well as in law, but the process of reasoning involved can be perceived more clearly in legal decision making. This is because in a legal system the nature of the discussion, the arguments, and the positions taken are controlled by procedural rules that oblige the parties to respond to each other so that adverse arguments and conclusions must be refuted and cannot be simply ignored.

The most interesting moral, political, or philosophical problems concern what is just and unjust in a way that goes beyond questions of facts and classification to challenge the very rules that have allegedly been violated. In these cases, arguments go beyond questions of the application of rules to challenge the very principles designed to guide individuals and societies.

While the critique of rules takes place on a purely juridical plane, we must also take account of institutions that determine the separation, the hierarchy, and the balance of powers, for not everyone is entitled to modify a law that is considered to be unjust. In order to act as a judge or a legislator, one must have authority. Those who do not have that authority can merely attempt to influence the holders of judicial or legislative power. It is only in leaving juridical perspectives — when one considers an action or a rule as morally or politically unjust — that one can disregard all the questions of jurisdiction and authority that are so essential in the law.

III

What are the techniques of argument that make possible the criticism of the rules themselves?

In the first place, criticism could once again rely on the rule of justice. It would then, however, no longer be designed to demonstrate that some legal provisions have been violated, or that the law has not been impartially applied with due respect for the principle of equality before the law. Rather, such criticism would be directed at provisions of the law itself that establish an unjustified discrimination or neglect distinctions that are considered essential. Criticism would be addressed to the absence of a proportional relation between delicts and penalties, or it could underline the unnecessary cruelty and the ineffectiveness of legal provisions that fail to realize the social purposes for which they had been designed.

Besides the criticism that bears on the ineffectiveness of legislative measures and points to importance of legal sociology for the legislator, all other criticism presupposes agreement on value judgments having to do with the necessary or trivial character of distinctions involving the seriousness of offenses and penalties. The weight given to certain distinctions and to the seriousness of some offenses can be assessed in different fashions, bearing in mind the political, social, and economic conditions of a country as well as conflicting ideologies.

In order to say that a rule is unjust, it is not enough to show its injustice in the light of one's own perspective, for it may appear to be just from the viewpoint of the opponent. One must also be in a position to show why one's own perspective is preferable to that of the opponent. To do this it will be necessary to obtain the support of public opinion for one's own thesis and, more specifically, the support of an important part of those who defend the established order. This explains the significance of all ideological discussions, be they of a political, philosophical, or religious nature. By discrediting the opponent's ideology, one weakens the moral authority of those who wield power under it, so that they appear merely as spokesmen for special interests hiding behind a garb of respectability. Challenging the justice of rules frequently leads to the criticism of an ideology and to the challenge of the authority that that ideology seeks to legitimize. Persons in positions of authority may then appear merely as usurpers who, failing everything else, rely on naked coercion to retain power.

When a chain of reasoning leads from premises that are accepted as true to a necessary conclusion, neither authority nor force can be resorted to either in support or in opposition. However, when the premises are contested or furnish only more or less compelling reasons in support of an argument, or when competing arguments can be reasonably entertained and no single conclusion imposes itself, then the role of authority and conceivably even the legitimate use of force become crucial to secure compliance with an existing order.

In that connection we must observe that juridical techniques can attempt to limit the use of force through legislative and judicial institutions, which provide agreed procedures for the elaboration of norms and the settlement of conflicts. If, however, these institutions are to function without too many difficulties so as to bring about agreement in contested matters through their authority, there must be a recognition of the legitimacy of the decision makers. But the role of these authoritative decision makers is not so vital when the question is not one of intervening in contested claims but rather of recognizing the customs and general principles that form part of the culture of a civilization and are, moreover, generally accepted as such.

There is indeed a complementary relationship between the doubtful character of rules and the authority of those providing for their acceptance. The more that rules and decisions are questionable and questioned, the greater must be the authority of those who would like to see them accepted by the community. There is no need for the authorities to secure the acceptance of generally acknowledged moral or equitable principles or to inculcate respect for traditionally recognized values and institutions, principles and values that indeed the authorities could not oppose without seriously jeopardizing their prestige and courting disobedience.

This is the meaning of the opposition sparked in Antigone by Creon's order, which did violence to divine laws traditionally respected. This is the meaning and the weight of the claims of the advocates of natural rights, according to whom the rights of man do not flow from any positive authority, which could then arbitrarily revoke them, but exist independently of positive authority, whose task is to respect and to protect them. Even in this field, however, in which the existence of norms generally accepted in a society or in a civilization does not depend upon the decision of a positive authority, such authorities nevertheless have an undeniable role to play in their interpretation and in determinations of their applicability. These fundamental norms must not be equated with mathematical premises that are self-evident and unequivocal, but rather with 'commonplaces,' that is, vague but commonly accepted principles requiring a clarification of their mode of application, which may in some cases conflict with other principles. It is the role of the authorities to determine the reach of every one of these principles and their hierarchy, so as to solve conflicts arising from their application in concrete cases.

What kind of reasoning could be resorted to in order to justify decisions taken in such cases? It can be described as dialectic reasoning, because resort must be had to arguments of all kinds that cannot be reduced either to deductive schemes or to simple induction. They frequently combine analogical reasoning and pragmatic arguments with appeals to the rule of justice requiring the like treatment of like situations.

A systematic analysis of the relations between the rules of positive law, the general principles of law, the rules of morality, and the techniques resorted to by legislators and judges to back their statements and their decisions, makes it possible to enumerate, classify, and systematize the models of argument to which lawyers resort when it is necessary to reason in terms of justice. If, then, in the light of the outcome of such investigations, moral philosophers were to reflect on the task expected of them, they would realize that it must not be limited to the establishment of general principles, which lend themselves to a multitude of interpretations. They cannot avoid the study of concrete situations or disregard techniques of argumentation that must necessarily be resorted to if practical reason is to succeed in guiding men of goodwill and in limiting to some degree unbridled reliance on arbitrariness and violence.

NOTES

* Reprinted by permission of New York University Press from *Law, Reason and Justice: Essays in Legal Philosophy*, edited by Graham Hughes, © 1969 by New York University.
[1] See Perelman, *The Idea of Justice and the Problem of Argument* (1963), pp. 79–87; Perelman, *Justice* (1967), Chap. 2. (Chapter 3 of the present volume.)
[2] For example, a person may have a general right to hunt on his rural property even if the noise of the guns should cause some annoyance to his neighbors. However, if the court takes the view that the predominant purpose of the hunting was to interfere with the neighbor's quiet enjoyment of his property and was actuated by malice, it may award damages. See the English case of *Hollywood Silver Fox Farm v. Emmett* [1936] 2 K.B. 468.
[3] The operation of this principle can be illustrated from the laws about bigamy. If a Moroccan, already polygamously married, should come to France, the French criminal law does not pretend to extend its jurisdiction so as to prosecute him. However, if a Moroccan, not yet polygamously married, should come to France, the French civil authorities will not recognize the law of his domicile to the extent of officiating at a polygamous ceremony.

CHAPTER EIGHT

EQUALITY AND JUSTICE*

Although the concept of justice seems to be one of the most controversial, since conflicting parties usually claim that their cause alone is just, the concept of equality is capable of a formal and uncontroversial definition. It is tempting to bring the two concepts together and elucidate one by means of the other. Certain popularisers of socialism, such as Bernard Shaw, whose lectures on equality were published in 1971,[1] have indeed attempted this. There he treats equality as an ideal to be brought about by the socialist revolution. On page 62 we read 'Through revolutions we may get the perfect State, the criterion of perfection being equality'. In a lecture given in 1884 with the title 'The Socialist Movement is only the assertion of our last honesty', he says that 'honesty' means that 'when one man has worked an hour for another, that other shall work not less than one hour for him (p.1)'. Finally, in a lecture entitled 'Equality,' he said 'Ask the first comer what Socialism is, he will tell you that it is a state of society in which the entire income of the country is divided between all the people in exactly equal shares, without regard to their industry, their character, or any other consideration except the consideration that they are living human beings (p.155)'.

These few examples, which identify equal and just treatment, show at once how the idea of equality is transformed when it is related to justice.

The notion of equality as formally defined in arithmetic enables us to demonstrate that $2 + 2 = 4$ but that $2 + 2 \neq 5$. We can show that we have here two true propositions in which there is no question of preferring equality or inequality. Here it is enough to note that if the sum of two numbers is equal to a third, it is not equal to any number different from the latter. There is no question in this context of bringing about an equality which does not already exist.

The kind of equality which, since Aristotle, has been related to the notion of justice is that of equality of treatment. It is a matter, as Bernard Shaw puts it, of treating living human beings equally.

In the same spirit, but less dogmatically, I. Berlin writes in his paper 'Equality',[2] 'Equality needs no reasons; only inequality does'. Equality is not to be justified, for it is presumed just; inequality, on the other hand, if not justified, will appear arbitrary and so unjust. In exactly the same spirit John

Rawls, in his theory of justice writes 'All social values — liberty and opportunity, income and wealth, and the bases of self-respect — are to be distributed equally unless unequal distribution of any, or all, of these values is to everyone's advantage.'[3]

It is admitted, in these two cases, that reasons may justify unequal treatment, and consequently that equality is not a value which has to be satisfied in every case.

In my first work on justice I distinguished six formulae of distributive justice: To each the same thing; to each according to his merit; according his work; according to his needs; according to his rank; according to what the law sanctions.[4] In seeking the element common to these I was able to isolate a formal rule of justice defined as a principle of acting in accordance with which beings of the same essential type (i.e. which are essentially similar) should be treated in the same way.[5] These different formulae of distributive justice indicate severally the criteria determining those differences which are relevant or irrelevant to the essential similarity of beings and situations. The merit of the final formula, treating each according to the law, lies in its legal imposition of the relevant criteria, for it obliges us to treat as equals all those among whom the law fails to distinguish: *in paribus causis, paria jura*.

Some claim that the rule of formal justice is no more than a law of logic, requiring equal treatment for all those to whom the same rule applies. But there are two objections to this view.

The first is that a law of logic being necessarily valid, admits of no exceptions. But we may, in the name of equity, reject formal justice. Thus if I became a supreme legislator in Saudi Arabia, where for more than a thousand years thieves have had their left hands cut off in accordance with the Koran, I would oppose the administration of this penalty for theft. In modifying this rule I would have produced a break between the past and the future, and so a different treatment for essentially similar cases. It is true that the rule of law makes jurists conservative, for it requires them to look for precedents, and in the absence of good reasons for not doing so, to treat present cases in the same way as essentially similar cases in the past. But every jurist will admit that one can discount precedent for good reasons.

The second objection to the assimilation of a rule of formal justice to a formal law, is that it is a rule of *justice*, and is only applicable when considerations of justice can be invoked. If the farmer's wife chooses a single hen out of a hundred to be killed and served for Sunday lunch, she is under no obligation to treat the remaining 99 which are indistinguishable from it in the same way. Considerations of justice do not enter into her dealings with the chickens, and she is not obliged to treat them equally.

The Belgian Constitution asserts, in article 6, that 'All Belgians are equal before the law', and thus rejects those privileges concerning taxes, access to public employment and the law which the 'Ancien Régime' granted to the nobility and clergy. Yet for nearly a century women were denied access to the bench, and to the bar, and for more than a century were denied the right to vote, despite the existence of this article. Thus we see that the general requirement of equality never consists of anything but a rejection of *certain* specific inequalities, and not of all conceivable inequalities.

Some constitutions, such as that of Austria in 1934, go further in prescribing not only to judges that they treat similarly those situations where the legislator makes no distinction; but also forbid the introduction of arbitrary distinctions into the law themselves, which are not justified by objective reasons. Again, 'numerous decisions of the Constitutional Tribunal of the Federal Republic of Germany forbid legislators from treating differently cases which are essentially similar. A difference is treated as arbitrary when there is no clear or good reason, conforming to the nature of things or one that is reasonable, relevant or at least not unreasonable, to support it'.[6] But what constitutes a good reason justifying an inequality of treatment varies with the society and the age. Though it seemed natural to the Supreme Court of Belgium, in its verdict of 11 November 1889, to exclude women from the bar on the grounds that legislators 'regarded it as an axiom too obvious to require stating that the administration of justice was reserved for men', such an argument would appear to us today not merely unacceptable, but even completely unreasonable. It is interesting to note in the legislation and jurisprudence of different legal systems the ways in which the underlying reasons for justifying discrimination have evolved. Since such developments are linked to those of ideologies, these modes of supporting inequalities will throw light on the development of attitudes of mind in any given society.

One will see, in these cases, which values are regarded as prior to equality of treatment, conceived as a form of justice. N. Rescher in his book *Distributive Justice* has examined in this way the conflicts that can arise between justice and utilitarianism.

It is plain that on grounds of justice, or equal treatment, we will prefer a distribution of 2,2,2 to one of 3,3,0 when sharing 6 units of positive value among three persons, A,B,C among whom there is no essential difference. It is plain that on utilitarian grounds we will prefer a distribution of 3,3,3 to a distribution of 2,2,2. But in terms of what criterion should we prefer a distribution 3,3,x to 2,2,2?

Rescher gives an example where justice – equality of treatment – may be abandoned for utilitarian reasons rather than on the grounds of equity.

But the most delicate problems arise in connection with the category which calls for equality of treatment. Traditionally, in our individualistic civilisation, equality of treatment concerns human beings. But this point of view is quite special. Can one not conceive an equality of treatment required for families, cities, nations, races, states, universities, professions, social classes etc?

In the USA admission to some universities is determined not just by selecting the best candidates, which would eliminate nearly all black students, but by allocating a quota of places to the black students, even if by so doing some more deserving white students are rejected. Again, if one wants to treat two communities equally (such as the Flemish and French speaking communities in Belgium) it will turn out necessarily that individuals on one side will be favoured over the other. In a federal system such as the USA's the same number of senators is elected by each state whether they have only a hundred thousand inhabitants or more than twenty million. But this inequality is compensated for by electing representatives in proportion to their population. It can be seen in this example how different applications of the principle of equality can be in conflict and reconciled by means of every sort of compromise.

But the real difficulty in this issue results from the opposition between two concepts of equality, equality of treatment and equality of situations.

Equality, as conceived by the French Revolution and in the 19th century, was equality of treatment and manifested in the abolition of privilege; whence the principle, generally accepted in liberal democracies, of equality before the law. But today the idea which is increasingly accepted is that of reducing inequalities between members of a society, or between nations and states whose development is backward, by giving privileges to those in the inferior position. Facilities, grants, and special aid are given to those who are disadvantaged either by nature or by society. In commercial treaties between states, such privileges are given to those whose economies are precarious or underdeveloped. What concerns people today is less justice conceived as equality of treatment than justice conceived as reducing glaring inequalities in the situations.

Even so quick an examination of the conditions in which equality as a value is applied shows how incongruous it is to consider social equality as a mark of perfection. In so doing one is concealing not only the existence of other values, such as efficiency or social utility, but also the fact that equality can be applied not only to individuals but to groups of every kind, and that equality of treatment can be opposed by equality of situations.

It is for these reasons not satisfactory to identify equality with justice in the absence of good reasons justifying inequality. For it is first necessary to make clear which sort of equality is in question.

We have seen that the equal treatment of essentially similar situations, supporting considerations of precedent, makes jurists conservative, if one so defines those for whom only change needs to be justified, while the status quo has no need of justification. No reasonable person questions rules and accepted values without good reasons; and one of these is an inadmissible disparity of circumstances.

The conclusion which emerges from this analysis is that one has only to examine the ways in which various social values are applied in practice through morality, law or religion, to uncover an irreducible plurality of viewpoints and of goals. Such a plurality does not allow us to aim at a unique truth which applies at all times to everyone, but instead only at a complex account which may help us to understand that plurality of cultures, ideologies, religions and philosophies. This plurality implies a diversified approach to the idea of equality as an approach to just action or the ideal vision of a just society.

NOTES

* Presented at the Stirling Conference of the Scottish Philosophical Club in September 1975. French original text published in *Egalité V*, Bruylant, Brussels, 1978, pp. 324–330.
[1] G. B. Shaw, *Road to Equality*. Ten unpublished Lectures and Essays 1887–1914. Beacon Press, 1971.
[2] I. Berlin, 'Equality,' *Proceedings of the Aristotelian Society* 56 (1956), p. 305.
[3] Harvard University Press, 1971, p. 62.
[4] See in the present volume Chapter 1, pp. 2–6.
[5] *Ibid.*, p. 11.
[6] Cf. Werner Bockenförde, *Der Allgemeine Gleichheitssatz und die Aufgabe des Richters*, De Gruyter, Berlin, 1957, pp. 62–63; see my article 'Egalité et valeurs', in *Egalité I*, Bruylant, Brussels, 1971, p. 323.

CHAPTER NINE

JUSTICE RE-EXAMINED*

Philosophical analysis of the notion of justice must begin with the question: 'Is justice the sole virtue concerning our relations with others or is it merely one of the virtues, in competition with others, such as equity, mercy and generosity?' Plato chose the first of these alternatives in his works, while Aristotle has shown a distinct preference for the second. The choice made by each of them is by no means arbitrary, since it is explained by the difference between their philosophies.

For Plato, the philosopher with his skill in dialectics can attain knowledge of the realm of ideas, and especially of the idea of justice. Accepting the existence of a realm, an order universal, harmonious and just, the wise man will draw upon this to present the ideal of a just political community for which he will formulate just laws which in his capacity as judge he will be able to apply in an unequivocal way, without giving rise to criticism or controversy. From this standpoint, nothing is more justified than the maxim *pereat mundus, fiat justitia,* that justice be done, though the world perishes; no consequence, whatever it may be, may hold us back from carrying out the requirements of justice.

Almost thirty years ago, at an International Philosophical Conference in Amsterdam, a Calvinist judge confided to me that he conceived his role as searching out in every case the just solution as known to God. In this he expressed the Christian, Augustinian, version of Platonism: the world of ideas being located in the divine understanding, man will strive to find what is just in the eyes of God. This end being achieved, the man who allows himself to be guided by God in his judgments and decisions can have no good reason for departing from the just solution. The person who knows the absolutely just answer to every human problem, wholly in accordance with truth, ought not under any circumstances to deviate from it. Each and every concession will be unworthy of an upright judge who will not allow himself to be corrupted, intimidated, or even moved by pity: *dura lex, sed lex.*

Against this absolutist view of justice, inspired on the one hand by the spirit of mathematics, and by a religious ideal on the other, Aristotle has set the ideal of practical wisdom φρόνησις, which is derived from long experience of how human institutions function. When called upon to judge, to reach a deliberate decision, the wise man is unable to find in matters of human endeavour the unique solution based on intuition or incontestable proof. Thus, in the domain of practical reason, he has no recourse beyond dialectical arguments which at best merely produce a reasonable solution. The norm on which the judge will draw is neither divine, nor absolute since it is the man of practical wisdom who will be his only model. The rule formulated by the human legislator, even if it is just, is merely adapted to habitual situations. When faced with the situation which is out of the ordinary and which has not been foreseen by the legislator, the judge will have to seek, on the basis of equity, a solution which is more just than that of the law, and better adapted to the problem. When it is required, Aristotle opposes to justice conceived as conformity to the law a superior justice based on equity.

Human justice, consequently imperfect, cannot impose unconditional submission: it will be normal to temper its excesses by recourse to equity, charity, and generosity.

In the debate between Plato and Aristotle, I have no hesitation in placing myself on the side of Aristotle. For if I had the temerity thirty years ago to write that philosophy is the systematic study of confused ideas,[1] it is the idea of justice which seems to illustrate this thesis best.

At first glance, it seems that a decision will be just if it conforms to a rule of formal justice requiring the same treatment for essentially similar cases. But this rule requires to be refined and even amended on important points.

We can begin by recognising, with Norman C. Gillespie,[2] that it is not always unjust to treat essentially similar cases differently. For instance, if I give £1 to a passing beggar and an hour later give merely a quarter of this sum to a second beggar, I have not acted unjustly since the rule of justice does not transform at a stroke an act which I am free to do or omit into an obligatory one. If justice requires me to act in a determinate way in a certain situation, I must act in the same way in an essentially similar situation. But if I am left completely free to act as I wish in the first situation, I retain this freedom of action in an essentially similar situation. My way of acting has not then set a precedent to which I will be held to be bound in virtue of the rule of formal justice.

I would add however that in my view there are few situations in which the act one was free to do or omit does not tend to become an obligatory act, in so far as it generates an expectation in the mind of the beneficiary. One knows how quickly a voluntary bonus awarded to an employee at the end of the year by his employer, is transformed into an obligation, a custom, from which it is difficult to disengage onself.

We should also note that conforming to a rule or precedent will be considered just only if the rule or precedent is itself accepted. One would never say that the doctor carrying out the selections at Auschwitz and scrupulously following the rule directing him to send Jewish children under fourteen years of age to the gas chamber, had acted in a just manner by punctually and zealously carrying out a criminal order or precedent.

It is necessary then, for an act to be just in virtue of the rule of formal justice, not only that the new case be essentially similar to the previous case, but also that the decision which furnished the precedent be equally accepted. But that these two conditions have been met is rarely beyond challenge.

When are two situations essentially similar? In other words, when is one to say that what differentiates the two situations is negligible?

In 1944, in my first work on justice, I listed six principles of justice which present different criteria on this point. These were:

1. To each the same thing.
2. To each according to his merits.
3. To each according to his works.
4. To each according to his needs.
5. To each according to his rank.
6. To each according to his legal entitlement (*cuique suum*).

The choice of one or other of these principles will make situations which appear essentially similar according to one principle appear different according to others. Do differences of sex, age, or race need to be taken into account when it is a matter of working out the just wage? Is it necessary or not to take family responsibilities into account? Or productivity? One sees immediately that controversies can rage on such issues, and that even if the solution adopted in a given context is the one we prefer, and seems reasonable, it is not necessarily the unique solution, imposing itself as just in a way beyond dispute.

The second condition, determining the rule to which it is just to conform, or the recognised precedent, poses a problem which cannot be solved in any way that is absolute.

So, when is a rule just or a precedent recognised? One could reply that this is the case when the rule or the precedent is justified or does not stand in need of justification. The latter case arises when the one who sets the rule or precedent is not open to criticism. When is the matter of laying down rule or an act open to criticism? When the rule or act is in opposition to a recognised norm or value.

From this standpoint, Patrick Day has shown in a stimulating paper entitled 'Presumptions'[3] that presumptions exist with regard to some principles, which absolve those who adhere to them from having to present any justification, but which demand a justification from those who go against them. What is characteristic is that these principles do not amount to universally valid truths, but represent different attitudes which the author describes as conservative, liberal, or socialist.

The conservative presumption works in favour of what exists: only change, always, everywhere and in anything, requires justification.[4] The liberal presumption demands the justification of every restriction of liberty: 'leaving people to themselves is always better, *ceteris paribus,* than controlling them' (J. S. Mill, 'On Liberty', ch. V; in *Utilitarianism,* (ed.) M. Warnock, Collins, 1964, p. 228). The socialist presumption on the other hand demands that inequalities be justified. As Isaiah Berlin affirms, 'equality needs no reasons, only inequality does'.[5]

In this way, adherence to particular principles or values will result in dispensing with justification for any rule or action which conforms to them: this is an approach of the same sort as that of *consensus,* which supplies jurists with a criterion frequently employed as a basis for justice. Three variants of this criterion can be distinguished, in terms of whether it is a matter of personal and express consent, or a collective and implicit consensus, or finally an indirect consent, not to the rule, but to the authority which proclaims it.

(a) The first form of *consensus,* giving rise to rights and obligations which it is just to recognise, is that which is found in one or several wills expressed in a promise or agreement. It is just to respect every arrangement which stems from a promise, contract, or pact. Well known legal maxims follow from this: *volenti, non fit injuria,* no injustice is done to him who consents, and *pacta sunt servanda,* contractual agreements are to be respected.

(b) the communal, implicit form of *consensus* is to be found in custom which, because it has been followed by the members of a community for a long time, seems to express a consensus to which it is just to conform.

(c) the final form of *consensus* is indirect: the question of agreement upon a rule or precedent considered as just does not enter into it, rather it is a matter of a trust placed in an authority which is accepted by the members of a community, whose decisions are binding and to which it will accordingly be just to conform. This will be a matter of a religious authority such as God or his spokesmen for a religious community, or of a political authority such as a monarch, parliament or judge, whose powers will be admitted within the framework of an accepted ideology in the political community.

The study of legal institutions shows how the various bases of *consensus* can be contested. Some have sought to show in certain cases that the accepted commitment does not amount to a freely given consent, since it was obtained under constraint or was given as a result of false information. Or that the custom is unclear, or has been overtaken by a legal ruling which runs contrary to it. Or that the religion or ideology, treated as accepted, is in fact contested or has been perverted in application to particular situations. Or that the justice of a rule or decision, even if it is presumed just when emanating from a recognised authority, may be contested when the rule or decision is in flagrant conflict with a principle which expresses established values.

In such a debate where it is normal for divergent points of view to be manifest, it is rare for unanimous agreement to be reached. Thus, the arguments put forward on one side or the other are more or less strong, more or less pertinent, and although this does not mean that they all have the same value, they are never compelling. In the practical domain where it is a matter of morals, law or politics, one has recourse to arguments which are dialectical in the sense of Aristotle who contrasted them with analytical arguments. Such arguments allow certain decisions to be dismissed as unreasonable, but they almost never amount to demonstrating, in a way which is beyond dispute, that the envisaged solution is the only reasonable one.

It is important to notice here that the category of the *reasonable* which plays an essential part in argument, in what I have called the *new rhetoric,* differs from the *rational.* While the rational refers, in a way which varies according to individual writers, to eternal immutable truths, to a law or morality of universal validity, to compelling proofs, to the appeal for system, to the use of the best means to a given end, the reasonable is a more flexible notion with a content influenced by the history, traditions, and culture of a community. What is considered reasonable in one society, at one period, may not be regarded as such at another period or in another society.

An example taken from the law of Belgium illustrate this. On 11th November, 1889, the Belgian Supreme Court refused a Belgian woman access to the bar although she was a doctor of laws who fulfilled all the requirements for admission set out in the law. While article 6 of the Belgian Constitution proclaims the equality of Belgians before the law, the Supreme Court nonetheless ruled that if the legislator had no explicitly excluded women from the bar, it was 'an axiom too evident to require legal pronouncement that the administration of law was reserved for men'. What was evident and therefore reasonable in those days, can appear unreasonable and even ridiculous today. I might also add in this connection, that it was not until 1922 that a law admitted women to the bar in Belgium, and it was not until after the last war that they were admitted to the bench.

For all that the notion of the unreasonable is a fluid changing notion, it sets, in every state based on law, a limit to the exercise of legally recognised discretionary power. Wherever it applies, such a power confers the right to choose among the different options which are open, but only on condition that the choice is not unreasonable, because otherwise it will be considered contrary to law, whatever the precise grounds may be which result in this choice being refused legal recognition.[6]

Moreover, the idea that there are principles of justice analogous to principles of mathematics, which will always provide just solutions when correctly applied, whatever the circumstances may be, proves itself to be contrary to reality.

Legal history shows how long-standing precedents lead, in special situations or changing conditions, to decisions contrary to equity. To obviate what seems unacceptable several solutions have been adopted: sometimes distinctions have been introduced into the *ratio decidendi,* into the rule which furnishes the decision; sometimes there has been recourse to a fiction, that is to say a false construction of facts; sometimes the rule on which the decision is based has been reinterpreted; and sometimes there has been recourse to a 'court of equity' in which an injunction is demanded against the carrying out of an iniquitous measure. Finally, the most radical solution is recourse to the legislator who will replace by statute the rule which was followed previously. The change introduced in this way prevents the application of the rule of formal justice requiring the same treatment for essentially similar cases: the same situations will in future no longer be treated as in the past; what had been considered to be just will cease to be so after the adoption of the new law.

If jurists have been accused of being conservative, it is because they refuse to accept any unjustified change in the law: the stability of rules and decisions stemming from them contributes indeed to important values such as legal security, the predictability and reliability of the law. But if they think that every arbitrary, unjustified change in the law is unjust and partial, they nonetheless admit that there can be good reasons for modifying a previous rule, though it is very rare for these reasons to be recognised by everyone as having most weight. That is why some recognized procedure such as a majority vote in competent instances will be indispensable to decide the lawful character of the change, to which it will be just to conform in future.

This rapid examination of problems involved in the pursuit of justice in human institutions, shows what is imperfect and open to question in the solutions adopted. The administration of justice, a human and imperfect affair, will never be the sort of absolute and divine justice before which all objections must evaporate. This is why it is very necessary to recognise along-side justice in the functioning of human societies, a place for other virtues such as equity, mercy, and generosity.

NOTES

* *Austin Lecture* delivered at Durham on March 30, 1979. First published in *Archiv für Rechts- und sozialphilosophie*, Bd LXVI/1, 1980.
[1] See Ch. Perelman, 'Concerning Justice' (1945) in *The Idea of Justice and the Problem of Argument*, p. 4.
[2] Norman C. Gillespie, 'On treating like cases differently, *Philosophical Quarterly* 25 (1975), 151–158.
[3] *Actes du XIVe Congrès International de Philosophie*, Herder, Vienna, 1970, Vol. V, pp. 137–143.
[4] *Ibid.*, p. 139, following B. Wootton, *Social Foundations of Wage Policy*, London, 1958, p. 162.
[5] I. Berlin, 'Equality', *Proceedings of the Aristotelian Society* 56 (1955–56), p. 305.
[6] See Ch. Perelman, 'Le raisonnable et le déraisonnable en droit', *Archives de Philo-sophie du Droit* 23 (1978), 35–42.

CHAPTER TEN

THE USE AND ABUSE OF CONFUSED NOTIONS*

The title of this chapter might seem, to one raised in the rationalist tradition of the West, not only paradoxical, but even provocative. Can there be a defensible use of confused notions? Is not the act of utilising a confused notion, without attempting to make it more precise, to clarify it, always an abuse to be condemned?

Allow me to illustrate this normal reaction with an anecdote which you will excuse me for drawing from my own past.

In 1962, before receiving the Prix Francqui from the King of Belgium for my work on argumentation and rhetoric, I delivered a short speech in which I expressed my gratitude to those who had contributed to my intellectual formation. On this occasion, I thanked my mentor Eugène Dupréel for having made me understand the importance of confused notions. This statement so intrigued the King that, at the reception following the ceremony, the first thing he asked me was to explain the importance of confused ideas. After hearing my explanation, he told me that he was going to recommend to all his ministers that they read my 'new rhetoric.' The reaction of King Baudoin prompted me to speak to you about the subject which I am treating here tonight.

The philosophical tradition of the West, at least since the seventeenth century, has been profoundly influenced by the development of mathematical physics and the natural sciences, both based on experimentation, measurement, weight, and calculation. Everything that was not reducible to a quantifiable value was, by that very fact, considered to be vague and confused, something foreign to clear and distinct knowledge.

For the rationalists of the seventeenth century, God was a perfect Being, hence rational, and the world, that divine creation or emanation, could only be rational. The philosophy of Spinoza was inspired by this ideal of universal rationality. Leibniz is the author of the formula 'dum Deus calculat, fit mundus' (the world is accomplished according to divine calculations). If God is a mathematician and the world conforms to a plan, mathematical in character, the role of men of science is to discover the divine equations according to which the laws of nature are formulated. The role of philosophers is to underscore the confused and uncertain character of all those opinions and ideas which cannot be quantified. Disagreements among men result from the fact that, instead of being guided by the clear and distinct ideas of their reason, a faculty common to all men, an imperfect reflection of divine reason, they are carried away by their passions and their interests, their prejudices and their imagination.

We can see, from this perspective, that all confused ideas are condemned, that there is always reason to dissipate confusion, to replace confused notions with clear ideas, the only usable ones in science and rationalist philosophy.

The logical positivism of the twentieth century has again taken up the demands of rationalism for clarity and rigor, but by expressing them not in terms of reason and clear, distinct ideas, but rather in terms of language: scientific philosophy must accomplish the goal of constructing an ideal language.[1] This ideal language, in order to be an instrument of *effective* communication, giving rise to no misunderstanding, no disagreement, must conform to certain laws for the construction of a formal language: one must enumerate all the basic symbols of the language, indicate the way of combining these basic symbols in order to obtain well-formulated statements, designate from among these formulae the axioms of the system (the expressions that one considers valid from the outset) and, finally, indicate the rules of inference which permit one, on the basis of these axioms, to prove the theorems.[2]

The drawback to this attempt to reduce natural language to a perfect language is the assumption that natural language has only one usage, that of an instrument of perfect communication, giving rise to no ambiguity, to no controversy. But, can we say that glass constitutes a perfect material because it is transparent and cannot be deformed. Who would want to make shirts and pants from this material? Let us not forget, in effect, that natural language has more than one use and that certain of these usages force us to depart from the conditions that logicians and mathematicians impose on an artificial language such as formal logic.[3]

In order to demonstrate this, let us consider a certain number of concrete situations where, in order to achieve different objectives, one is obliged to introduce ambiguities and confusion, or to use confused notions, or to attempt to specify a confused notion in a determined context, which would assign a new use to it and thereby increase the confusion with regard to that notion as it is perceived outside the specific context in which it was clarified.

Let us begin with the example of Holy Scripture, the Bible and the Gospels. For all believers, these texts which reveal the word of God can contain no error: for the Jewish people, the Bible contains, in addition, legislation the just nature of which cannot be contested. However, whoever wishes to safeguard one or the other of the two values, truth and justice, will sometimes be obliged to reinterpret the texts and accept, together with the literal or habitual interpretation, another more satisfying interpretation.

In this connection, let us consider one of Pascal's 'pensées': 'Quand la parole de Dieu, qui est véritable, est fausse littéralement, elle est vraie spirit-uellement.'[4] (When the word of God, which is true, is literally false, it is spiritually true.)

The necessity of recourse to a metaphorical interpretation in order to safe-guard the truth of the text, prompts us to search for a new meaning, perhaps debatable, which can only harm the clarity and unequivocalness of the text. In an analogous spirit, the talmudists, for whom the Bible furnishes the immutable law of the Hebrew people, were forced to interpret it in such a way that the judicial rule drawn from it be acceptable to the society to which it was supposed to apply. They were thus led to distinguish from the literal interpretation (the 'pshat'), an interpretation indispensable to their judicial construction (the 'drash').

Let us pass from the particular example of the sacred texts to examples where it is a question of human communication. When one finds oneself confronted with the affirmation of another person, whom one supposes to be saying nothing obviously absurd or devoid of all interest, one seeks to reinterpret the text which, at first glance, might seem contradictory or tautological.

Confronted with the famous fragment of Heraclitus, 'We enter and we do not enter twice in the same river,' one attempts to understand the text in such a way as to avoid a contradiction: one assigns two different meanings to the expression 'the same river': we enter the same river twice if that river is identified by its banks: but we never enter twice in the same river if the river is identified by the waters which flow in it.

In the same way when one says 'Business is business,' 'war is war,' 'children are children,' one does not see in these expressions an application of the prin-ciple of identity (A is A) but, in order for these affirmations to become mean-ingful, one gives to the same words, stated twice, different meanings, which will make the expression ambiguous and contradictory.

We can see, from these few examples, that, when it is a question of expres-sions formulated in a natural language, the necessity for unequivocalness can disappear before necessities considered to have priority.

This is often the case with judicial texts: the one who must justify, in law, an acceptable solution, is led, upon occasion, to deviate from the letter of the law in order to furnish another interpretation which conforms more to the spirit.

In Belgium, a ruling forbade agreements between companies attempting to cause the rise in price of a product. Is this ruling applicable if the companies form an agreement in order to avoid the lowering of prices following the lowering of the price of raw materials? If the judge is of this opinion, the expression 'rise in price' will acquire a new meaning which it did not have in ordinary usage, a meaning which can only render the expression more confused.

Article 4 of the Napoleonic Code obliges the judge to adjudicate: 'The judge who refuses to adjudicate, under pretext of the silence, the obscurity or the insufficiency of the law, can be prosecuted as guilty of denial of justice.'

The judge who must pronounce the law, each time that he is competent to render a decision, cannot declare, like the mathematician, that a problem is irresolvable: He must both decide and justify his decision. He is granted, by this very fact, the power to interpret the text in such a way as to eliminate obscuritites, antinomies and gaps in the law. If, while exercising this power, he happens to clarify the text by deciding for one of the possible inter- pretations, he can also, in order to fill a gap or eliminate an antimony, provide from a text an interpretation contrary to habitual usage. Such an act will increase the confusion of a notion, by adding to it an unexpected inter- pretation, like that of 'rise in price.'

If the reinterpretation of a text can increase the confusion of a term which figures therein, there are cases where the legislator, unable to work out an unambiguous text, introduces a confused notion, such as equity or moral standards, by charging the judge to decide, in each concrete case, what does or does not conform to equity or to moral standards. Recourse to a vague or confused notion increases, in itself, the power of interpretation of the one who must apply it. Inversely, by specifying a notion, perferably owing to indications of a quantitative nature, we decrease the evaluative power of the judge. Thus when the very delicate problem of drunk driving, a principal cause of traffic accidents, arose, we began by taking this notion from the law concerning public drunkenness, but very quickly it was realized that it was necessary to decrease the judge's power of evaluation. He was too indulgent in the eyes of the legislator, who replaced the notion of drunkenness with a specific degree of intoxication, a degree of alcohol in the blood, which can be detected with precision thanks to chemical techniques.

The recourse to confused notions which is sometimes indispensable in internal law proves to be completely inevitable in public international law when the confusion of notions is an indispensable condition for achieving agreement on a text between States having different, if not incompatible, ideologies. In 1948, how could the agreement on the text of the Universal Declaration of the Rights of Man have been achieved? Jacques Maritain, in his introduction to the text of the declaration published by UNESCO, pointed out that those involved were able to formulate rules which, though justified differently by each one, are to all parties analogically common principles of action.[5] In other words, the signers agreed on texts containing confused notions, susceptible to varied interpretations, each one reserving to himself the right to interpret these notions in his own way. But when a tribunal such as the European Court of the Rights of Man is charged with applying such texts, the individual intentions of the signers must give way before the authorized interpretation given by the Court. Confused notions thus permit a reconciliation between agreement on the formulae and disagreement on their interpretation. In effect, it is necessary, for the declaration to become effective, that one agree to submit to the ruling of the court which provides an authorized interpretation of the text.

These examples borrowed from law serve to illustrate some of the techniques of reasoning concerning confused notions, which could be transposed to other domains and particularly to philosophy, the specific task of which consists, as I stated more than thirty years ago, in the systematic study of confused notions.[6]

It was in 1944 that I undertook my first study of a confused notion, the idea of justice. At that time, I was still imbued with positivist philosophy. I believed that the only acceptable method for studying this idea was to clarify it by emptying it of its emotive aspect which shows itself every time one discusses the notion of justice, because this notion designates a universal value which everyone respects but which everyone conceives in his own way. In my positivistic analysis of the notion of justice, I identified a structure common to all those who hand down a rule of justice, a structure which I designated *formal justice,* according to which it is necessary to treat situations which are essentially the same in the same way.[7] In law, this principle is expressed in the Latin formula *in paribus causis, paria jura* which provides the basis for recourse to judiciary precedent.

But this principle cannot be applied, in concrete cases, without the intervention of value judgments: in effect, it is necessary, in each case, to answer the question, 'are the two situations being compared essentially similar or not?' In order to answer, it is necessary to determine the similarities and differences, thus bringing to bear judgments of value and importance with which one is frequently not in agreement, in the absence of unequivocal criteria which permit us to arrive at a consensus with the help of recognized techniques.

This fact was already noted by Plato in a dialogue entitled 'Euthyphron or Of Piety.' In the course of a discussion on piety, another confused notion, Socrates remarks that, when disagreement is over number (eggs in a basket), weight (an object in gold), measurement (a piece of material), agreement is quickly reached thanks to calculation, weight, or measurement. But as soon as the disagreement centers on right and wrong, the beautiful or the ugly, the good and the bad, that is, on what we consider to be values and which are expressed as confused notions, in the absence of decision-making criteria, one must resort to dialectic (Euthyphron, 7–8). Aristotle took up again, in the same spirit, the distinction between analytical reasoning and dialectical reasoning, the latter proceeding from accepted opinions and attempting to justify, through controversy, the best, the most reasonable opinion.

Aristotle emphasized that, when it is a question of dialectical reasoning, it is necessary to begin with what is accepted by the listeners, with what constitutes an accepted opinion, a recognized value. In rhetorical and philosophical tradition, this point of departure has been defined as commonplace. Commonplaces such as 'all men are seeking happiness,' 'justice is preferable to injustice,' and 'liberty is worth more than slavery' form the point of departure for dialectical and rhetorical reasoning which aim at obtaining the listener's agreement to certain controversial propositions. In this way, commonplaces play a role analogous to the axioms of deductive systems, but while the latter are established and unequivocal, commonplaces are accepted by the interlocutors; but it is rare that a controversy is not engaged when it becomes a matter of applying these common places in concrete situations.

This point is well illustrated in the following passage of the *Dialogues* of Epictetus, a stoic philosopher of the second century A.D. The commonplaces here are designated as 'prenotions' which, according to the stoics, are present in the mind of man from the age of seven years.

'Prenotions are common to all men. No prenotion is in contradiction with any other. Who among us does not accept that good is something useful and desirable, to be sought and pursued in all circumstances? Who does not accept that right is something beautiful and suitable? Then, at what point is there a contradiction? When one applies the prenotions to the particular realities, when one says: 'He acted honestly, he is a courageous man' and another says, 'No, he is a fool.' There is thus conflict between them. Such is the conflict which opposes Jews, Syrians, Egyptians and Romans: that it is necessary above all to respect holiness and to seek it in everything is not in question; but one wonders whether the act of eating pork conforms to holiness or not. Such is the conflict which opposes Agammenon and Achilles. Call them before you. What will you say to Agammenon? Is it not necessary to act as one should and with honesty? It is necessary. And you, Achilles, what do you say? Are you not of the opinion that one must act honestly? I am totally of that opinion. Now, apply these prenotions: here is where the conflict begins (Dialogues I, XXII).

Just and honest conduct is approved by all men, but each one conceives justice in a manner which conforms to his passions and his interests. It is here that the philosopher such as Socrates traditionally intervenes. From among the multiplicity of meanings, he seeks to identify the true meaning, that which conforms to the ideas of justice, piety and courage. His effort aims for clarity and truth. Such goals will permit him to deviate from the habitual meaning, from the confused meaning built up by common opinion, the insufficiencies of which he will show, in order that a well-defined meaning which conforms to the adequate idea possessed by the philosopher might prevail. It is thus that Spinoza conceives, in his Ethics, the philosophical enterprise to which he was dedicated. After having provided us, in the third book of the Ethics, with the true definition of twenty different feelings, he adds the following explanation: 'I know that these names (of the feelings) have, in common usage, another meaning. Thus my plan is to explain, not the meaning of words, but the nature of things, and to designate those things by terms whose usual meaning is not completely removed from the way in which I wish to use them.'

Spinoza does not feel overly bound by the habitual usage of confused notions, for he seeks to understand them and to define them in clear terms, which conform to his own philosophy. But whoever does not share the mystic rationalism of Spinoza, whoever does not believe in the existence of objective criteria which permit one to describe in an adequate manner the realities to which the confused notions relate, will say rather that Spinoza abuses the notion of truth when he qualifies as true the definitions which constitute the framework of his system. Spinoza is using a rhetorical technique, well-known since the article of Ch. Stevenson devoted to persuasive definitions.[8]

This technique consists in modifying the conceptual meaning of an idea while maintaining its emotive meaning. In so far as we consider justice, liberty and democracy to be positive values, it will suffice for us to furnish our own definition of these notions and attempt to obtain the agreement of our listener to the content which we give to these uncontested values. We will disqualify the habitual usage of these confused notions by saying that this usage designates apparent justice, liberty and democracy. In contrast, the definitions that we ourselves propose conform to true justice, liberty and democracy. Such an opposition between appearance and reality points out the specific effort of the philosophers and ideologues to establish their point of view on the subject.

But along with the notions which designate uncontested values, there are others, such as the notions of reason and natural law, which are defended by some and attacked by others.

Whoever contests the value of reason, by showing that it takes into consideration only abstractions opposed to life and the concrete, will seek to devaluate reason by comparing it to a schematic and static vision of reality which corresponds only to an apparent knowledge. In contrast, the rationalist who sets himself up as defender of reason will seek to make the idea we have of it more flexible, showing how reason adapts itself to the most diverse situations and circumstances, how it shows itself, from the point of view of what is rational, to be logical and systematic and indifferent to particular cases, how from a reasonable point of view, which takes into account concrete elements, and seeks an adequate solution to each human problem, reason shows itself as presenting an equitable solution because it is reasonable. By making a notion more flexible, one enlarges its field of application, one permits it to escape criticism; but at the same time one blurs the notion and makes it more confused. In contrast, by making the notion more precise, one clarifies it, but one rigidifies it and makes it inapplicable in any number of cases.

It is thus that the idea of justice can be specified if one defines it in conformity to the law in effect: He who violates the law is unjust. This static and conformist conception of the notion of justice leaves us without a response to the question: 'Is the law to which one demands you conform in itself a just law?' What criteria do we have to decide this question? Whoever recognizes the value of natural law will find in it a criterium, as vague as it may be, to which one can refer when one opposes natural law to the arbitrariness and injustice of the actual law. But whoever sees in the idea of natural law only an ideological conception which is strongly questionable will note the well-known plurality of conceptions of natural law in order to show that natural law cannot render the services that one expects from it, for truth does not exist in this area.

The notion of truth itself, which is clear in certain of its usages, is supposed to be unique, the same for all, prevailing over all opinions. In its ideological usage, it becomes a confused notion, for one takes advantage of the common idea that all must bow before the truth in order to attempt to impose an opinion which is in no way compelling, by qualifying it as true.

The qualification 'true,' applied to an opinion which does not possess recognized criteria for acceptance leads from the use to the abuse of a notion, whose confusion one creates or increases. When the truth must be recognized, owing to techniques of demonstration and verification, it happens that one takes advantage of the unquestioned unicity of truth in order to impose forcibly an opinion which cannot avail itself of compelling proofs. Such a qualification is abusive and constitutes what Jerémy Bentham defined in his treatise on political sophisms as ' "petitio principii" hidden in a single word.'[9]

The passage from use to abuse, from permitted usage to the condemned use of a notion, as with everything else, supposes the existence of a separation between the two, a border which one cannot cross without giving rise to opposition. If one is not in agreement with the line of this border, to designate a usage as an abuse can also constitute a 'petitio principii' hidden in a single word. In effect, the act of recognizing the existence of an accepted distinction between use and abuse does not mean that in any particular case one finds oneself in the presence of a marked abuse.

These last reflections will perhaps permit us to see more clearly what distinguishes the handling of confused notions from that of notions which seem clear and unequivocal. One cannot abuse mathematical notions, which have been formally defined, as long as one conforms to the rules which determine their correct handling. In this case, abuse is defined by error, that is, by the violation of a known rule. In correctly effecting a mathematical operation, there is never abuse, whatever the result of the operation. But, when it is a question of the application of a confused notion, there exists no unanimously accepted procedure concerning its handling, which is not to say that its handling is entirely arbitrary. Even then there is a limit not to be transgressed, that of *unreasonable* usage.

Let us note, in this connection, that even if one does not always agree on the manner in which to act in a given situation, for several solutions can be equally reasonable, there normally exists, in a human community at any given moment, general agreement about what would be *unreasonable* and, in consequence, unacceptable or intolerable. This application does not result from the nonconformity to rules, but rather from an appreciation of the result, the end to be sought, to which end the unreasonable or abusive action is manifestly opposed.

A simple example of this concerns the use or abuse of food; it is good to nourish oneself but the use of food or medicine, as soon as it harms our health, is qualified as unreasonable and thus abusive.

It is in law that the distinction between use and abuse, between the reasonable and unreasonable use of a right, has been demonstrated by doctrine and jurisprudence. It is in the case of the abuse of the right of property that the theory of the abuse of rights has been developed. There is abuse when the exercise of this right aims essentially at harming another: the right of property, which was once considered to be absolute, ceases in this case to be protected by the Courts and Tribunals. For example the act of erecting large poles at the approaches to an airport, with the single intention of creating an artificial obstacle to the passage of the planes, was considered to be an abuse of rights.

But this theory of the abuse of rights can be generalized. Any unreasonable use of a discretionary power will be censured as abusive, in all branches of the law.

In granting discretionary power to any authority, one allows it to judge the expediency of the decisions to be made. But if these decisions seem arbitrary, clearly contrary to the general interest, the competent tribunal will seek to rescind them as abuse, excess or abduction of power.

The Supreme Court of Appeals of Belgium normally intervenes only in cases of violation of the law; it declares itself incompetent when it is a question of fact which the Court surrenders to the sovereign determination of the lower courts. But if this determination appears to be unreasonable because clearly erroneous, because it is incompatible with the elements on which it is based, the Supreme Court will intervene: it will always find good reasons which will permit it to set aside an unreasonable judgment.

Normally, in the general assembly of a society, the decisions reached by the majority are valid in law, unless there is abuse, that is, when they can only be explained by the will to act to the detriment of the minority.

Article 1854 of the Napoleonic Code states in its first paragraph: 'If the parties have agreed to rely on one of themsleves or a third party for the regulation of their interests this regulation cannot be attacked if it is not clearly contrary to equity.'

This exception can be generalized: when one entrusts a mission to anyone,

one grants him a right but one can imply the condition that he fulfill his mission in a reasonable manner: unreasonable conduct cannot be considered as valid in law, whatever the judicial grounds invoked to invalidate it in each particular case.

In law, there are judges to decide, in each case, if there has or has not been an abuse of rights. But how can one decide if there is abuse when the problem does not involve the law? If in morality, in philosophy, or in political debates, recourse to confused notions is inevitable, when will the use one makes of them be considered abusive? The question is difficult, for we do not have at our disposal objective criteria in this area. The only observation that one can make in this connection is that the users of a common language, which is employed as an instrument of communication, cannot use it with the goal of leading their interlocutor into error, for this would be to act in a manner similar to the counterfeiter, abusing the confidence that one accords to legal money.

Is it necessary in this case to forbid a philosopher to give a new meaning to a confused notion, such as liberty or justice, expressions of unquestioned value. Must one accuse Spinoza of abuse of language because he defined liberty in his own way, deviating from the common usage? I don't believe so. In effect, having clearly kept his distance in relation to the common usage, he certainly did not seek to deceive his readers. On the contrary, he explained himself at length on this subject by showing why the habitual usage which defines liberty as liberty of choice must be discarded and replaced with the meaning that he advocated. He thus did not commit 'petitio principii' because he endeavored to justify the new meaning instead of substituting it, without warning, for the common and habitual meaning of the notion. There is abuse once there is deceit, voluntary or involuntary, for it can happen that whoever introduces the new usage does not realize it himself, for lack of a critical mind.

This critical mind is not innate, and it could not be acquired by an education which limited itself to a rigorous tuition of a mathematical nature. Confused notions constitute, in the theory and practice of action, especially public action, instruments of communication and persuasion which cannot be eliminated. But it is necessary to handle them with caution. It is the role of rhetoric, as I conceive it, that is the role of a theory of argumentation, which encompasses moreover the dialectic of the Ancients, that of Socrates, Plato and Aristotle, to arm us against the abusive use of confused notions. It is through the study of argumentational, rhetorical and dialectical procedures that we will learn to distinguish acceptable reasoning from sophistic reasoning, to distinguish reasoning in which one seeks to persuade and to convince from reasoning in which one seeks to deceive and to lead into error. This is the reason, moreover, that I consider the teaching of rhetoric to be included as a principal element of any liberal education.

NOTES

* Presented at the Iowa Colloquium on Rhetoric and Public Policy in January 1978. First published in *ETC*. 1979, 4, pp. 313–324.
[1] cf. J. Sinnreich, *Zur Philosophie der idealen Sprache*, D.T.W., Munich, 1972.
[2] cf. A. Church, *Introduction to Mathematical Logic*, vol. I, Princeton University Press, 1956, pp. 50–52.
[3] cf. for this and what follows, my article 'Rhetorical Perspectives on Semantical Problems', *The New Rhetoric and the Humanities*, Reidel, Dordrecht, 1979, pp. 82–90.
[4] Pascal, *Pensées* in *Oeuvre*, Bibl. de la Pléiade, p. 1003 (687, ed. Brunschvicg).
[5] J. Maritain, *Autour de la nouvelle déclaration universelle des droits de l'homme*, texts compiled by UNESCO, Paris, Sagittaire, 1949, p. 12.
[6] *The Idea of Justice and the Problem of Argument*, p. 4.
[7] *Ibid.*, p. 16. In the present Volume, p. 11.
[8] cf. C. L. Stevenson, 'Persuasive Definitions', *Mind* (1938).
[9] J. Bentham, *Oeuvre*, Brussels, 1840, Vol. I, p. 481.

CHAPTER ELEVEN

THE JUSTIFICATION OF NORMS*

It is only in the last ten years that logicians have been concerned with the problem of justification, a term still absent in the majority of logic manuals. What traditionally concerns the logician is induction or deduction. Deontic logic treats the obligatory, the permitted or prohibited, i.e., what is regulated by norms, and is not concerned at all with justification. Even if it is mentioned, it is only to be assimilated to a deduction, where a norm may figure among the premises. To justify a norm, in this case, would be to deduce it from a more general and fundamental norm. Concerning the latter, unless it is based upon self-evidence or an intuition *sui generis*, it will be considered only as the expression of our aspirations, propensities or passions; it means that all rationality is discarded. From this latter perspective, the justification of norms does not arise from philosophy, but from psychology, sociology, history and always supposes an improper passage from what is to what should be. This negation of the possibility of a practical philosophy leads to scepticism; certain people admit it, with a smile, as inevitable, but console themselves by showing that it is not a disadvantage. We can find a characteristic expression of this point of view in Leonard G. Miller's article 'Moral Scepticism' (*Philosophy and Phenomenological Research* 22 (1961) 239–245). Professor Miller defends the thesis that it is meaningless to ask for justifications in the sphere of moral principles. His attitude seems to correspond to a very widely shared point of view and which he justifies by saying that the justification of normative assertions with the help of other normative assertions has limits which he would qualify as 'moral principles' and to the degree that it can be applied in morality the concept of justification does not apply to principles or to morality as such.[1] In fact, according to Professor Miller moral principles play an analogous role to that of axioms in a deductive system, a role that does not require their demonstration.

Can we find a foundation for norms instead of a justification? The very idea of an ontological foundation presupposes the possibility of deriving what must be from what is, i.e., arguments of value from arguments of fact. Since the celebrated Humean critique and the more recent analyses of Moore unmasking the 'naturalistic fallacy' such deduction is condemned in principle. Unable to have recourse either to justification or to the search for a foundation of fundamental norms, practical philosophy seems hopelessly at an impasse.

Before opposed practical philosophies, in which the logician saw only the expression of arbitrary assumed positions, he would have to limit himself to an internal critique, concerning the coherence of the given system. The different coherent systems would be of the same value for the logician, who would be incapable of deciding between them. The result is that every controversy and discussion concerning fundamental theses escapes not only formal logic but also methods of analytical thought. But we cannot limit ourselves to these methods. In reality, if there is nothing more rational than the method of critical discussion, which is to Popper[2] the method of science itself, then we must enlarge the domain of the logician's investigations, particularly of one who is interested in the techniques of reasoning. This enlargement would complete formal logic by the study of what, since Socrates, has been called *dialectics*. To avoid all misunderstanding about the meaning of this term, I prefer to qualify it as argumentation, and contrast it to formal logic conceived as the theory of demonstrative proof.

Argumentation is the technique that we use in controversy when we are concerned with criticizing and justifying, objecting and refuting, of asking and giving reasons. It is to argumentation that we have recourse when we discuss and deliberate, when we try to convince or persuade, when we give reasons for or against, when we justify our choices and decisions. It is argumentation which furnishes this logic of action, this logic of value judgments, which philosophy in the first half of the 20th century lacked, obligated, as it was, by its narrow conception of logic, to oscillate between absolutism and scepticism, between an irationalism and a positivism, both alien to the idea of the reasonable so important in law.[3]

Frege renewed modern logic by the analysis of mathematical reasoning; the analysis of legal reasoning and controversies allowed us to grasp the specificity of argumentation which is essential when we are concerned with justifying our actions, attitudes, decisions and choices. What characterizes the justification of norms are the reasons that we have for formulating or modifying them, for proposing or criticizing them, for adopting or rejecting them, for interpreting them one way or another, for conforming to them or violating them. These are the diverse modalities of justification for human behavior relative to the norms that we characterize, in an outrageously simplified and basically inexact way, as justification of norms. It is because of this simplification that the problems of human behavior are reduced to those posited by the search for truth, that the justification of norms is assimilated to the demonstration of propositions and that we ask serious questions about the truth of the norms. Such a question would have appeared senseless, or at least without relevance, if we had seen that the justification only concerns the modalities of our actions concerning norms. Our actions and decisions are never 'true'; they are correct, conform to a moral or legal order, are expedient, just, equitable or reasonable. It is obvious that the truth or falsity of information, the exact or erroneous character of facts, is at the base of our decisions and can influence them in one sense or another, but only on the condition that these truths and facts are appreciated as a function of values and norms which transform them into reasons for pragmatically determined decisions and actions.

When we discuss fundamental norms we are concerned much less with their truth than with their interpretation. When article 6 of the Belgian Constitution affirms that 'All Belgians are equal before the law' it will not occur to anyone to ask if this affirmation is true, but we will ask if only the judge is concerned with equal treatment or if the legislature is also bound by it and what are the reasons which would justify a departure in this matter. In this connection, norms, in law, are most often presented as expressing facts, but usually metaphorically.[4]

A fundamental norm of Belgian law and of many contemporary legal systems is given in article 25 of the Constitution: 'All powers emanate from the nation.' This norm, an expression of democratic ideology, is opposed to the fundamental norm of the Old Régime: 'All powers emanate from God.' Is it meaningful to ask which one is true? Is it the nation or is it God that legitimizes political power? In fact, instead of opposing these two norms one to another, we can synthesize them by the maxim 'Vox populi vox dei.' By saying that powers emanate from the nation or God, as heat from a fireplace, we are allowed to organize the diverse powers which represent either the national will or the divine will by referring them to their source (another metaphor).

Let us note that constitutional law is satisfied to posit article 25 without justifying it. Only the political philosophy and the ideologies which it develops connects this norm to the principles of freedom, equality, utility, assumed or presumed by their authors. This notion of presumption, characteristic of legal reasoning is essential for stabilizing situations. In fact, where presumption plays a favorable role we can dispense with the burden of proof: 'The mother's husband is presumed to be the child's father.' 'Every man is presumed to be innocent.' The burden of proof falls upon the one who wants to rebut a presumption.

In a paper called 'Presumptions' and presented in 1968 at the International Congress of Philosophy,[5] Patrick Day showed that along with presumptions bearing on fact, well known in legal reasoning, there are presumptions concerning *principles* which free all who assume them from the need of justification. He shows that these presumptions can bear upon different principles which characterize conservative, liberal and socialist attitudes. The conservative presumption is in favor of what exists: only change, always, everywhere, and in everything, requires a justification.[6] The liberal presumption asks for the justification of all constraint. It is Mill's presumptions: 'Leaving people to themselves is always better, *caeteris paribus*, than controlling them' (*On Liberty*, Chap. V, in *Utilitarianism*, Warnock, Collins, 1962, p. 228). The socialist presumption asks for the justification of inequalities. As I. Berlin asserts: 'Equality needs no reasons, only inequality does.'[7]

In three studies on justice, John Rawls combines the last two presumptions while extolling the following principle which seems rational to him: 'Each person participating in an institution or affected by it has an equal right to the most extended freedom compatible with a like freedom for all.'[8] As we have seen, in the conservative conception only change must be justified. With Mill, only the legitimate defense of the individual or of society justifies the use of a constraining power against a member of the community.[9] The same for Rawls: 'Inequalities as defined by the institutional structure or fostered by it are arbitrary, unless it is reasonable to expect that they will work out to everyone's advantage and provided that the positions and offices to which they attach or from which they may be gained are open to all.'[10]

Justifications are required when our conduct or a rule which inspires it violates an admitted principle and can, for this reason, be criticized. We see from this that justification is always a secondary phenomenon. If a behavior is not opposed to an admitted principle or does not sin in some way, if we do not find reason to criticize it, we do not ask that it be justified. Whoever excuses himself accuses himself, whoever justifies himself recognizes that his action falls under the threat of an eventual or real criticism.

We see immediately that conflicts arise when we have to justify a change, a constraint or an inequality. When we are concerned with principles which do not admit, from their author's perspective, of exception, such as Kant's categorical imperative or Bentham's utilitarian principle, then controversies will arise when we are concerned with specifying the rule and the path from abstract principle to specific cases.

In this connection, it should be noted, that philosophers who present their theses as non-temporal and a-historical are hardly concerned with cases of application, as if, like a formal principle, the fundamental norm were characterized by a clarity and a distinction which makes it self-evident. But as soon as we go from the abstract principle to cases of application, this illusion disappears at once. When we think of the libraries of commentaries caused by article 1382 of the Code Napoleon: 'Every act of man which causes damage to another obligates the former through whose fault it occurred to redress it,' we are surprised that philosophers can be content with enunciations whose application would incite interminable controversy. This is why jurists seeking security, be they of the left or the right, all accept, contrary to the philosophers, the conservative principle requiring the justification of change. Because of this stabilizing principle jurists will not accept the justification of change on account of general principles of freedom or equality which are, indeed, very vague, but on account of a pertinent interpretation of liberty or equality in a particular context. In fact, freedom and equality, and the principles which proclaim them, are not sufficiently precise propositions to be considered true or false, valid or not: they are commonplaces, generally admitted but very equivocal and cannot be assimilated to axioms or to formal language formulae. It is only in a fixed context, when we can show which concrete consequences the application of these principles, values and interests tends to favor or to oppose that we will be able to take a position in their regard. It is difficult to accept or to reject without further ado the principle of freedom if we know (as the secular controversy between liberal and socialist conceptions of freedom has taught us) that constraints, imposed upon some, guarantee the freedom of others. Similarly, for certain theoreticians, the principle of equality demands an equality of treatment, when for others it implies the equality of conditions even at the price of incontestable privileges.[11]

The assimilation of fundamental norms to mathematical axioms has created the illusion that the unique problem of practical philosophy, be it a concern with morality, law or politics, consists in extracting principles from which we can deduce theorems relative to action. But these norms are closer to the general principles of law whose bearing or field of application, and whose relationship to other norms, with which they may be incompatible, can be given precision only after a discussion in which values of a given society are confronted in a dialectical debate, where opposed, though reasonable, positions will surely occur.

When general principles are applied in a normative context, they play a very different role from mathematical rules. We can develop an arithmetic or

112 CHAPTER ELEVEN

geometry independent of the objects we counted or measured, by putting into operation rules of a correct deduction; in contrast the norms of our behavior contain vague elements that can only be specified in concrete situations. This is what is fundamentally right in the Hegelian dialectic which ties the usage of practical notions and principles to their historical manifestation. The notions and principles of practical philosophy are for this reason indeed, closer to legal notions and principles than to the notions and axioms of the formal sciences.

When we are concerned with the justification of norms, we must, together with the rules for their formulation, proposal and acceptance, also be concerned with their application and interpretation. A philosopher who takes his role seriously should not be content to elaborate some commonplaces which would be the most acceptable, general principles of behavior, like those of Kant and Bentham, but should examine the repercussions of the controversies which would arise from their application and interpretation in situations which are always open to conflict.

When it is a question of behavior, the philosopher will take into account not only the fact that principles govern individual situations, but that the regulation of the latter reacts upon the interpretation of the principles as ends and values. Examining the procedures of argumentation in this dialectic, the logician appeals to the non-constraining reasoning which endeavors to convince and persuade in contrast to the traditional techniques of deduction and induction. The modern limitation of logic to formal and analytical proofs has eliminated, unfortunately, this non-constraining reasoning from our concerns.[12] But once we have recognized that this kind of dialectical reasoning, argumentation in all its forms, is indispensable wherever problems of choice and decision-making occur, we'll recognize the indispensable role of what I call the new rhetoric, as the theory of persuasive and convincing communication, that should regain the place it had in antiquity, at the center of every liberal education.

NOTES

* The original French text appeared in *Human Sciences and the Problem of Values*, Entretiens in Amsterdam of the International Institute of Philosophy, Nijhoff, The Hague, 1971.

[1] '... the justification of "ought" statements in terms of other "ought" statements comes to an end in what I call "moral ultimates," and insofar as it does the concept of justification does not apply to ultimates or to morality as such,' p. 239.

[2] K. R. Popper, 'Conjectural knowledge' in *Revue Internationale de Philosophie* 95–96 1971, p. 193.

³ See in the present volume Chapter 17.
⁴ A. Giuliani, 'Nouvelle rhétorique et logique du language normatif' in *Etudes de logique juridique* **IV** (1970), 66.
⁵ Presented at the Congress in Vienna, *Proceedings of the Fourteenth International Congress of Philosophy*, Vienna, 1970, Vol. V, pp. 137–143.
⁶ Op. cit., p. 139, according to B. Wootton, *Social Foundations of Wage Policy*, London, 1958, p. 162.
⁷ I. Berlin, 'Equality', *Proceedings of the Aristotelian Society* **56** (1956), p. 305.
⁸ J. Rawls, 'Constitutional liberty and the concept of justice' in *Nomos,* **6,** ed. Carl Friedrich, New York, 1963, p. 100.
⁹ Mill, *Utilitarianism*, op. cit., p. 135.
¹⁰ Rawls, p. 100.
¹¹ *L'Egalité*, vol. 1, published by the Centre de Philosophie du Droit of the Free University of Brussels and in particular my article 'Egalité et valeurs', Brussels, 1970, pp. 319–326.
¹² See Ch. Perelman and L. Olbrechts-Tyteca, *The New Rhetoric*, Notre Dame, 1969; my *Le Champ de l'argumentation*, Brussels, 1970 and *The New Rhetoric and the Humanities*, Reidel, Dordrecht, 1979.

CHAPTER TWELVE

LAW AND MORALITY*

Traditionally, studies dedicated to the relations between law and morality insisted, from a Kantian orientation, upon the following distinctions: law governs external behavior, morality emphasizes intention, law establishes a correlation between rights and obligations, morality prescribes duties which do not bring forth subjective rights; law establishes obligations sanctioned by power, morality escapes organized sanctions.

Jurists unhappy with a formalistic, statist and positivistic conception of law, insist upon the importance of a moral element in the functioning of the law, upon the role played in law by 'good and bad faith', 'good and bad intentions', 'equity' and many other notions whose ethical aspect cannot be neglected.

On the other hand, those who recommend the study of law as an object of meditation, and at times, even of inspiration for the moralist, are indeed rare. It is, however, on this latter aspect of the relations between law and morality that I would like to dwell.

Along with constitutional principles which vary from one legal system to another, with laws derived from transitory circumstances or justified by opportunistic considerations, the multiple systems of Western law contain many common rules which remain binding for very long periods of time and are often derived from Roman law.

Certain of these rules had been designated as 'general principles of law' and jurists did not hesitate considering them as obligatory even in the absence of legislation which would accord them the formal status of a positive law, such as the principle affirming the rights of defense, that is expressed by the maxim *'audiatur et altera pars.'* Others are enunciated by several articles of the civil or penal codes, or by procedures concerning responsibility, different kinds of crimes, the admissibility of witnesses, different forms of presumptions and so many others, common to countries having an old legal tradition.

It is in thinking of these more or less permanent rules of legal thought that I would like to advance the following thesis: before undertaking the elaboration of a very abstract formula — such as the categorical imperative or the utilitarian principle — from which moral rules should be derived, should not the moralist be interested in showing, amidst all the legal rules those which, by their perennity and generality express values which force themselves upon jurists? It seems to me reasonable to admit that these laws and the values they guard, the distinctions they establish, are pertinent for the moralist's thinking.

These rules and all that they teach, could play, for the moralist, the same role that ordinary language and its analysis plays for a philosopher of the Oxford School, such as John Austin, without asserting that the lessons that one could draw from such an analysis would constitute the last word in philosophy. Yet there would be no cause to set them aside without good reason. If the ordinary use of the language brings forth distinctions, there is presumption in favor of its philosophical importance. The philosopher should not neglect this and cannot hold it to be erroneous or superficial without proving his objections. The moralist must proceed in the same way with regard to legal rules. It may be evident that such or such rule or presumption corresponds to the finality of law and not to that of morality. The moralist may, for this reason, neglect it, but at least he will justify not taking it into account. In certain cases it is normal that legal rules differ from moral ones, but such a divergence is not presumed; this must be explained.

To make myself better understood, I would like to recall the discussion that recently took place at the Congress of French Language Societies of Philosophy (at Geneva, Sept., 1966) concerning the moral and immoral usage of language. For some, the immoral usage of language was limited to the violation of the obligation to speak the truth. But if it is analyzed, a propos modern legislation, the problem of moral or immoral usage of language shows itself to be infinitely more complex. In law the central notion is promise; the witness who lies is punished essentially because he promised to speak the truth, the whole truth and nothing but the truth. But if it is a question of parents or the conjoined of one of the parties he cannot be obligated to testify under oath; if these people are heard without administering the oath we cannot condemn them for false testimony or false declaration when they testify in favor of the accused or the charged (Art. 268 of the Belgian Code of Civil procedure). The legislator admits that there is no reason to violate the sentiments of affection presumed to exist between near relatives by obligating them to testify under oath against an accused or charged father, son or husband.

But there are more flagrant cases where legal prescriptions do not oblige truth telling, by not punishing the lie, but where they punish the person who tells the truth in a circumstance where there is cause to guard the secret. In fact, violation of the professional secret can be punishable by law. Professions on which the professional secret is imposed may vary in the course of the centuries, but the existence of a parallel obligation is found in the most diverse systems. It is the same in all cases of the denunciation to the enemy. The denunciation to the state authorities is at times recommended both morally and legally but at other times, even if the law prescribes it, it can be morally condemnable. The variations in this matter are very instructive in terms of the relations which exist in a given society between its members and the authorities.

We can, by lying, injure the honor and the esteem of people; it is normal that the person who cannot bring authorized proof of his allegations, exposing another person to public contempt, is guilty of slander and condemned by this indictment. But, there are cases where the proof of the alleged facts is not allowed and, one may lie or speak the truth, but one is nevertheless guilty of defamation. In addition, a person will be rendered guilty of sinister divulgence who will impute to another facts for which legal proof exists but which he advances for the unique aim of injury.

We have seen that the witness under oath is obliged to speak the truth; yet in other cases, one is bound by professional secrecy. When the two obligations enter into conflict the person held to secrecy, when called to testify, can decide with a free conscience, which obligation is dominant on this occasion.

We can assume that the laws can oblige us to be silent but never to lie. This is not always so. There are cases, in fact, where silence equals denunciation and the sole honorable action is to lie. A person faced with an enemy's question whether he was hiding a fugitive, would be acting in a less honorable way if he responded with silence than if he would lie, because silence would not fail to be interpreted as an affirmation and would constitute a form of denunciation. Likewise, we could not condemn the patriot who had recourse to lying because he was unable to resist torture and, refused to denounce his comrades.

These examples are sufficient to show that legal prescription, placing emphasis on the pluralism of norms and their values and conflicts to which they can, in concrete circumstances, lead, obliges the moralist to recognize the inadequacy of strict ethical formalism. It is not sufficient to enunciate general principles, the moralist must be concerned with problems which their application poses in the most varied cases.

The moralist can be usefully inspired by the legal model in his attempt to clarify the dialectic of the relations between general rules and particular cases.

In fact, the general principles of law such as article 1382 of the Code Napoleon concerning civil responsibility (whatever action of a man causes harm to another obliges the one through whose fault it occurred to rectify it) enunciates rules which no one disputes but whose application has led to innumerable controversies about which a library of legal studies has sought solutions.

Would it not be the same in ethics? The fundamental principles of morality, either deontological or teleological, either formalistic or utilitarian, and should the acts be judged by their conformity to rules or by their consequences, all of them can be uncontested in *abstract*. As soon as it is a question of application in concrete circumstances, there is infinite controversy. In these circumstances, the methods and criteria of interpretation, allowing for the application of the rules, acquire even more importance than the rules themselves in their abstract and more or less vague formulation. In limiting himself solely to enunciating these rules, the moralist renounces the essential role attributed by law to doctrine and jurisprudence. The moralist is content with the role of legislator and even of a legislator who does not declare very precise rules, trusting the judge to apply them. The example of law convinces us immediately of the insufficiency of this point of view, because does not the moralist renounce the task that is essential for jurisprudence?

These reflections in no way signify that law does not possess a specificity by which it is distinguished from points of view proper to ethics. In fact, the particular importance accorded by law to legal security explains the specific role of the legislator and the judge. This is opposed to the autonomy of conscience which characterizes modern ethical theories. With the multiplicity of norms and values, the law, wishing to guarantee legal security, which would fix the rights and obligations of everyone, must allow certain people, legislators, the authority to elaborate rules which can be imposed on everyone, and then assign to other people, the judges, the right and obligation of applying and interpreting them.

Similarly, to avoid the disputes which question existing situations, the law reserves an important place to all sorts of presumptions which exempt from all proofs those they benefit. Along with irrefutable presumptions which guarantee the stability of certain institutions by preventing all contrary proof (stability of legal decisions protected by the authority of the *res judicata*, family stability where the disavowal of paternity is no longer possible after a very short delay) other presumptions *juris tantum* admit contrary proof but impose the burden of proof upon the person wanting to reverse them (presumptions of innocence, of ownership for the possessors of personal

property). Reasons of legal certainty impose limits of admissibility for proof
(certain types of proof only being admitted to prove the existence of
important legal acts and obligations), institute special procedures guaranteeing the satisfactory course of suits, both civil and penal. Similarly, to avoid
parties having recourse to judges who would be partisan to them, precise rules
of procedure predetermine which judges are competent to handle each type
of litigation, which are qualified in appeal cases or for procedures of cassa-
tion.

Preoccupation with legal certainty prevents, with the help of the techniques and procedures which I have just mentioned, the development of
zones of incertitude and penumbrae which escape legal regulation. Is such a
person honorable? Can we have confidence in his courage, discretion and
loyalty? To these questions posed in purely moral terms, the most varied
responses can and are effectively given. But in law one is innocent or guilty,
acquitted or condemned. According to temperament and mores we judge
more or less severely a past crime. In law a misdemeanor falls under the
statute of limitations or it does not; it doesn't waver some-place in between.
We can judge the maturity of a young man in various ways, but his majority is
determined by precise conditions fixed to the day.

We can multiply the examples of the effects of legal certainty. Nothing is
more normal but that in many cases a very different treatment of the same
situation comes about as a result of either a moral or legal point of view. The
treatment of euthanasia provides an excellent illustration of this.

People who admit euthanasia, for reasons which they consider morally
justifiable, i.e., the right to accelerate or provoke the death of a dear one, to
end the suffering caused by an incurable sickness or to terminate the miserable existence of a child monstrosity, are scandalized by the fact that
euthanasia, from a legal point of view, may be purely and simply identified
with murder.

Supposing, from a moral point of view, we admit euthanasia by not
attaching an absolute value to human life, whatever may be the miserable
conditions in which life is prolonged. Is it then necessary to place legal texts
parallel with the moral judgments? This would be a dangerous solution
because in law doubt is usually in favor of the accused. We would risk grave
abuse in promulgating an indulgent legislation in this matter of life and death.
But we have stated that when the judged case appeals rather to pity than to
chastisement, the jury does not hesitate to have recourse to a fiction, by
qualifying facts in a way contrary to reality, by declaring that the accused has
not committed murder, and it does this to avoid applying the law.[1] It seems to

me that this recourse to fiction, which allows, in exceptional cases, the avoidance of the application of the law — a procedure inconceivable in morality — is better than providing expressly, in law, for the fact that euthanasia is a case for justification or excuse.

We see by this particular example that even if it is not a flagrant violation by the legislature of a moral rule, there can be good reasons why the moral rules are not entirely in conformity with legal ones, these being subject to conditions of security, to presumptions and the techniques of proof which the moral judgment hardly embraces.

The general rule, or at least the presumption, is the conformity of moral and legal rules. It is for this reason that the study of law, recognizing its usual relevance to morality, prevents the theoretician from indulging in extreme simplifications concerning both the content of rules and their application in concrete situations. He will see that the diverse principles which the philosophers have presented as supreme norms in ethics are in reality only commonplaces, in the meaning of classical rhetoric, that they give reasons which are to be considered in each concrete situation rather than as axioms like those of geometry whose consequences can be drawn by simple deduction. Practical reasoning, applicable in morality, must not be inspired by the mathematical model, which is not applicable in changing circumstances, but by a knowledge characterized by reasonableness and by the taking into consideration diverse aspirations and multiple interests, defined by Aristotle as *phronesis* or prudence, and which is so brilliantly manifested in law, in Roman *jurisprudentia*.

NOTES

* Presented at the XIVth International Congress of Philosophy, Vienna, Sept. 1968, *Proceedings*, Vienna, 1970, vol. V, pp. 153–158.
[1] See Chapter 3 p. 41 of the present volume.

CHAPTER THIRTEEN

LAW AND RHETORIC*

There are two limitations to the application of Aristotle's doctrine of rhetoric which he interpreted as the study of persuasive discourse and its modalities. On the one hand, where the admitted thesis is self-evident and imposes upon every attentive mind there is no cause for argumentation. When truth is manifestly clear, when self-evidence leaves no room for willful choice, all rhetoric is superfluous. On the other hand, when the thesis is shown to be arbitrary and there is no reason to favor it, the demand for submission to a constraining power can come about only through brutal force, without any concern for intellectual acceptance. These two extremes are indeed rare; the field of rhetoric is thus immense.[1]

Every man of common sense is inclined to accept self-evidence that necessarily leads to the same conclusion. When we are involved in an arithmetic addition, the question of competence is no longer at issue. To arrive at the conclusion that two plus two equals four, we don't need to refer to a judge. The judge is indispensable only when there is reason to make a decision and not when the result can be had from a calculator.

Similarly, if judges were only docile instruments as Montesquieu described them: 'the mouth that pronounces the words of the law, mere passive beings, incapable of moderating either its force or vigor'[2], then judiciary reasoning would be foreign to all concepts of rhetoric.

If argumentation does not intervene where there is no cause to evaluate, to interpret or to judge and where there is submission to self-evidence or force, the role and importance of rhetoric clearly increases with the growth and independance of the judiciary power. This occurs when the judiciary power attempts to motivate its decisons and not forcibly impose them. It is the same with the legislative power. When the latter recognizes that the laws which it enacts are not self-evident — and not wishing to arbitrarily impose them — it furnishes reasons which would give them public acceptance. Parliamentary debates are often preceded by exchange of opinions in both the press and in specialized journals, and this clarifies for the public the arguments which merit approval or rejection for the projected law, and the evils and advantages which would result from its enactment. The role of argumentation and rhetoric grows with every controversy in which self-deliberation and the interchange of thoughts help to achieve a reasonable decision.

The discipline of rhetoric, in the Aristotelian concept of the term, probably arose at the time when litigations began to take place over properties that were confiscated during periods of political changes. The old property holders, many years later, claimed restitutions when the former government returned to power. It is conceivable that these successive political changes, with all the legal complications which occurred in the intervals, caused difficulties which no legislation could foresee and which the simple application of laws could hardly resolve equitably. We know what a pivotal role law and judicial form played in Greece and Rome among the principal theoreticians of rhetoric from Aristotle to Hermagoras, to Cicero and Quintillian. In Greece, Rome, the Middle Ages and the Modern Era legal development went hand in hand with rhetorical development. Several general principles of law, as well as numerous rules of Civil and Criminal procedure, bear squarely the mark of their rhetorical origin.[3] It is thanks to rhetoric and to the introduction into law of such notions as 'good faith' or 'equity' that the highly formalistic ancient Roman law was transformed and became a better instrument in the service of justice.

In a less authoritarian and more democratic concept of law, the role of rhetoric becomes more and more indispensable. This happens also when jurists insist upon the importance of judicial peace, upon the idea that law must not only be obeyed, but recognized, that it will be even better observed when it is more extensively accepted.

The acceptance of a legal system implies a recognition of the authorities who have the power to legislate, to govern and to judge. This legitimacy is based on tradition, religion, and the most varied ideologies and political philosophies. There is abuse of power when the decisions taken by the existing power seem unreasonable, contrary to the common good and if they are not accepted, but imposed by constraint. Power in this situation risks the loss of its authority; it can make itself feared, but it will not make itself respected.

The role of the judge, servant of existing laws, is to contribute to the acceptance of the system. He shows that the decisions which he is led to take are not only legal, but are acceptable because they are reasonable. Each time he must settle conflict of opinions, interpretations, interests and values, he must seek those solutions which are both in conformity to the law and acceptable.

Law does not govern everything: it does not foresee everything. In extraordinary situations, in case of *force majeure*, the strict application of the law could be in conflict with reason and equity. The judge must make the law pliable to make it acceptable.[4]

In a trial, it is normal for the contesting parties to present all legal and factual elements, all types of considerations, legal documents, jurisprudential judgements, doctrinal precepts and legal topics, i.e., the general forms of argumentation which show what values and interests should prevail and for what reasons. The judge having to bring the litigation to a conclusion will indicate what values and considerations have a bearing in law and equity. After hearing the contestants' pros and cons he will present the reasons which determine his decision. He will seek to provide the motivation which will allow his final decision to be accepted by the parties to the litigation, by public opinion and by higher judicial tribunals.

From this perspective the best lawyers' argument is the one which the judge uses in his own deliberations and the best motivation of a decision will be the one that is not contested or, at least, confirmed in appeal.

If each time a question is submitted to deliberation and discussion, there is a necessary recourse to argumentation, very often the discourse does not end in a decision but creates an attitude of mind, a disposition to react in one manner or another. This happens with theoretical, political and philosophical discussions. Doctrinal and theoretical works, even when we are concerned with legal doctrine, attempt to influence public opinion but do not lead necessarily to decisions.

When a question is submitted to a body qualified to clarify a legal text, it will decide upon its applicability and it will adopt an argumentation suitable for a highly restricted audience: legislators or judges. In fact, one of the characteristics of law is that it provides procedures to which conformity is necessary if we are to arrive at a valid legislative, administrative or judicial decision and it also provides a qualified body to make decisions in each case. Legal, and more often, constitutional dispositions will regulate problems relative to the relationships among the power structures in the hierarchy or their relative independence. The qualified bodies which must make authorized decisions ought not be challenged and if they are, there must be a final tribunal empowered to settle conflicts. In the absence of such dispositions, the settlement of litigations does not fall in the realm of law; they become political questions whose settlement will be imposed by force.

Is it necessary that every legally valid decision have an effective practical consequence and if there is cause, be sanctioned and imposed by force? Generally it is true and it is desirable that decisions be applied effectively, otherwise legal institutions cannot preserve their authority. I, however, do not believe that a formally valid legal decision, taken by competent authorities, loses its stature as a legal act by the fact that it remains without effect. A decree of the Belgian Council of State which annulled an adjudication, does not lose its legal validity because it intervened too late to modify purchasing operations already in effect subsequent to the adjudication.[5] The essential element in this matter is the existence of competent authorities to speak the law whether this be by way of general dispositions (legislative and regulatory power) or in each specific case (executive or judiciary power).

Is the judiciary power entirely subordinate to the legislative? If that were so, then the implication is that law coincides with statutes. The judge's role would be limited to the establishment of facts, their subsumption under a legal text and the drawing of a conclusion in the form of a judiciary syllogism. Argumentation would play a role only in the judge's intimate conviction, but apart from that, subsumption and deduction would suffice. Argumentation would not intervene in the application of the legal rule.

In this regard there has been considerable development since 1790 when the Ideologues of the French Revolution wanted to subject the whole judiciary system to the national will, which would now express itself through statute. After the quickly abandoned attempt forcing judges to refer (each doubtful legal interpretation) to the legislature, the compilers of the Code Napoleon granted the judges a complementary power in the formation of the law. The celebrated Article 4 of the Code Napoleon states: 'The judge who refuses to judge under pretext of the silence, obscurity or insufficiency of law can be prosecuted, as guilty for the denial of justice.'

The obligation to judge goes hand in hand with the judge's power to make decisions, to fill the law's lacunae, to resolve antinomies and to choose one or another interpretation of the text.

The judge's power of interpretation now clearly stated in Article 4 of the Code Napoleon will be increased if recourse to the will of the legislator allows the legislator's sought for aims to be opposed to the text of the law. This is done in view of an extension or restriction of the import of the law. The judge will apply the letter as well as the spirit of the law without bringing overtly into play considerations of equity.

Since the last World War there has been fewer scruples in these matters. More and more the general principles of law are considered to be legal rules which the judge will take into account even independently of a legal text which authorized them. We have noticed the increasing role which 'juridical topics' — arguments considered to be pertinent for the application and clarification of law and accepted societal values — have played, and have seen that a right that is held to be reasonable cannot be put aside.

In a democratic vision of law, where statutes themselves are not considered only an act of power, the decisions of justice should not only be legal but also acceptable because they do not oppose socially recognized values. In this respect the role of the European judge has markedly grown and approaches that of his Anglo-Saxon colleague. At the same time the role of argumentation and rhetoric has grown in the application and evolution of law. This reality concerns the judge more than the lawyer. The judge who is more and more compelled to motivate his decision is less and less content to provide only formal correctness but tends to give his decisions a more persuasive character. The motivation will be different when there is cause to convince public opinion of the decision's reasonableness than when a Court of Appeals must be shown that the decision does not violate the law. A less formalistic vision of the law is rising in legal positivism. This vision insists upon the acceptance of judicial decisions in the social milieu in which the legal system is applicable.

In view of post World War II developments, we can better understand and appreciate the importance of Professor Viehweg's work in the evolution of Western European legal ideas.

NOTES

* To be published in German in the *Festschrift Th. Viehweg.*
[1] Ch. Perelman, *Le Champ de l'argumentation*, Brussels, 1970; *L'Empire rhétorique*, Vrin, Paris, 1977; *The New Rhetoric and the Humanities*, Reidel, Dordrecht, 1979.
[2] Montesquieu, *The Spirit of the Laws*, Book XI, Chap. 6, trans. T. Nugent, New York, 1949, p. 158.
[3] J. Stroux, *Römische Rechtswissenschaft und Rhetorik*, Potsdam, 1949, and A. Giuliani, *Il concetto di prova, contributo alla logica giuridica*, Milano, 1961.
[4] Ch. Perelman, *Logique juridique*, Paris, 1976, pp. 167–169.
[5] Ch. Perelman, 'A propos de la règle de droit, réflexions de méthode,' in *La règle de droit*, Brussels, 1971, p. 313.

CHAPTER FOURTEEN

LEGAL REASONING*

The present Congress is dedicated to what is traditionally known as legal logic. Both words 'legal logic' have been avoided in indicating the theme. In fact, the theoreticians of contemporary law reproach each other for inadequately using this expression.

Those who are influenced by the terminology of the modern logicians and would like to keep the name logic for formal logic, which is tied to the structures of reasoning, pretend that there is no material logic and that if we are concerned with the material conditions of reasoning, we leave logic and occupy ourselves with rhetoric, with dialectic, with argumentation and eventually with methodology but not with logic properly speaking.[1] When, like Kalinowski and Klug, they understand legal logic as the analysis of notions and structures of formal logic, which are used in the jurist's reasoning, and limit legal logic to formal logic as applied to law[2], they feel censured because they turn this expression away from its traditional meaning, which was the study of the essential forms of *legal* reasoning.[3] To the degree that jurists only use schemas of ordinary reasoning such as the syllogism or the *modus ponens,* there is as little cause to speak of legal logic as there is to call zoological logic, the reasoning which from the fact that an elephant is larger than a fox and a fox larger than a mouse, concludes that an elephant is larger than a mouse. If it is the same logic which is at work in all domains, the expression 'legal logic' is as unusual as legal arithmetic when it is a question of adding the number of records of sales drawn up by the nation's statisticians. The first theoreticians blame the second for employing the word 'logic' in an improper sense; the second blame the first for specifying as 'legal' operations those which are in no way specific.

Doubtlessly, the jurists' techniques of reasoning, like those of the philosophers, are characterized by controversies[4] where some competent men defend one position, others another, a situation clearly different from the constraining demonstrations of the logicians and mathematicians. To this the logicians reply that the controversies are not at all surprising because they result from the adversaries implying opposing premises. But is not the jurist's reasoning characterized by the fact that it proposes to justify the preference given to certain premises and not to others? Must not judges who complete a trial by their decision motivate it, i.e., show that their judgment is based on fact and law? Can we then not consider that legal reasoning is shown at work essentially in judgments and decrees of courts and tribunals?

Does formal logic allow us to resolve juridical controversies? Certainly not. It is quite exceptional that the controversies come about from the fact that one of the antagonists commits an error in formal logic. It would suffice to show him the error so that he may retract it, like every normal person who has been shown his mistake in additions. If it is so, if effectively the laws of logic are never in question in legal controversies, why do many jurists dislike logic and oppose it to equity, to good sense or to experience? We would find it certainly bizarre that a customer wishing to purchase three yards of cloth at $17 a yard and from whom was asked the sum of $51, finds it too expensive and accuses the arithmetic of being responsible for the cost of living. Why impute to logic the reasoning of the jurists which affects not the form but the matter of reasoning? It is in fact, supporters of what we call 'le formalisme juridique,' 'Begriffsjurisprudenz' or 'mechanical jurisprudence' who would like to make logic the heart of law and who, for this reason, are identified with logicians; but in fact, they are jurists whose 'logical' reasoning, since they take part in legal controversies, goes beyond the limits of formal logic.

In fact, the rules of logic, to be applicable, require that certain conditions be observed. The first of these conditions, preliminary to the application of logical formalism, demands that the same signs preserve always the same meaning without which the most self-evident logical laws cease to be valid, i.e., an identity is no longer true and a contradiction no longer necessarily false.

The statement 'business is business' is not a tautology and is in no way admitted by those who contest commercial practices. Heraclitus' statement 'we enter and do not enter twice in the same stream' is not a contradiction and even reveals a profound truth if the expression 'the same stream' relates as well to the bed of the stream as to the waters which flow in it.

The partisans of mechanical jurisprudence, those who would like to reserve to logic the central place in law are led to require the univocity of signs and legal concepts, to demand that a concept defined in one legal text keep the same meaning in all branches of law and in all situations, thus guaranteeing a certain legal stability and a security for legal deductions. They seek to impose a univocity upon legal language which is indispensable to the rigorous language of formalism.

In a similar way, the principle which affirms what is valid in all cases must be valid in each, will be used by the formalists for not admitting departures unforeseen in the law text, but required by good sense, equity or humanity. A police officer charged with enforcing the communal ordinance which prohibits the entrance of vehicles to a public park would allow a baby carriage or an invalid's wheel chair to enter, but would prohibit, in the name of logic, the entrance of an ambulance coming for a pedestrian stricken with a heart attack. The ambulance doubtlessly is a vehicle. Obviously it is not the logic that is on trial but the policeman's formalistic interpretation, tied to the letter of the ordinance, misconceiving the spirit, forgetting the existence of cases of irresistible circumstances, i.e., of *force majeure*.

This opposition between letter and spirit is the stumbling block of mechanical jurisprudence. In fact, when in mathematics the unison of signs is perfectly reconcilable with the spirit of the system which is defined equally by reference to formal criteria, i.e., rules of substitution and deduction, the systematic unity of law is made by reference to values and to value hierarchies which allow the *ratio juris* to be defined. It is in reference to the finality of law, or to the diverse hierarchical ends which each legal system proposes, that the spirit will be opposed to the letter of the law.

When in certain situations the text does not furnish adequate means for the sought ends, when it admits antinomies that the judge is obliged to resolve and lacunae which he must fill, when he has the obligations to judge and justify his decision, when deductive, purely analytical reasoning is insufficient, there is cause to refer to what Aristotle, who in his analyses is greatly inspired by law, has designated as dialectical reasoning and which I personally characterize as a recourse to argumentation.[5]

The oppositions between the spirit of the law and the letter of the norm in certain cases limit the scope of law as well as the taking into account of exceptional situations, of cases of *force majeure*. These, however, compel recognition if we recognize that legislative rationality, the spirit of the system, is relative to ends, and to a hierarchy of values, which a given society considers as reasonable.

No one will deny that in our society, a human life is more important than the inconveniences caused by an ambulance's entry into a public park. It is obvious that in less flagrant cases a controversy can arise. Can a car be allowed to enter a park which comes for a pregnant woman, a convalescent or an old man? Legal security requires that the rules of law determine what is permitted, required and prohibited behavior. It hopes to achieve this through precise and adequate specifications. Yet must we, to remain faithful to the letter of the law, forget its spirit, i.e., its goal?

In an interesting article written to honor the eminent American jurist

Roscoe Pound,[6] Recaséns-Siches, a spokesman for the reasonable in law, relates an incident which illustrates the controversy which had been previously pointed out by Petrazycki, and which caused some stir in Poland at the beginning of the century.

At a station entrance a sign prohibited access to the stairways to people accompanied by a dog. A peasant with a bear on a leash became very indignant when he was refused access to the stairs. He claimed that no one would take his bear for a dog and that only dogs were indicated on the sign. We see in this example that recourse to the spirit of the law or to the spirit of the system causes us at times to limit the scope of the law and at times to extend it.

The fact is that controversies may arise concerning the interpretation of a text which question the primacy of the surety or of finality in a particular situation, and which concern the precise values at stake and how they are scaled. These are strange problems irrelevant to formal or mathematical logic, but are frequent in the application of the law and it is indispensable to have recourse to the judge's authority to solve them.

There are domains other than law which are characterized by controversies and conflicts. I am thinking more particularly of philosophy and politics. Nothing prevents the debates among the philosophical schools from becoming eternal and remaining without solutions. The *philosophia perennis* would consider as an inadmissable show of force the intervention of any authority and power other than reason to end a philosophical debate. This is the meaning of Socrates' words in the first book of the *Republic* which oppose to debates settled by judges, the philosophical dialectic, where those who discuss must convince each other, playing simultaneously the role of the judge and lawyer.[7] On the other hand, political conflicts are settled more often by the sword or the ballot — the latter in democratic society replaces the recourse to violence.

What is specific in the way matters are resolved in law is that decision is obtained by recourse to a judge, normally designated in advance and who, in the procedure of modern states, cannot be satisfied only with a decision which settles the conflict, but must in addition justify it and show that it is in conformity to the law that is in force. The pronounced judgement is not given as a collection of premises from which a conclusion is deduced, but as a decision justified by adduced reasons. In a formal deduction the conclusions flow in a constrained and impersonal way from the premises. But when the judge makes a decision, his responsibility and his integrity are at stake, the reasons he gives to justify his decision and to refute the real or eventual objections which could be made against him, furnish a sample of practical reasoning, showing that his decision is just and conforms to the law, i.e., that the decision takes account of all the directives which the legal system has given, and that he is responsible to apply — a system from which he draws his authority and competence — without putting aside the obligations which his conscience, as an honest man, imposes on him. In fact, to the degree that the judge is not a calculator entirely programmed by a third party, but a social being charged with confronting values belonging to the spirit of the system, a sensibility for values is an indispensable condition for the exercise of his functions.

Legal reasoning is thus a very elaborated individual case of practical reasoning, which is not a formal demonstration, but an argumentation aiming to persuade and convince those whom it addresses, that such a choice, decision or attitude is preferable to concurrent choices, decisions and attitudes. The reasons given in practical argumentation, the 'good' reasons, can be moral, political, social, economic or religious according to the field from which the decision is drawn. For the judge, they will be essentially legal, for his reasoning must show the conformity of the decision to the law which he is responsible for applying.

What characterizes an argumentation is its non-constraining character. If we admit certain presuppositions and methodological rules, we can show the inadequate character of certain solutions, but, even there, the accepted solution rarely can impose itself in all its details. It is rare when the judge does not have to exercise a power of appraisal, which his authority will have to impose on the issues before him as the expression of the law, although his practical reasoning is so closely rule bound.

If the decision were assuredly the same, whatever be the judge's personality, questions of competence would not have the fundamental importance they have in law. The judge's decision, based as it is upon explicit legal argumentation, remains, nevertheless, a personal decision: it is to the judge's convictions that we refer for questions of fact; it is to his judgment that we appeal for questions of characterization, it is his legal knowledge and his sense of equity that will settle legal questions. It is he whom the parties must convince; it is he to whom the lawyer's indictment and pleadings are addressed.

The jurist who elaborates legal theories, who furnishes a justified interpretation of a text or who proposes new legislation will measure the success of his enterprise by the approval of the courts or that of the legislator. From this perspective, legal theories do not have the task of stating the truth but of preparing and justifying decisions.

When the jurist interpreting a text invokes the will of the legislator or the sense of the law, it is not sufficient for him conscientiously to do the work of the legal historian, because then his demonstration would be addressed, not to the judge, but to other legal historians better qualified in the matter to decide the value of his demonstration. If he addresses the judge it is not as a legal historian but as a jurist attempting to convince the judge that in there is reason now to interpret the law in a certain way.[8] The submission of the judge to the will of the legislator does not concern essentially the legislature which voted the law as much as the presumed will of the present legislator. The latter supposedly indicates his accord with law he has not expressly abrogated. To conclude from this that he would interpret the laws, in every case, in the same manner that the former legislature did, is doubtful. If political, social, economic or even linguistic changes make new interpretation of an old text reasonable, jurisprudence can hardly go immediately from the letter of the law to its interpretation. Rarely is it the case that there is an explanatory law or that the legislature gives the judges interpretive directives. Thus Article 4 of the Polish Civil Code of 23 April 1964 which expressly declares that 'the dispositions of the Civil Code must be interpreted and applied in conformity with the principles of the social system and the goals of the People's Republic of Poland,'[9] expressly implies that all Polish legislation previous to the new regime, to the extent that it has not been abrogated, must be interpreted in a different spirit from that of the bourgeois legislator. It is obvious that this directive is hardly favorable to juridical security and that it is better, at the time of a revolutionary change, to replace the texts considered to have lapsed in conformity with the new legal spirit. It is conceivable that as a transitory measure the ancient texts that have not been abrogated subsist and the judge has the obligation to interpret them in the spirit of present legislator. It is true that political considerations determine the spirit of a legal system, but it is the task of the jurist, using the methods of legal reasoning, to reconcile the spirit with the letter of the law, in conformity to the values that the legal system tries to promote. Legal reasoning is thus a specific application of the theory of argumentation, a generalization of the Greco-Roman dialectic and rhetoric.

According to the values that prevail in a society (respect for the divine word, or human law, the search for equity or the common good, the dignity of the individual and the veneration of certain institutions) such arguments give good reasons for the justification of a given decision. Such a precedent or law will have more or less authority for the judge, jurist and public according to the societal place and importance of the legislator and judge.

This takes into account the predominance of such jurisdiction in the legal hierarchy.

Legal reasoning, which the judge uses to justify his judgment in particular cases, and which furnishes the reasons for convincing the contesting parties, the hierarchically superior tribunals, and the qualified public, of the merit of his decision, is not presented as a formally valid deduction from non-temporal truths. If this were the case we would understand neither the nature of legal problems nor the structure of legal controversies. Reasons considered good at one period of time and in one milieu are not in another; they are socially and culturally conditioned as are the convictions and the aspirations of the audience they must convince. Any preliminary study of legal history and jurisprudence suffices to show this.

Under the influence of a mathematically inspired rationalism, and especially of Cartesianism, the modern theories of natural law were developed and they presented the role of the legislator as being under the obligation to provide the universally valid relations of an objective justice through the promulgation of positive laws.[10] To this vision of law there was, at first, opposed the historical school, then positivism, which saw in legal relationships only the expression of the will of the nation or the sovereign legislator and to which the judges must blindly conform. In the Cartesian vision of the universe, the divine will is entirely free, not being bound by logical or mathematical truths but, once posited, these truths bind, by their self-evidence, every rational being. Similarly the sovereign's will has to account to no one, knowing no limitation, and once expressed in law, the citizens and more particularly, the judges, must submit uniformly to it. Already in the ideology of the French Revolution the absolute respect for the will of the legislative power was combined with confidence in its capacity to express itself clearly and all need for interpretation became, for them, superfluous in the vast majority of cases. They foresaw, by Article 12 of the law of 16–24 August 1790 concerning the judiciary organization in France, the obligation to refer to the legislature. 'The courts may not make regulations but will address themselves to a legislative body every time that they believe may be necessary, either to interpret a law or to make a new one.'[11]

The good functioning of this institution presupposed the exceptional character of this procedure because normally the legal texts were supposed to be sufficiently clear so as not to necessitate any interpretation (*interpretatio cessat in claris*). Very quickly this type of legislative procedure was abandoned and replaced in the Code Napoleon by Article 4 imposing upon the judge the obligation to decide even in cases of the law's silence, obscurity or inadequacy. In fact, to decide that a text is clear, we must see if any reasonable interpretation of it that could be given would lead to a similar solution for all other individual cases. But we are never sure that all concrete situations have been examined. A text considered clear in relation to known cases could pose a problem of interpretation in a new situation. Thus Article 617 of the Civil Code foresaw, among other things, that usufruct was ended by the natural death of the usufructuary or by the right's non-usage for 30 years. If the advances of biological technique would allow a man to be maintained indefinitely in a state of hibernation, if the usufructuary was to ask to remain in this state for a century, would it be necessary to wait 30 years before ceding his rights to the title holder? If the usufructuary wished to affect the product of the usufruct by being in a state of hibernation indefinitely, will we allow the new proprietor to be deprived, actually for ever, of the right to the good of which he is proprietor? Doubtless, new possibilities for prolonging life indefinitely in a state of hibernation would pose problems for the interpretation of a text which previously could be considered clear.

It is obvious that with the obscurity of law, the antinomies and lacunae, no purely deductive reasoning, which supposes the existence of a clear text and single applicable rule, would furnish the judge the legal solution that he is obliged to give if he does not want to be liable for a denial of justice. Only recourse to argumentation could give him the reasons sufficient to justify his legal decision.

The argumentative procedures to which legal argumentation has recourse are numerous. Several have sought to formalize some of them, such as reasoning by analogy, a *pari, a contrario, a fortiori,* as well as their diverse variants.[12] I do not believe in the success of such attempts. I do not believe, that uniform solutions can be found to controversies where the spirit is opposed to the letter of the law, that we can reduce to formulas, to a univocal application all the commonplaces, 'topoi', to which jurists have had recourse for centuries to justify their adoption of a position. The appeal to reason, to the nature of things, to equity or equality, all these notions and their conditions of application suppose an agreement of a philosophic nature on general perspectives, without which the commonplace can no longer play its role as a principle of common action and at the end, ceases to be comprehensible.

Every effort to convince presupposes the existence of an agreement on certain notions and principles. What is well-known and is the object of a general consensus does not have to be proved; similarly, this is true with what is presumed. It is the existence of an elaborated technique of the usage of presumptions and of the burden of proof which furnishes one of the characteristics of legal reasoning.[13] He who appeals to a presumption in his favor is freed from the burden of proof which is only admitted against presumptions *juris tantum*. At times, the contrary proof is inadmissible, at times, it is strictly regulated, such as the action which would attempt to reverse the presumption designating the wife's husband as the child's father.

Presumptions, normally, aim at protecting an existent state of affairs because it is presumed that the fact conforms to the law. It is thus that Article 2279 of the Civil Code affirms that possession presumes the right to possess. At times presumptions protect the individual against the abuses of power, e.g., the presumption of innocence; at times, they protect an institution like legal marriage, e.g., the presumption of paternity. Presumptions have a great variety of applications, but in every system the more a situation endures the more it seems to conform to the law. At a given moment different according to cases and systems, the statute of limitations comes into play and prevents every proof contrary to the factual situation. Because a presumption *juris et de jure* is imposed by this statute, fact becomes consolidated into law.

If an institution has functioned in a certain manner for years it will be difficult for the courts to admit that its function has been illegal or unconstitutional. Thus the Court of Accounts, which contrary to Article 97 of the Belgian Constitution, gave judgments, did not issue them publicly. It escapes this obligation by a judgment of the Supreme Court of Belgium of 2 January 1880 (Pas. 1880, I, 145) although a satisfactory justification for this non-public procedure was not given until the judgment of the Supreme Court of the 9 October 1959 (Pas. 1960, I, 170).[14] In an analogous way, Article 6 of the Belgian Constitution provides for the equality of Belgians before the law. The first Belgian female doctor of law who wished to become a lawyer was refused the right to the lawyer's oath, although she filled all the conditions stated in the law. The Supreme Court supported its decision in a judgment of 11 November 1889 (Pas. 1890, I, 10) affirming that if the legislator had not excluded, by a formal disposition, women from the bar, it was because it held it to be too evident an axiom for it to have to enunciate: 'that the service of justice was reserved to men.' The Court had not hesitated to interpret an explicit constitutional text in terms of a traditionally accepted state of affairs.[15]

A presumption *juris et de jure* protects an assumption and assimilates it to an unquestionable truth. A judiciary power when it is not submitted to the control of a superior court can even have recourse to fictions and determine facts in a way contrary to evidence so as not to hand down a sentence which is repugnant to it, but which the text of the law made inevitable without this subterfuge. This recourse to fiction permitted juries to acquit the accused in many cases of euthanasia.

In principle, and conforming to the rule of formal justice which requires equal treatment for essentially similar situations, a decision in conformity with an established precedent is presumed just without further justification. However, to put aside precedents or to modify jurisprudence, there is the necessity to justify change. It is one of the characteristics of the judicial spirit, desirous of security and stability, to presume that conformity to precedents, custom, and tradition is conformity to law and justice.[16] From this perspective change only requires justification. This is the reason why jurists have been accused of being conservatives; giving great value to order and security, they require good reasons for all innovation. Thus, judges subordinated, in fact, to the will of the present legislator and not to the ancient legislator which can no longer react, presume that the two wills coincide unless there are major reasons justifying an interpretation of the ancient texts in a new light. Without this presumption of continuity, the present legislator would be put aside and the judges would substitute their will for its will.

This occurs in legal systems where God, through the intermediary of prophets such as Moses or Mohammed, institutes legislation. His work being perfect, there is no question of changing it; therefore it is incumbent upon the interpretors to adapt it to the needs of society. Their theological-juridical reasoning brings together great respect for the letter of the law with an extraordinary freedom in interpretation. The prohibition of all new legislation obliges the interpretor to be an intellectual gymnast, which at times make the uninitiated smile, and this in view of elaborating equitable and utilizable solutions in relation to texts whose strict application has become practically impossible.

In all cases, recourse to presumption, with or without the admissibility of contrary proof, allows an escape from anarchy, which would result without it, i.e., from the absence of a logical or empirical proof. The diverse ways of utilizing presumptions and the multiple domains in which jurists used them should become an object of an analytic and historical study which would be of the highest interest. It would furnish an inventory of situations and values which the several legal systems have sought to protect.

Legal reasoning shows all the tensions created by the desire to conciliate stability with change, the need for continuity with adaptation and security with equity and the common good. The essential value of legal security distinguishes legal reasoning from other forms of practical reasoning. In this type of reasoning one has always sought to minimize the intervention of the will which is very often identified with the arbitrary and the irrational. But the personal factor cannot be eliminated from legal reasoning. Like all argumentation, being the function of the people who argue, its value will depend, in the final analysis, upon the integrity and intelligence of the judges who determine its specific nature.

NOTES

* French text in *Archives for Philosophy of Law and Social Philosophy*, Proceedings of the World Congress of the International Association for Legal Political Philosophy, on Juridical Reasoning, Brussels 29. 8 − 3. 9, 1971, Wiesbaden, 1972. Beiheft N.F. 7 pp. 1−15.

[1] G. Kalinowski, *Introduction à la logique juridique*, Paris, 1965, pp. 38−39.

[2] U. Klug, *Juristische Logik,* Berlin, 1966, p. 7.

[3] Ch. Perelman, 'Qu'est-ce que la logique juridique?', in *Le champ de l'argumentation*, Brussels, 1970, p. 133.

[4] See A. Giuliani, 'La logique juridique comme théorie de la controverse,' in *Archives de philosophie du droit*, 1966, pp. 87−113, et *La Controversia*, Pubblicazioni della Università di Pavia, 1966.

[5] See my article 'Raisonnement juridique et logique juridique,' in *Le champ de l'argumentation*, op. cit, pp. 123−130.

[6] 'The Logic of the Reasonable as differentiated from the Logic of the Rational' in *Essays in Honor of Roscoe Pound*, Indianapolis, 1962, p. 205.

[7] Plato, *Republic* p. 348 a−b.

[8] My article 'A propos de la règle de droit, réflexions de méthode' in *La règle de droit*, Brussels, 1971. pp. 320−321.

[9] Z. Ziembiński, 'Les lacunes de la loi dans le système juridique polonais et les méthodes utilisées pour les combler' in *Le problème des lacunes en droit.* Studies published by Ch. Perelman, Bruylant, Brussels, 1968, pp. 140−141.

[10] Montesquieu, *The Spirit of the Laws*, Book I, Ch. I. Trans. T. Nugent, N.Y., 1949.

[11] Huberlant, 'Les mécanismes institués pour combler les lacunes de la loi' in *Le problème des lacunes en droit*, Brussels, 1968, pp. 48−9.

[12] U. Klug, *Juristische Logik*, pp. 118−138.

[13] My article, 'La spécificité de la preuve juridique', *Justice et Raison*, Brussels, 1963, pp. 212−15. In English in *The Idea of Justice and the Problem of Argument*, London, 1963, pp. 98−108.

[14] J. Miedzianagora, *Philosophies positivistes du droit et droit positif*, Paris, 1970, pp. 7−10.

[15] Perelman, 'Essai de synthèse' in *Le problème les lacunes en droit* pp. 547−8.

[16] Perelman, *Justice*, New York, 1967, pp. 9−10. Chapter 2 pp. 27−28 of the present volume.

CHAPTER FIFTEEN

LAW, LOGIC AND EPISTEMOLOGY*

In examining or discussing the relations between law and other disciplines, the concept of law has not been adequately examined. However, our conception of law can determine these same relations in completely different ways. This is true with the relations of law and logic. It is for this reason that I would like to begin by recalling the idea of legal reasoning. I would like to show you how this idea is tied to a certain ideological conception of law and how by changing this conception we will come to a completely different conception of its relations to logic and, in addition, to a completely different conception of logic. The difficulty is that we are involved in the study of relations among non-static concepts and this leads us to study the problem dialectically and not analytically.

The idea of law which, since the French Revolution, has prevailed on the continent is related both to the doctrine of the separation of powers and to a psychology of human faculties (emotion, will and knowledge). Let me explain. The separation of powers means that there is a power, the legislative, which by its will determines the law which is to govern a certain society. The law is the expression of the will of the people given through the decisions of the legislature. The judicial power, on the other hand, declares, but does not elaborate, the law. Accordingly, the judge simply applies the law that is entrusted to him.

The doctrine of the separation of powers parallels the doctrine which distinguishes will from knowledge. Law is the expression of the legislator's will which judges must enforce, and in no way, modify. This leads to a legalistic vision of the law; it expresses uniquely the will of the legislator, and the judge's passivity satisfies our need for legal certainty. Law is a given which must be recognized by everyone in a similar fashion. This vision of law leads to a similarity between science and law. If we consider law as a deductive system or if we compare the rendering of justice to 'weighing', then the judge seems to be participating in an impersonal operation which allows him to weigh the pretentions of the parties and the gravity of the crimes, etc. This process should be impartial and passionless, i.e., without fear, hate or pity; justice must have its eyes covered and not see the consequences of its actions: *dura lex sed lex*. This is an attempt to reconcile law with a calculation, a weighing, in any case with something whose reassuring exactness can protect us from the abuses of the corrupted justice of the Old Regime, and makes us think that we are not at the mercy of men, but are protected by more or less impersonal institutions.

Traditionally, and this is still the case for those who know the law only from a distance, the judge's decision was schematized by what we call the judicial syllogism. Its major premise is the rule of law, the minor states the facts established by the trial, and the conclusion is identical with the legal consequences derived from them in respect to the system of law in force. A logician would prefer, in this case, not to speak of syllogism, since it is a question of the application not of a syllogism, but of *modus ponens*. This is the schema of deduction: each time A, i.e., certain conditions are united, then B, certain legal consequences follow; A is so, then B must be applied. The major premise is given to the judge, it is the rule of law which must govern the facts in question; the minor premise states the facts which he himself must establish, and the consequences result by simple deduction.

What is the role of jurisprudence in this conception? It is to transform the totality of laws, regulations and positively admitted norms into a system. The role of jurisprudence is to systematize the law and to elaborate juridical dogma which furnishes the judge with all the major premises needed to expound the law and to put at the disposition of the judges and the parties as perfect an instrument as possible.

For this instrument to play its role the system of law should be as close as possible to a formal system; so that for each situation there is a legal rule and this rule is one and unambiguous. In a formal axiomatic system there are thus three requirements: (1) the elimination of all ambiguity in relation to the rules of formation of significant expressions as well as the rules of their governance; (2) the system be coherent, that it not permit at the same time the affirmation and negation of a proposition; and (3) the system be complete, i.e., that for each proposition that is to be formulated in this system we must be ready to prove its truth or falsity, that the system furnishes a definite response. No problems must arise in the system that can be declared to be insoluble. In formal logic the first condition, the elimination of ambiguity, is always realized, but at what price? The price is the creation of an artificial language similar to the mathematical one and the presentation of rules of demonstration and proof which in their application leave no doubt nor controversy. This takes place in mathematics and in logic when conceived as formalized deductive systems. The second requirement, coherence, is almost always, and for a simple and good reason, realized. If there is incoherence the system is abandoned and replaced by another, free from this incoherence. This is no guarantee that on another occasion some incoherence will not reappear. Those who know the history of logic are aware of the many systems which have been formulated, abandoned, improved, etc., etc. As for the third requirement, i.e., completeness, this can be fulfilled only in very simple systems. Therefore, we can show that a system equivalent to elementary algebra, for example, is not complete and we cannot resolve every problem which it can bring forth. There is a general tendency to say that every system having a certain richness of expression is necessarily incomplete. This means that we can show that sufficiently rich systems necessarily contain undecidable propositions which can be neither affirmatively nor negatively demonstrated.

The question must now be asked as to what must be done if the system used by the judge or at his disposal is not a perfect system; that it does not respond to the three exigencies of non-ambiguity, coherence and complete-ness? This is the case of every legal system however perfect it may appear to be. The French Revolution sought a solution to this problem with the enact-ment of law of the 24 August 1790 which dealt with the legal system. It in-stituted an obligation to refer to the legislature each time a judge had doubts concerning a legal interpretation or a legal application. The legislator was to interpret or complete the law in doubt which thus allowed the judge to make his decision. It was believed that only in very rare cases would the judge have to refer to the legislature. Had they believed that in all cases where there were questions of law, but not questions of fact, the interpretation of the law would require legislative advice, they would have eliminated the courts and replaced them by ten thousand legislatures which would be in constant session responding to all questions. It was sufficient that the judge be hesitant and believe that his doubts were real for him, to refer to the legislator. This system prevented the judge from intervening as legislator. To improve the law the judge could neither complete nor interpret it. Thus, very quickly as a result of this bottleneck, this solution became impossible and the idea of obligatory legislative referal was abandoned, and replaced by another solution. This obligation to refer to the legislature, besides having practical inadequacies, brought about another confusion of powers. In interpreting the law retroactively — all legal interpretations being retroactive — they settled, at the same time, the litigation by giving the decision. The legislator became, from then on, the judge, and this was contrary to the principle of the separa-tion of powers. A certain confusion of powers is inevitable, but the procedure of obligatory legislative referal led to unending delays, and another solution had to be found. The judge must have certain legislative powers allowing him to complete, clarify, explain and perhaps also modify the law. The celebrated Article 4 of the Code Napoleon was enacted: 'The judge who will refuse to judge under the pretext of silence, obscurity or of legal insufficiency will be held guilty for denial of justice.' In other words, this article institutes the obligation to judge. In instituting this obligation the legal system, which had been assimilated to a deductive and formal one, was transformed. Why? Because if the judge is obliged to judge and also to seek motivation for his decision, because he cannot decide arbitrarily, he must justify his decision from the law he applies. The judge must then be given the means, the intellectual instruments, which are indispensable for the achievement of his task. If there is ambiguity, he must resolve it. His decisions are not indifferent as they would be by the rule of formal justice which is valid in every legal system, i.e., to be just we must treat in the same way essentially similar cases. For the judges who apply the law, treating essentially similar cases in the same way, there had to be knowledge of how other judges decided in similar cases. They had to confer together and publish a *pasicrisie*,[1] they had to know precedents. To the degree that judges decide in law they must cite legal precedent. If there is no reason to set it aside, it is reasonable that later judges use the same criteria as earlier ones. This manner of behavior, although not obligatory, constitutes a guarantee of judicial security in law. What role will the judge play? He will have to eliminate ambiguities. If there are different applicable laws he must avoid conflicts, either by placing them hierarchically while finding general rules for the solution of the conflicts, or if he cannot find general rules, because we are dealing with laws having the same bearing, emanating from the same authority, he will have to limit the applicable extent of each law so that in the future we may know how to proceed. Yet, if there is no applicable rule, one which can be drawn from the whole system, then two solutions are possible. The judge can apply the rule declaring that if the plaintiff does not find the rule establishing his suit, his case must be set aside by virtue of the rule of freedom, according to which one is free to do what the law does not prohibit. This solution, however, is not possible nor equitable in every case. For example, one agrees to a settlement for the payment of back interest, without taking into account the interest rate; the agreement is incomplete, it has lacunae, the judge has to complete it and find the means to determine a just rate of interest, and the laws which allow him to give his decision. In each of these cases, formal logic cannot help him. In the first case, because of ambiguity of the notion, formal logic cannot guide us when we are concerned with the content and not with form of reasoning.

If the question concerns the preciseness of the notion of urgency, formal logic cannot help us. Formal logic cannot help us eliminate an antinomy or fill lacunae. On the contrary, formal logic would eventually contribute to the existence of an antinomy or of a lacuna, but it could neither eliminate the one or fill the other. For that we must have recourse to other techniques, such as those of legal logic. It is clear from the above that the idea of legal logic is not, as we have believed, the application of formal logic to law. We are dealing with instruments — *methodological* ones — intellectual techniques placed at the disposal of the jurist, and especially at the judge's disposal, to accomplish his task. These are reasoning by analogy, arguments *a ratione legis,* by the finality of law, *a pari, a contrario,* etc., and which traditionally and for centuries, were recognized as forming part of legal logic. Until the 18th century works were published entitled *the juridical topics* which showed the methodology of the jurist.

I have shown up till now that even though there is a precise regard for the systematic aspect of law, the result of the intervention of Article 4 and the latitude which it gave to the judge, provided the judge with the obligation to use these intellectual instruments which could no longer be placed under the sign of truth or of formal logic. The judge accomplishes his task under the guidance of other values: the reasonable, the acceptable, the socially efficacious, the legal security and its warrant formal justice, but also the value of material justice, id est equity. We see immediately that values which are not purely those of theoretical knowledge intervene as guides for the judge's decision.

To show what is characteristic in the judge's reasoning, let us take as simple a case as possible. We will take a law which offers no possibility of dispute, no ambiguity, a rule as clear and as non-equivocal as possible. Let us suppose a police regulation stipulated on a sign at the entrance of a public park, 'Vehicles are forbidden to enter the park.' The last time I used this example I spoke of traffic in the park but let's simplify and say, 'Vehicles are forbidden to enter the park.' Let us suppose a police officer stationed before the park gates is the first judge. He sees someone enter with a baby carriage. He asks himself: 'Is it a vehicle?' 'No', he says to himself, 'a baby carriage is not a vehicle; it can go.' Then a child with an electric auto enters. 'Good, it can enter', he says to himself, 'a vehicle is an automobile or a motorcycle, everything that makes noise, pollutes the air, nuisances we want to eliminate.' This is the first interpretation of the word vehicle defined for a certain regulatory purpose. We ask why this limitation? Then an ambulance arrives; someone had a heart attack: Must the ambulance be allowed in the park? What will the judge say, even if the law is clear and unambiguous? He will say it is a case of circumstances outside one's control, *force majeure*. Then a child falls and breaks his leg and a taxi is called to take him to a hospital. A pregnant woman in the park unexpectedly has to be driven to the hospital. What are the problems which the police officer must resolve? Is it a question of interpreting the word vehicle? There is more to it. The judge does not judge from the meaning of a line in the text. He asks what value we want to protect and what value is competing with it. Which is the most important? Suddenly, we see that instead of being a simple calculator, the judge — be he the first or a subsequent judge is of little importance — has to face values and all at once we are reminded that for this purpose, the judge's role is not simply to bow to a pre-determined conclusion but that he is obligated to judge and this means to make a decision. This decision must be legally motivated. The most interesting examples of legal reasoning and of the confrontation of law and logic are those furnished by legal decisions. I am not saying that there are not others, for example, administrative decisions, but what is interesting in the case of legal decisions is that they are published, they can be compared, they furnish precedents, they are part of a system of law, they may be either judgements of lower courts, decrees of the Council of State or judgments of the Supreme Court. What is interesting is that we have a decision preceded by an explanation which is published and known and which provides the material for the study of legal reasoning. These decisions concern values which are, at times, respect for truth — truth is at the base of these legal decisions — but not always.

If law knows fiction — which is not an invention of a civilization or of a culture, fiction being found in all legal systems — it is because fiction is a decision by which facts are qualified in a way contrary to reality, so that a desirable result is achieved and one which will be more in conformity to equity, justice or social efficacy. I would like to give some examples. The best known example of fiction, which was taught to all students of law, is the fiction of the Roman praetor who to apply Civil (roman) law to foreigners, assimilated them to Roman citizens for whom this law was normally reserved. But how should foreigners be judged? It was necessary to find rules by which to judge them and the fiction allowed the assimilation of the foreigner to the Roman citizen. Let us illustrate another fiction. A few years ago before a jury of a criminal court at Liège, they judged the trial of a Catholic mother, who with the agreement of her doctor, also Catholic, had decided actually to kill her fifth and last born child, monstrously deformed as a result of the effects of the thalidomide which she had absorbed. She thought that by allowing this monstrous child to live she would cause misfortune for her other children, for the whole family. She was a very honorable woman, all Belgium took pity on her, but she had committed a criminal act. Our legal code foresees no other designation, in a similar case, than murder or assassination. The jury decided that the woman did not commit murder. This decision led to her acquittal, but it was a consequence of a fiction; the act was qualified contrary to the established evidence. A third example of fiction is in English law at the end of the 18th century and its recognition of the crime of grand larceny, a serious misdeed that was punishable by death. In the enumeration of what constituted a grand larceny was included every theft of 40 shillings or more. Very quickly English judges revolted against this prescription and regularly, even when the thief stole a large sum of money, estimated every serious theft at 39 shillings. If there is fiction, this is the most obvious case. The judges, however, were justified by the result. The English parliament decided to abolish this law and no longer included such thefts in the category of grand larceny. Here is an example of the way the judge, not being able to change the law, and finding that it leads to iniquitous or inefficacious consequences, introduces a fiction allowing him to decide in a manner that seems equitable. These examples show that the judge, in certain cases, can use other techniques and is not limited to provide means to supplement the lack of legal clarity, because in certain cases the law is very clear.

Let us take another example. There was a law in Imperial Germany before 1914 which punished with a prison sentence those who on May 1 walked in procession behind a red flag. On May 1 the police intervened, arrested some people and confiscated their flag. The trial took place several weeks later. The flag was on the table in the court; it was not red but lilac —. Should they to be condemned or not? Were the factual conditions fulfilled or not? Had they walked behind a red flag? Can it be said that for the needs of the cause lilac should be assimilated to red? But then the scope of the law is broadened. Is not the interpretation of penal law restrictive? In reality, judges are not content simply to apply the law; very often they extend it by analogy, but they can also restrict it. This is the reason for legal theories. Great legal constructions have a purpose; they aim at the modification of the law's application. When the theory of legal abuse was created, the proprietor no longer was protected in the exercise of his property rights if he wished to use it for the purpose of injuring another. The right of property conceived as an absolute right was replaced, was referred back to its social function and protected only when it fulfilled this function. This theory eliminated the protection accorded the proprietor in every case where he wanted to use his property rights in a way that was no longer in conformity to its social function. A whole theory is elaborated to say that the proprietor is not protected in certain cases.

International private law tells us that the conditions governing the status of persons is derived from the national legislation of the interested parties. Suppose a Moroccan comes to Belgium, he already has two wives and he would like to marry a third. His law allows him to marry four women. Would he be given the right to have his national law taken into account since bigamy is punishable by the penal code? This is an illustration of what is called the international public order. This notion opposes the application of a foreign law when it is too flagrantly opposed to the national public order. But if, for example, a Moroccan has two wives and he is killed in an automobile accident, is the first wife alone entitled to the indemnity and not the second? Belgian Courts have recently decided that the second wife also has indemnity rights, although bigamy may be involved, because here there is no violation of the international public order. All these theories oppose one value to another; thus, restraining or extending the scope of the law and not merely clarifying it. The judge's mission is to speak the law but in a way that conforms to the sensibilities of society. Why? Because his role is to establish legal peace and this peace comes about only when he can convince the parties, the public and his superiors that he has adjudicated in an equitable way. Let us not forget that justice is the *ars aequi et boni* according to the old traditional Roman definition. Another element intervenes when the judge applies the techniques of legal logic, confronts values and comes to a decision. We affirm that these techniques do not have the rigor and the non-ambiguity of formal logic. By introducing these techniques we introduce a degree of insecurity into the law in the name of other values such as equity, efficacy. etc. We maintain that legal logic must furnish good reasons for its decisions: *good legal* reasons. The notion of a good legal reason can change evidently according to the system and the times, etc. We can be in disagreement concerning the force of arguments; they can lead parties to different decisions. Here a personal element is introduced; the judge is not an automaton; he is involved in the value of reasons. The judge decides after having listened to the parties, and the opposing legal points of view. Each party seeks not only to clarify its position but also to convince by means of argumentation; because of the non-compelling character of this argumentation the judge's role is indispensable. We do not need a judge to know that two plus two equal four, nor to resolve problems where calculators or measurement give the solution.

There is no need of a judge where the rules lead everyone, provided no errors are committed, to the same solution, and where correct rules of reasoning from indisputable premises exist. We need a judge when these rules are *equivocal*, when reasoning does not end in a conclusion, but justifies a decision. We can reach contrary decisions according to the importance we accord to this or that type of argument, and it is for this reason that we turn to a judge who will have the power to decide. When the judges do not agree, we need a criterium, e.g., the majority who will hand down the decision and which in the last instance *pro veritate habetur,* will be presumed in conformity with truth. There is no truth in fact, but only recourse to a power that makes the decision binding. From this perspective we understand the importance of this power and also the fact that this power is recognized and its authority admitted. It is the same with legislative power. The legislator also exercises a power because laws can be conceived in different ways and men must have the power to establish which is the applicable law, which is the law in force. Concerning both the legislator and the judge, and recognizing that neither laws nor legal decisions are imposed self-evidently, recourse to power and recognized authority must supplement the absence of unanimity. Without it we risk anarchy. If we think that only questions of knowledge, on which there is unanimous agreement, should be taken into account then when faced with choice, decision and opinion, we would feel as if we were before a void. The application of the calculus of probabilities would give us no response, because the questions of law involve decisions, as Jean Carbonnier[2] has aptly pointed out. The lawyer seeks to influence and to convince the judge that the case he is defending is the best; he presents arguments from which the judge decides. The lawyer's triumph is when the judge embodies his arguments in his decision; the lawyer thus collaborates in the exercise of justice.

There are cases where a lawyer to a client who asks about his chance of winning a case replies, 'you have no chance'. Here he no longer intervenes as a practitioner, he forecasts what we would call legal sociology. In other terms, he considers the situation from the outside and he sees what his client's chances are for a favorable decision, given precedent and the jurisprudence in force. In this instance the lawyer responds to what we call a theoretical consultation since he does not intervene to influence the decision. The legal practitioner has different roles to play. At times, he participates directly or indirectly in a decision; at others, he regards the problem from the outside and states the situation as he sees it. Is it the role of jurisprudence to declare what is true? In the past, jurisprudence formulated the law just as the legislator had wished it, and legal dogmatics — the name reveals the reality —

spoke truth in legal matters. In my conception, the legal theoreticians, those who formulate jurisprudence, should rather be considered counsellors, whose role is to enlighten the judges and others who have power to make a decision. They are there to show them what the most reasonable and most equitable decision would be, to furnish them with all the arguments for a given solution. They prepare the judge's work, but like the judge they must not say solely the truth but also the just, the equitable, the reasonable; their role is to prepare in the same spirit, decisions of justice. Consequently, I take the opposite view of Hans Kelsen's pure theory of the law for whom the role of jurisprudence is solely scientific, i.e., we can conceive jurisprudence as if it were a concern of a theoretician who studies the legal system from the outside, who takes the law as a scientific object. In reality, and traditionally, jurisprudence has a different role. It is to prepare by its reflections, its analyses, its considerations, its motivations, the legal decisions which in every case might be presented before the judges.

I would like to end with a few very general considerations. If we have forgotten that the techniques of the jurist and, in particular, of the judge are argumentative ones, consisting in giving good reasons, replying to objections, so as to end controversies and obtain legal peace, i.e., the consent of the interested parties, the public and other qualified people, etc., if we have forgotten this, it is because for centuries the theory of law was modeled on the sciences. We have not taken into account the fact that law is a practical activity and not a purely theoretical reflection. But if you ask me if it is possible to transform practice into theory, I would say yes, it is very easy. I have published an article on practical reasoning[3] showing that by introducing a supplementary premise a practical controversy can be transformed into a purely formal logical deduction, but, the debate will concern the premise that has been introduced. Is there or is there not cause to introduce this premise? This is the objection that I made to Kalinowski[4] at a recent debate on legal reasoning. In it he sought to show that to resolve the problem of legal lacunae it would simply suffice to introduce new premises. I told him that the question was whether there was cause or not to introduce these new premises.[5] We can always transform practical into theoretical reasoning by introducing, without reason, a disputed premise, but then, evidently, the argument ceases.

This conception brings continental law close to Anglo-Saxon law because if we see fundamentals, if we see that law is basically a discussion of values, all the rest becomes technique. It is in terms of techniques that French, English, American, Roman, Talmudic law, etc., can be compared.

All these are variable techniques, exercised within a general function of law.

If law has suffered much from being too influenced by the sciences, I believe the same reproach can be addressed to philosophy. The latter has also wanted to be like a deductive or an inductive science, think of Hume who proposed an inductive philosophy, or Spinoza who proposed a deductive one. Actually it is a baited trap. Philosophy is also concerned with values. Ontology in philosophy is not only a descriptive study of the actual but, to some degree, an evaluation of it. If the new concept of law spreads, which is basically a very old one, and which has been forgotten for centuries, philosophers will have much to learn from it. They will look to the techniques of the jurist to learn how to reason about values, how to realize an equilibrium, how to bring about a synthesis of values. We will then see that in philosophy, reasons in the plural are at least as important as reason in the singular. Reasons in the plural are put into history, they vary, depend upon the social structure and the existential reality of the individual. All the historical and existential elements are introduced into this philosophical vision. I do not know what Gueroult[6] who has studied the idea of reason and reasons, will think of this new approach. I believe, however, that there is a reality here that can entirely modify our perspective of reasoning in general.

I would like to end by saying that if formal logic has conquered almost all the world's universities, except perhaps certain Italian and French ones, the teaching of argumentation on the other hand, has been entirely neglected for centuries. Argumentation is the ancient dialectic and rhetoric of Socrates, Plato, Aristotle. It is not the dialectic of Kant and Hegel, and it would be a very interesting thesis subject to know how one could go from one to the other. But there is a revival of the theory of argumentation. Three years ago the Faculty of Law of the University of Brussels in the process of organizing its program, asked me to teach a new course that was entitled 'Logic and Argumentation' to underscore the importance of argumentation for the training of jurists. This example should be followed.

NOTES

* *XXIXe Semaine de Synthèse, Le Droit, Les Sciences Humaines et La Philosophie*, Vrin, Paris, 1973.
[1] A record of significant legal decisions in every country.
[2] Leading French sociologist of law.

[3] 'Le raisonnement pratique', in *Le Champ de l'argumentation*, Brussels, 1970, pp. 183–192.
[4] Polish logician living in France.
[5] *Etudes de logique juridique IV*, Bruylant, Brussels, 1970, pp. 25–31.
[6] Professor at the College de France who elaborated a theory of philosophical systems.

CHAPTER SIXTEEN

LAW, PHILOSOPHY AND ARGUMENTATION*

Every practical man is thoroughly convinced that the proper method of legal reasoning is an argumentation through which we discuss, with regard to each problem, reasons for or against an attitude or a decision. This is equally true for cases of motivated judgment, doctrinal study, a pleading or an indictment. Most works, however, called 'legal logic' present a theory of formal logic, illustrated, as the case may be, by schematic examples of deductive reasoning applied to law.[1]

There is widespread agreement among modern logicians to reserve the name 'logic' for formal logic, and to ignore every other form of reasoning: even, in relation to induction, to display only techniques which allow us to invalidate or confirm hypotheses and to say nothing of their elaboration. This attitude has intimidated jurists who don't dare use the words 'legal logic' to qualify proper legal modes of reasoning and who are content to speak of legal reasoning or legal thought.[2] Not even those who see that legal reasoning goes beyond the limits of formal logic have placed their analyses within the framework of a general theory of argumentation, yet without this the particularities of legal reasoning are unintelligible.

The role of philosophers in our culture with respect to legal reasoning is plain to see. Their theories open new horizons to us, individual problems are placed in a total perspective, yet the philosophers prevent us from seeing what is incompatible with their vision of things. Philosophy has been able, since Descartes, to extend to all aspects of life a *Weltanschauung* which has been inspired by the methodology of the exact sciences, but has not given to law, nor, in a more general way, to practice, such a place in philosophy as to embrace action and its problems.

The theory of argumentation which concerns both set speeches and controversy has its origins in ancient Graeco-Roman rhetoric and dialectic, its tradition going from Gorgias and Protagoras to Quintillian and including Socrates, Plato, Aristotle, the ancient teachers of rhetoric and sophistry, and continuing through the Middle Ages and Renaissance. In its contemporary aspects, it constitutes an attempt to free western philosophy from the impasse which it has faced since Hume because of the absence of a logic of value judgments. Contemporary philosophy, in its desire to oppose value to reality, the subjective to the objective, will to knowledge, and passions to reason, has led to the rejection of practical philosophy, including every theory of choice, decision and reasonable action: this it has done to the degree that it has totally dismissed nonverifiable intuitions.

If the application of means to ends is the sole object of rational investigation and the ends themselves are viewed as the results of irrational choices which reasoning does not allow us to decide, then our highly qualitative technological civilization will be put in the service of irrationally uncontrollable passions, desires and aspirations. Without practical philosophy, man becomes a plaything of his unconscious, or even a slave of cultural, political and religious traditions which, lacking adequate method, he can neither transcend nor adapt to new needs and situations.

As a result of my first studies concerning justice, I reached the conclusion that the only formula for justice that can be acceptable to a positivist is that of formal justice: essentially similar cases must be treated in the same manner. It is obvious that value judgments are indispensable for the application of this formula, because without them we cannot say which cases are essentially similar nor how they are to be handled. These judgements seem arbitrary because they can be based neither on experience nor on calculation.[3]

Faced with the impossibility of admitting this last conclusion, especially after the years of Nazi rule inspired by the 'Myth of the 20th Century' and the cult of violence, I, in collaboration with Mrs. L. Olbrechts-Tyteca, began a search for a logic of value judgments. After many years, during which we analyzed, as minutely as possible, hundreds of arguments concerning values, we found that this specific logic of value judgments did not exist. What we found, however, was the ancient tradition, today almost completely forgotten, of rhetoric and of Graeco-Roman dialectic.[4]

Modern logic, which is the result of the analysis of mathematical reasoning, was conceived as a collection of structures without subject or object, as a logical syntax of language (Carnap). Time was needed before logic, including semantics, could define the function of denotation, the basis of material truth and falsity. Over the course of the years the field of investigation was extended to plurivalent, modal and deontic logics. Then, having seen that language is a means of human communication, logicians became interested in the practical, and recognized that language is a means of action by which we involve and obligate ourselves (Austin's performative).

The history of logic might have been richer and less reductive if modern logic had started from the analysis not only of mathematical reasoning but also of other forms of reasoning such as those used in practical experience, e.g., when we deliberate, criticize, justify, give positive or negative reasons, and attempt individually or in groups, to make a reasoned decision or adopt a rule of action. Practical reasoning that justifies a decision is rarely the simple conclusion of a syllogism. If men oppose each other concerning a decision to be taken, it is not because some commit an error of logic or calculation. They discuss apropos the applicable rule, the ends to be considered, the meaning to be given to values, the interpretation and the characterization of facts. When engaged in a controversy on each of these points they reason, and their reasoning deserves as much analysis as the reasoning of the mathematician.

Lacking knowledge of other forms of reasoning, the formalist conception of law is forced to refer every decision about justice to a judicial syllogism; the major premise declares the rule of law, the minor subsumes the given facts under the rule and the conclusion draws the resulting judicial consequences. With the judicial syllogism we lose sight of the fact that the judge's intellectual effort has already been achieved, his deliberation finished, and there remains only the question of form. The important thing is not the passage from premises to conclusion but the way the judge justifies his premises both in fact and in law. This justification does not consist in a formally correct demonstration but in an argument guided by rules of legal application.

Since Descartes, however, only mathematical demonstration, the compelling proof, imposed by its evidence on every reasonable being, has been judged worthy of our attention. If men do not agree about some matter, and one cannot show the other that he is wrong, it is probable that no one knows the truth or has clear and distinct ideas about the matter.[5] Disagreement disappears before self-evidence, which suppresses the possibility of choice and disagreement, and even makes the idea of reasonable choice seem contradictory. Arguments which justify our options, choices, and decisions are never as compelling as demonstrative proofs; they are more or less strong, relevant or convincing. A demonstration is correct or incorrect, it is imposed absolutely or lacks value; but in argumentation it is always possible to plead for or against, because arguments which support one thesis do not entirely exclude those supporting the opposite one; this in no way means that all arguments are of the same value.

The noncompelling character of argumentation has caused the rationalists to neglect this form of reasoning and has made them favor intuition, calculation and experimentation. When we must justify preferences, deliberate about a decision, or discuss values, then argumentation and recourse to dialectics are indispensable. This is what Plato had already affirmed in the *Euthyphro* (7b–d) according to Moreau's paraphrase:

We do not discuss what can be objectively determined by incontestable procedures. If we differ in opinion, you and me, says Socrates to Euthyphro, about the number of eggs in the basket, about the length of a piece of cloth or about the weight of a sack of corn we will not argue about it, we will not discuss it; it will be sufficient to count, to measure, to weigh and our difference is resolved. Differences are prolonged and poisoned when such procedures and objective criteria are lacking. This is precisely the case, Euthyphro, when we disagree on the just, the unjust, the beautiful and the ugly, the good and the bad: in one word, on values.[6]

If philosophy is the field of controversy concerning values, where inter-locutors seek to convince each other without necessarily reaching agreement, law organizes the controversies and the procedures to bring about a decision imposed by a judge.[7] It is the judge, competent to settle disputes – a specialized judge or any other authority filling these functions – who allows us to distinguish law from morality and philosophy. The elaboration of judicial rules and procedures makes it possible to see in law a group of social techniques able to guide those subject to jurisdiction, to prevent, and as the case may be, to settle conflicts by a decision motivated by a competent authority. A judgment so motivated is like a decision supported by an argu-mentation showing that the decision is in conformity to law.

The purpose of this argumentation, as of all argumentation, is to obtain or intensify the adherence of an audience to theses given to them for their approval. For the judge, this audience is made up by the parties, superior Courts, and enlightened public opinion. When the Supreme Court justifies its interpretation of a law it should avoid opposing the will of the legislator. There are two conceptions of interpretation, one is designated as 'static' and requires that the interpretation be in conformity with the will of the legisla-ture that has approved the law; the other is 'dynamic' and requires that the interpretation conform to what the public interest demands in the circum-stances. Both conceptions seem insufficient. The first because the ancient legislator no longer has legal existence and there is no possibility for him to manifest his agreement or nonagreement with the Court's interpretation; the second because given the freedom of presenting its conception of 'the public interest', the Court would suppress every distinction between decisions *de lege lata* and those *de lege ferenda*, and become a substitute for the legislator whenever it seemed useful to do so. This is the reason why I prefer to under-stand the submission of the Court to the will of the legislator as signifying a submission to the presumed will of the present legislature which normally decides for the public interest and could always react if the Court's decisions were opposed to its views. It happens that for reasons of legal certainty the

Court's decision follows the terms of the law, although it says that its decision does not conform to what it believes is in the public interest. The legislature is thus made aware of the fact that it has to amend the law.

A judge-legislator dialectic begins where the respective roles of judge and legislature depend, either on the Supreme Court's greater or lesser timidity to take the initiative, or on the greater or lesser procedural difficulty of modifying and amending legislatively the legal rule. The greater the procedural difficulty is, the more the judges will become substitutes for the legislature. In Muslim and Jewish law, where the legislator is presumed perfect and cannot manifest himself again, the judges and doctors of law must invent ingenious techniques of interpretation in order to adapt ancient and immutable texts to new needs and situations.

In a trial, each time the argument turns to questions of law, at least two points of view are opposed to each other. Each refers in its argumentation to different values. Legal certainty will as often be invoked against considerations of equality, utility or humanity as the public interest will be opposed to the rights of the individual; similarly a theory which speaks of the abuse of the law to limit its scope will be opposed to the absoluteness of law conferred by the legal text, etc.

It would be interesting to discover in each legal controversy the value conflict which each side expresses. The judge will have to, in each case, decide or choose among the parties by taking part in the controversy; his judgment settles an individual case but it also, because of legal precedents, influences the legal order to which it will now belong. The cases are rare where only the consideration of a law is sufficient to determine his decision. The judge will allow himself to be guided, in his reasoning, by the spirit of the system, i.e., by the values which the legislative authority seeks to protect and advance.

Contrary to what happens in a formal system which is built from simple elements by the combination of signs structurally defined, the judicial system expresses not just a range of ends to be attained — for this would make it much too vague to provide legal certainty — but a range of ordered, permitted or prohibited behavior proposed to promote the ends in question. Assuming that the text is clear, as long as means are adapted to ends, legal interpretation poses no problem. But nothing forewarns us against the rise of a situation in which the prescribed means are inadequate for the spirit of the law or the spirit of the system, i.e., for the values which benefit from the protection of the legislature in texts other than those envisioned by the law in question. In this case, a conflict will emerge: conformity to either the letter of the law or to the spirit of the law.

A law is clear, we say, if several plausible interpretations lead to the same solution. We can conclude that a law which is clear in one situation can become unclear in a new and unexpected situation, in which prescribed and forbidden conduct are not in agreement with the sought for ends. Must we, in this case, conform to the text of law or have we to apply *a simili* or *a fortiori* reasoning?

Recaséns-Siches told of a case, already indicated by Petrazycki, which caused somewhat of a stir in Poland at the beginning of the century.[8] A sign before a railroad station prohibited the use of the stairway to people with dogs. A peasant with a bear on a leash was very annoyed because he was refused entrance. He imagined that no one would take his bear for a dog, but he could do nothing because the station master refused to be restricted by the letter of the regulation.

In another case, we limit the scope of the law; the judge decides that the law has in view only normal conditions and not unforeseen exceptional conditions.

In a celebrated decision of 11 February, 1919 (Pas., 1919, I., p. 9) the Supreme Court of Belgium decided that the administrative decrees taken by King Albert during 1914–1918 war without the consent of Parliament were in conformity to the constitution, although they undoubtedly violated article 26 of the Belgian Constitution which gives *the legislature and the King* legislative power. Article 130 of the Constitution expressly says that 'the Constitution can neither partly nor totally be suspended.' The Attorney General Terlinden justified the decision of the Court as follows:[9]

A law is never made for a period or for a determined regime. It adapts to circumstances which have motivated it and cannot go beyond. It is conceived in terms of its necessity and utility; a good law must not be intangible because its value is for the period of time it wishes to rule. Theory can envision abstractions. The law, an essentially practical act, applies only to essentially practical situations. This explains the fact that if jurisprudence can extend the application of a text, there are limits to this extension and these are arrived at when the situation which the author of the law envisioned is now superseded by other situations which he had not envisioned.

A Constitutional law or ordinary law is enacted only for normal periods – for periods that can be foreseen.

As work of man, it is subject, as all human things, to the force of things, to superior force, to necessity.

There are facts that human wisdom cannot foresee, situations which it cannot envision and in which – the norm being inapplicable – we must, as we can, though deviating the least from legal prescriptions, ward off the brutal necessities of the moment and oppose rough and tumble means to the invincible force of events.

A seemingly clear text might not be in force. This does not necessarily imply a dramatic national situation such as the occupation of a country and the impossibility of the legislative assemblies to be in session. Let us take an example given by the Hart-Fuller controversy concerning a local regulation prohibiting vehicles from entering a public park. Interpreting this text, which seems clear at first glance, it is not sufficient to agree on what is a vehicle but also to decide when we are or are not in the normal condition for its use. Will police, in charge of enforcing the regulations, allow an ambulance to enter and help a stroller suffering from a heart attack or a child who, while playing, breaks a leg? Will the police allow the entrance of a taxi called by a pregnant woman feeling the moment of childbirth, or an old man recovering from a grave illness? Every time there is a conflict of values, a decision about the exception to the rule must be made, which at first glance, is not permitted by the regulation.

In fact, however precise a law may be, it cannot enumerate all situations in which, for unforeseen reasons, it cannot be applied. At best, it will contain clauses such as 'case of superior force', 'the invincible force of events', 'extraordinary situation', which limit its application. In the end, therefore, it is the judge or the police who must interpret it in each concrete situation.

To see a legal text only as a means in terms of an end and not a statement which is applicable in any circumstance voids any assimilation of a legal rule to a game rule. The game rule evades all conflict and is, by definition and as long as it is uninterrupted artificially, isolated from reality. If we see in law only a normative structure and are unaware of the functions of law in society, then the pure theory of law, for methodological reasons, risks the separation of the legal system from its social and political context and background. In fact, in an abnormal situation, unforeseen by the legislature, we stand before a legal gap, which the responsible powers, the executive and then the judiciary, must, for better or worse, fill.

The whole problem of legal gaps, including also the solution of antinomies,[10] shows clearly the role that values, reasoning about values, and consequently argument, play in law. Having an obligation to judge (art. 4. de Code Napoleon) and, even in the silence of the law, to justify his judgment (art. 97 of the Belgian Constitution) the judge must fill the gaps of the law, by means of the techniques of legal reasoning, i.e., he must find and establish in law premises which are lacking in it. Otherwise, he uses a general rule which, in the case of a legal gap, orders throwing out the plaintiff, be it in civil or in criminal cases (*nullum crimen sine lege*).

It should be noted with apparently similar situations the judge can adopt different solutions in different branches of the law. If a contract between individuals anticipates indemnities for delivery delays and does not determine how the amount is to be established, the judge will, without hesitation, set the amount of the indemnity in a way which seems to him to be equitable. But, if some administration should fix a tax on artistic performances proportional to the ticket price and not establish the rate, the tax will be considered null and void. The fact is that the general principles dominating fiscal law and contract law impose diametrically opposite solutions; the judge in the case of the contract is able to fill the gap but he cannot do so in the fiscal regulation.

Argumentation generally, and contrary to demonstration, even if guided by methodological principles, and in particular when guided by the principle of equal treatment for essentially similar situations, does not impose a determined decision. Most often, argumentation allows us to put aside solutions that don't conform to principles and yet does not impose a unique solution. The reason for this is that reasoning about values appeals to *loci communes* not because of their self-evidence but because of their ambiguity.

The ability to join reasoning about values (controversial objects) to admitted themes enables us to avoid a *petitio principii.*[11] He who argues searches for *loci communes* and for this reason deemed to be admitted by the audience he addresses. *Loci communes* can in no way be assimilated to univocal notions or axioms and it is for this reason that it is useless to question their truth or validity. It is here that we discover a remarkable peculiarity in argumentation about values, and which in turn distinguishes it from deductive reasoning, from axioms; if it is true that *loci communes* furnish argumentation with points of departure commonly admitted by a cultural milieu, they yield divergences as soon as we go from general notions to their applications. Equality, reason and experience form *loci communes*; their interpretation and application are strongly disputed.

When article 6 of the Belgian Constitution affirms the equality of all Belgians before the law, no jurist would think of contesting this egalitarian principle, but would ask if the rule is imposed only on the Courts or equally on the legislature and he would want to know what reasons would allow us to put it aside. Thus, in spite of the principle of the legal equality of all Belgians, women were not treated as equals in public employment. It was in 1922 that the first women were admitted to the bar and in 1945 to certain judicial functions. If we conclude from this that the equality of Belgians before the law is an arbitrary statement, we would certainly provoke general indignation.

In logic, all signs are supposed to have a unique and invariable meaning and the fact of admitting an axiom implies agreement concerning the meaning we give to it; in argumentation, which always comes forth in natural language, agreement on words and even on phrases does in no way signify agreement on meaning. Natural language is in no way tied like the artificial languages of formalized systems to conventions about the univocal meaning of the employed signs. From artificial languages are excluded vagueness, imprecisions and analogic and metaphoric usage of notions. These constraints are absent in natural language and its communication. In natural language, primacy is accorded to the presumption that the average speaker says something that make sense and is worth saying, requiring the interpreter to expound an acceptable meaning from what he has heard. It is obvious that the effort of interpretation be proportional to the respect for the author who is communicating. In the case of an author divinely inspired and who cannot deceive, we will always seek an acceptable interpretation in what he says. Concerning Holy Scripture, Pascal says: 'When the word of God, which is really true, is false literally, it is true spiritually.'[12]

The same situation, only to a lesser degree, exists in a legislative text. We must find a useful and reasonable meaning for it. Analogically, all communication demands good will from the listening interpreter. As soon as the strict rules imposed artificially by language yield to the hermeneutic requirement, the same words will no longer have the same meaning; a significance given in one context can no longer be valid in all others; the use of analogy and metaphor can no longer be denied, but, on the contrary, imposed by the desire for communication and comprehension.

An agreement on *loci communes*, as appears from these considerations, and serving as a point of departure for an argumentation, be it a question of common values, e.g., freedom or justice, or of notions which are more objective, such as nature, reason or experience, does not allow for a similar agreement concerning the consequences which could result in practice. It is clear that the great problem of argumentation, including both legal and philosophical, will be, as the result of interpretation, to assure this transition.

The jurists are fully aware of this problem. It suffices to think of the library of commentaries devoted to a text such as article 1382 of the Napoleonic Code: 'Whatever is done by a man which causes damage to another obliges the one by whose fault it occurred to make amends for it.' Philosophers, on the other hand, accord their principles a nonexisting self-evidence. They assimilate their principles to mathematical propositions and not to the general principles of law to which they are indeed much closer, and they entirely neglect this indeterminate aspect of their declarations of principle.

Commonplaces fully understood cannot *a priori* be assimilated to either judgments of fact or judgments of value. According to how they are made precise or elaborated, and according to the methods used to verify or justify them, they will belong as well to a scientific methodology which tries to eliminate or place in parenthesis everything that is controversial, as to the philosophical methodology which implies controversial positions. Thus, some seek to make the study of justice positive by assimilating it to a group of rules and laws, i.e., reducing it to legality. In the same way we consider rational what conforms to a formalism; we identify an experiment with what can be recorded by a machine. It is immediately obvious that a more general conception of these notions can raise doubts about these identifications and the positivistic methodology which emerges from them. But in rejecting the positivistic reduction, we are deprived of controllable criteria and we must face controversies like those that are customary to traditional philosophy.

Philosophers usually present their first principles as self-evident. The latter are rather presumptions: *juris* and *de jure* if they admit no exceptions; *juris tantum* if they admit justifiable derogations.[13] Kant's Categorical Imperative which says, 'Act always according to a maxim such as you may wish that it become a universal law' and Bentham's utilitarian principle 'which approves or disapproves an action according to the tendency it seems to have to augment or diminish the happiness of the party whose interest is considered or according to its tendency to promote or to oppose this happiness,' provide examples of philosophic principles which seem to allow no exceptions. There seems to be no case permitting any derogation, but agreement on these principles can nevertheless imply divergences in application. What maxim merits being universalized? How do we conceive the happiness of those we consider? Disagreements here show clearly that these principles are not self-evident, but are assimilable to commonplaces requiring a constant elaboration.

Principles which Day qualifies as conservative, liberal and socialist presume the superiority of what exists, of freedom and of equality, while admitting, at the same time, the possibility of derogation. Therefore, according to the conservative principle, 'change — always everywhere, in everything, requires justification.'[14] To J. S. Mill the motto of liberal ideology is 'leaving people to themselves is always better, *caeteris paribus* than controlling them.'[15] To I. Berlin, 'equality needs no reasons, only inequality does.'[16]

These last three examples do not give us self-evident and eternal principles but rather general principles whose application must be rethought in each case. This is the obligation we have when we constantly confront principles with the concrete conditions of their employment and give them a statute closer to the general principles of law than to the formal laws of logic or of mathematics. The dialectic of the general and particular, central to the jurist's reasoning, is of equal significance apropos principles of practical philosophy. In this respect, Hegel is right, and not Kant, for Hegel holds that notions and philosophical principles be defined and made precise in strict relation to the historical concrete conditions of their elaboration.

Since philosophical commonplaces do not have a nontemporal significance and implication, their determination depends upon the concrete context in which they are to operate. For this reason, the principle of equality in law and morality cannot be defined or understood, like the formal and mathematical equality, abstractly and a-historically. In the same way, the idea of justice leads to different practical requirements in various and diverse societies and eras. For this reason, I believe that views and methods of jurists are more suggestive and useful than those of the mathematician for the comprehension and treatment of universal values and of practical philosophic principles.

Our concern is not for an identification of philosophic methods with legal methods because the role of authority in law does not have its counterpart in philosophy and the authority of *res judicata*, which is necessary in law in order to end controversy, is, in no way, recognized in philosophy. In fact, in philosophy where the controversies are such that each attempts to justify his own position, to convince his interlocutor, the controversies may continue indefinitely, and the decision of a third party cannot put an end to them. This is true because philosophic argumentation does not involve compelling demonstrations but all sorts of reasons. These reasons, although presupposing a certain knowledge of facts, go beyond simple experience and cannot simply be reduced to these same facts. Philosophical affirmations imply a position which is inseparable from explicit or implicit value judgments.

While common sense, not hesitating, employs to reach its end all the resources of argumentation, philosophy cannot do the same. For each philosophic vision of the real there corresponds a relevant argument which the philosopher uses by preference. While Bentham writes that only the argument from consequences or the pragmatic argument constitutes good reason,[17] Aristotle values the argument from essence, holding that what is essential is more important than the accidental, and neoplatonism turns freely to the argument by analogy. Similarly, legal reasoning, conforming to a climate of opinion and style, uses other types of arguments at different times. It calls as much on the will of the legislator, as on the finality of law, common good, natural law or the nature of things.

What is specific in legal argumentation and what distinguishes it from the political and moral is the eminent place given to legal certainty. The latter aims at specifying as much as possible each person's rights and obligations in order to restrain, if not eliminate completely, all arbitrariness in judicial decision-making. In this there is an attempt made to reduce as far as possible personal influence of the person under indictment: his power or weakness, his riches or poverty, his friendly or hostile relationship to the judge. Impartiality demands the respect for formal justice which requires equal treatment for essentially similar cases. Together with this problem goes the importance accorded to precedent, thus an inertia is opposed to every whim for change, as is the importance of custom, and accepted practice as source of law.

Law, through its techniques of presumption, tied to the burden of proof and, in the case of statute of limitations to the inadmissibility of the contrary proof, aims at fixing the existing situations, at transforming factual situations, especially when they are prolonged, into legal ones. This protects the social order, perpetuates what exists, provides a favorable prejudice to what is, and recognizes as normative value, 'Der normative Wert des Seienden.' A recognized practice of functioning institutions, even if it is counter to proclaimed principles, exercises such weight that if we bring the judge's attention to the anomaly, he is rather tempted to reinterpret the violated text than to modify the functioning of the institution. Thus, secular discrimination against women seemed to be in no way counter to the principle of the equality of citizens before the law, which corrected the abuses of which the middle classes complained, but they, at the same time, forgot other discriminations which they judged belonged to the nature of things.

It is true that ideologies have their own dynamism and that commonplaces, when social, political or economic conditions change, lend themselves to reinterpretation. We forget the intentions of those who previously proclaimed them and accuse of hypocrisy those who have not drawn from these principles the consequences which impose themselves today and whose misunderstanding seems to be unacceptable now, although it seemed previously, and even for centuries, natural. In this respect, vehement, and even at times violent, protestation causes a sensitivity to certain values whose miscomprehension seemed for the time to correspond to the nature of things. This occurs when rules govern situations in a way unacceptable to moral, political or ideological reasons. They are then elaborated by legal theories whose purpose is not to ascertain the truth, to explain or to anticipate, but to guide an action in a certain sense, and modify the import of the legal texts to avoid the inconveniences of strict jurisprudence or to find a better justification of the jurisprudence which prevails.

Thus, the theory of the abuse of law seeks to ward off the abuses which an absolutist conception of the right of property caused, e.g., as defined by art. 544 of the Civil Code; it tends to suppress the protection given to the right of property when it is made use of for an antisocial purpose. From this point of view, the theory of international public order attempts to restrain the application of foreign law concerning the personal status of foreigners, when this law may be incompatible with the fundamental principles of an indigenous legal system. Although a Moroccan can marry four wives he cannot do so in Belgium, since bigamy is excluded by public international order. If, however, he is a victim of an accident, each of his legitimate widows can obtain an indemnity from the insurance company.

Law aims essentially at practice, the values that it protects are practical ones, legal theories have the same purpose. Even respect for truth is considered in law as a practical value, as a condition of legal certainty. There are cases when the respect for truth is considered as less important than other values, where we would admit a twist of the law to the search for or the proclamation of truth. To favor family order, we limit strictly every action denying paternity. In the same way, in case of defamation the law punishes the guilty one by not allowing him to furnish proof of the alleged facts (art. 443 and 444 of the Belgian Penal Code). No system of law can dispense with the existence of fictions which consist in using characterizations contrary to reality and does this to obtain a socially desirable result.

The law is essentially pluralistic. It lives to realize many values simultaneoulsy and can, in concrete situations, protect incompatible ones. Those will carry the day which seem the best in the eyes of the judge and for which we have presented the best reasons. We must emphasize that the force of these reasons cannot be measured or weighed; like all argumentation it depends upon the convictions, aspirations of those who must take a position regarding them. In all judicial debate the issue depends upon the convictions and the values of the judge and the respect for the principles and methods which govern the professional activity of the magistrate. These elements can vary according to place, milieu, climate and ideology of public opinion, but also according to the judge's general and professional education, his character and temperament. When we take into account these characteristics of practical reasoning: strong arguments and good reasons are the strong arguments and reasons for the one who is to be convinced, we become aware that the judge's personality plays a central role in law and that there is cause to be on guard that nobody in any way be distracted from his natural judge.

Law, in the name of impartiality and legal certainty, like philosophy in the name of truth and reason, seeks to eliminate or at least conceal the intervention of the personal element, however closely involved it may be to decision and its justification. The existentialist reaction, although exaggerated, had the good effect of attracting our attention to the personal elements both in law and in philosophy. We have seen in Existentialism the expression of modern irrationalism because we had a limited conception of reason. We limited it to logic and scientific methodology. But the theory of argumentation causes us to extend the field of reason's application to the whole domain of the reasonable, the *eulogon* of Aristotle.

A reflection on law, its problems and its methods can reveal a philosophy of the reasonable which integrates the personal element, and seeks to elaborate perspectives which can be proposed to the universality of men.

NOTES

* French text appeared in *Handelingen van de Vereniging voor Wijsbegeerte des Rechts* 55 (1) Zwolle, 1971.
[1] G. Kalinowski, *Introduction à la logique juridique*, Paris, 1965, and U. Klug, *Juristische Logik*, Berlin, 1966.
[2] Ed. H. Levi, *An Introduction to Legal Reasoning*, Chicago, 1948 and K. Engisch, *Einführung in das Juristische Denken*, Stuttgart, 1956.
[3] C. Perelman, *The Idea of Justice and the Problem of Argument*, London, 1963, pp. 56–57.
[4] L. Olbrechts-Tyteca, 'Rencontre avec la rhétorique' in *La théorie de l'argumentation*, Louvain, 1963, pp. 3–18.
[5] Perelman, 'Self evidence and proof' in *The Idea of Justice and the Problem of Argument*, pp. 109–125.
[6] J. Moreau, 'Rhétorique, dialectique, et exigence première' in *La théorie de l'argumentation*, p. 207.
[7] A. Giuliani, 'La logique juridique comme théorie de la controverse' in *Archives de philosophie du droit*, 1966, pp. 84–113.
[8] 'The logic of the reasonable as differentiated from the logic of the rational' in *Essays in Jurisprudence in Honor of Roscoe Pound* (Indianapolis, 1962), p. 205.
[9] A. Van Welkenhuyzen, 'De quelques lacunes du droit constitutionnel belge,' in *Le problème des lacunes en droit*, studies published by Ch. Perelman, Brussels, 1968, pp. 347–349.
[10] See in addition to the already cited volume on lacunae, the publication of Centre National (Belge) de Recherches de Logique on *Les antinomies en droit*, Bruylant, Brussels, 1965.
[11] The *petitio principii* is the defect of argumentation which supposes a thesis to be

admitted which through argumentation we are asked to admit. In formal logic starting from a premise which is to be demonstrated is not to commit error but to apply a logical law, the principle of identity (if p, then p).

[12] Pascal, *Pensées*, trans. W. F. Trotter et al., Great Books of the Western World, Chicago, 1952, Vol. 33, p. 299.

[13] Patrick Day, 'Presumptions,' *Proceedings of the XIVth International Congress of Philosophy*, Vienna, 1970, Vol. V, pp. 137–143.

[14] *Ibid.*, p. 139, B. Wootton, *Social Foundations of Wage Policy*, London, 1958, 162.

[15] *Ibid.*, J. S. Mill, *On Liberty*, Chap. V.

[16] *Ibid.*, I. Berlin, 'Equality,' *Proceedings of the Aristotelian Society* 56 (1956), 305.

[17] Perelman, 'Pragmatic Arguments' in *The Idea of Justice and the Problem of Argument*, London, Routledge and Kegan Paul, 1963, p. 197.

CHAPTER SEVENTEEN

WHAT THE PHILOSOPHER MAY LEARN
FROM THE STUDY OF LAW*

At the entrance of the Academy, Plato had placed the inscription 'No one may enter unless he be trained in geometry'; in the same fashion, Descartes and Spinoza proposed the geometrical method to philosophers as a model of rationality. Leibniz dreamt of being able to terminate philosophical disputes by having recourse to counting – *calculemus* – and hoped to put an end to differences of opinion among philosophers by means of those procedures which bring mathematicians to agreement. Other thinkers with empirical tendencies, from Hume to Piaget, have proposed that philosophers follow the methods of the experimental sciences.

On the other hand, I know of hardly any philosopher who has proposed that one draw inspiration from the juridical model. On the contrary, philosophers, at least the rationalists, traditionally did not hesitate to express their scorn for law, its techniques and its practitioners. Instead of endlessly discussing the shadowy images of the just, Plato aspired to furnish us with the knowledge of true justice, which would enable the dialectician, who alone is qualified to involve himself with politics, to find rational solutions to any problem of justice.

It is worth noting that in all the utopian cities, which are supposedly rational, no place is reserved for the practitioners of law, even when these cities are the creations of jurists. This stands out clearly from the interesting paper, presented by my colleague Paul Foriers, at the Brussels conference on *Les Utopies à la Renaissance:*[1]

Constructors of ideal cities or visionary reformers, the Utopians drew plans which, by their very perfection, reduced the place of law, its role and its influence.

Because it is harmonious, the ideal city knows hardly any dissonances. Conflicts would thus be accidents, which utopian optimism would see only as such. Their multiplication would be avoided, such optimism believes, by condemning the jurists as a group and putting faith in the pre-excellence of human nature.[2]

In utopian countries there are only a few laws; simple and clear, they are immediately accessible to everyone and do not need to be interpreted in order to be understood: 'No lawyers from now on. Far from viewing them as instruments of justice, the Utopians regarded professional pleaders as men intent on twisting the meaning of the law and living by chicanery.'[3] This is certainly the opinion of Thomas More in his *Utopia*, and Eméric Crucé, in *Le Nouveau Cynée*, does not hesitate to accuse the lawyers of perverting the law:

The text of the laws is clear and intelligible. If there is something lacking, let the judges supply it with their wisdom and equity, without recourse to a thousand interpreters who agree no more amongst themselves than do clocks and who cause scruples and distractions of the spirit by the diversity of their opinions. It is this which engenders and nourishes litigations and makes them last so long that the end is lost from sight. This is why the Spanish peoples in the Indies were correct in begging their king not to send them any lawyers. Primitive people living naturally are more at ease than those who employ their subtlety in trickery.[4]

One hopes that in the ideal city the laws will be inscribed in the heart, conscience, and reason of each person; that each person's conduct will conform to them spontaneously; and that one will need neither judges nor lawyers. Does one imagine tribunals in Paradise?

The diversity of laws, their variation in time and space, provoked Pascal's celebrated comment:

Three degrees elevation of the pole upsets all jurisprudence; a meridian determines truth; after a few years' possession the fundamental laws change; law has its periods; Saturn entering Leo shows us the origin of a certain crime. Merry justice which is limited by a river! Truth this side of the Pyrenees, error on the other.[5]

The diversity of laws is proof of our ignorance of true justice. That which conforms to reason cannot be just here and unjust there, just today and unjust tomorrow, just for one and unjust for another. That which is just in reason should, like that which is true, be so universally. Disagreement is a sign of imperfection, of a lack of rationality.

If two interpretations of the same text are reasonably possible, it is because the law is ambiguous, therefore imperfect. If the law is clear, then at least one of the two interpreters disputes in bad faith. In any case, disagreement is a scandal, due either to the imperfection of the legislator or to the deceptive subtlety of the lawyers. The innate sense of justice, which each equitable judge certainly possesses, should permit the rapid reestablishment of correct order.

In the ideal city, where everything is rationally organized, the laws cannot present these defects; and lawyers who are too subtle must be removed from positions where they might be injurious. Why should not the agreement which is observed as to mathematical axioms and theorems be achieved in law? Divine reason in its omniscience knows the true and the just in all things: Should not men therefore, in conformity with divine reason, extend to all matters that clear and distinct knowledge which is the glory of geometry?

determining the unique correct solution of all problems, and thus eliminating all possibility of an enlightened choice.

The traditional role of law is to organize effectively and in various ways the dialectics of *imperfect* human will and human reason. It contrasts with the divine model of the rationalists which is inadequate precisely where it admits no room for the idea of rational decision.[8]

It was the geometrical method that inspired the classical rationalists with the ideal of reason. Beginning with self-evident axioms, imposing themselves on every rational person by means of rules of deduction equally undoubtable, a man is able to transfer the self-evidence of the axioms to all the theorems. Divine reason being capable of knowing the truth or the falsehood of every proposition, it is an understandable ideal to propose that men find, by correct use of the geometrical method, the truths which God has known throughout all eternity. By dismissing all the opinions about which there could be the slightest doubt, Descartes hopes to arrive at self-evident truths which, like a solid rock, will permit the founding of an unshakable philosophical system, serving as a basis for the universal community of rational beings. This ideal of rationality supposes humanity purged, through doubt, of all the prejudices, dogmas, values, and norms which a long history has deposited in the conscience of each constituted society. Any axiomatic system presents itself, in the same fashion, as independent of all context: Whether we should consider the axioms as evident or as arbitrary (and the will of the mathematician is supposed, in this case, in the manner of the divine will, not to know any obstacle and to determine both the first principles and the rules of inference), they are not, in the classical perspective, the object of a rational decision. Either the axioms impose themselves on the will of every rational being or, conforming to Carnap's principle of tolerance, each person elaborates, as he understands it, his axiomatic system. In the first case, conformity to reason eliminates all choice; in the second case, choice is arbitrary and without reason. This is why the axiomatic method, which is applied in geometry, and which served as a model for the classical rationalists, differs completely from juridical reasoning. We will see that by taking the latter as a model, one arrives at the conception of another type of rationality.

While Descartes wanted to construct his rational knowledge from the starting point of a universal doubt, marking a rupture with the past, all rationality for jurists is continuity. Rupture with preexisting order, the installation of a new regime, of a new constituitonal power, could be done in history only by violence or at least by the threat of the use of force. It is an illusion to believe that a new order imposes itself by its rationality alone. When it is recognized as being rational, it is because it conforms to a criterion of rationality previously accepted, and because it does not represent a complete rupture with the past. A thesis like Kelsen's, developing the pure theory of law by considering the system of law as separated from all nonjuridical contexts, could at best be considered only as a hypothetical-deductive system, the validity of the fundamental norm or of the constitutional principles always being presupposed. But whence does the fundamental norm receive its validity? Certainly not by its being self-evident. The initial theses of a juridical system, whatever they may be, whether it is a question of constitutional principles, of laws, of judiciary precedents in the *common law* system, or even of general principles of law, have never been considered as self-evident, as imposing themselves in an unambiguous fashion on all rational beings. But, on the other hand, neither have they ever been considered as arbitrary. Situated in a social, political, and historical context, they find, in this context, reasons which explain and justify their acceptance.

Acceptance of the fundamental theses of a juridical system is as rarely based on force alone as it is based on the self-evidence of the system. Ordinarily, what the clarity of juridical rules lacks is supplied by the *authority* of those who have presented them insofar as they are considered the legitimate possessors of constitutional or legislative power.

Every revolution that ended with a change of regime and not simply with a change of persons within the same regime, was preceded by a period, more or less lengthy, which furnished ideological justification for the new constitutional principles. As for new laws, they are normally preceded by a statement of motives which indicates the reasons for which the law has been advanced and admitted. By presenting the law as a means of permitting the realization of certain previously accepted ends, an effort is made to show its legitimacy — not merely its legality, i.e., that it had been voted according to the forms provided by the juridical system. When the law sanctions only the traditional rules, practices, and customs of the society to which it is applied, it benefits at the outset from the adhesion accorded these rules. The more legislation conforms to expectation, the less indispensable is recourse to authority in order to enforce it. Thus, for example, in 1919, the Belgian government was able to abolish the plural vote and establish egalitarian, universal suffrage (one man, one vote) by a means which violated the constitution in a flagrant fashion, but which corresponded so closely to the conceptions of the great mass of the population that the government's illegal action did not pose the least political problem and the legitimacy of the measure appeared in-contestable.[9]

The authority of judicial precedents in a society administered under *common law,* and, to a lesser degree, in any system of law whose legal decisions are published, is also founded on prejudice favoring conformity to past decisions.

As for the general principles of law, these express traditional values in the juridical consciousness of a given civilization. They formulate theses which the educated members of the society are tempted to admit spontaneously, and thus closely approach self-evident principles which hardly need a parti-cular authority to be admitted. Nevertheless, this authority is indispensable, inasmuch as these principles necessitate an interpretation and a delimitation of their field of application. The field of application can be much more con-troversial than the principles themselves, agreement on these having been achieved with ambiguity and vagueness.

The exigencies of the juridical order, which continues through all kinds of upheavals as long as it has not been entirely or partially replaced by a new order, clearly show us what is unfeasible in the advice of Descartes, asking us to make a *tabula rasa* of all our opinions. What normal man would put any one of his convictions into doubt if the reasons for doubt were not more solid than the opinion to which they were opposed? To shake a belief there is need, as with a lever, for a point of leverage more solid than what is to be moved. Nobody has ever seriously put in doubt the totality of his opinions, for they test each other reciprocally: One keeps those which, up to the present moment, have best resisted the testing. This, however, does not guar-antee them absolutely against all subsequent tests. While in absolutist meta-physics the spirit oscillates from absolute doubt to absolute certainty, we are in reality always in the 'in-between': The opinions to which we adhere con-stitute the last state of the evolution of our ideas, which does not necessarily signify a definitive state; but it would not be reasonable to abandon these ideas, unless they prove themselves to be incompatible with ideas to which we attach superior credit. To ask us to make a *tabula rasa* of our intellectual past is to act against the principle of inertia, upon which is founded, in fact, our spiritual life as well as our political and social organization. This principle manifests itself by the Rule of Justice, which asks us to treat in the same fashion beings and situations that are essentially similar,[10] and, more parti-cularly, by the conformity to precedents, which assures the continuity and the coherence of our thought and our action. One could formulate the principle of inertia as a directive: One should not change anything without reason. If one maintains that our ideas, our rules, and our behavior are devoid of an absolute foundation, and that for this reason, the pros and the cons are equally worthy, and that one must therefore in philosophy make a *tabula rasa* of our past, one expresses an exigency which comes from utopia and to which one can only conform fictitiously. It is true that even Descartes in his provisional ethic showed more realism, but must one, in order to build science and philosophy, adopt principles entirely opposed to those which are useful for the 'actions of life'? I believe, on the contrary, that (all use of violence being excluded by principle) the totality of our ideas is transformed from within, as is a juridical order which, in order to function as it adapts itself to new situations and aspirations, provides for procedures ensuring flexibility and allowing for reform.[11]

Thus rationality, as it presents itself in law, is always a form of continuity — conformity to previous rules or justification of the new by means of old values. That which is without attachment to the past can only be imposed by force, not by reason. As a result, the new and the old do not have to be treated in the same fashion, they do not have to be accepted if they are self-evident and ruled out in the contrary case. For if this were the case, all rules of action, which are never self-evident, should be dismissed. Even Descartes recognized this as impossible, for he could not do without a provisional ethic. But he did not see that it would be impossible for him to replace the provisional ethic with a definitive ethic, the principles of which would be both clear and self-evident.

Law teaches us, on the contrary, to abandon existing rules only if good reasons justify their replacement: Only change requires justification, presumption playing in favor of what exists, just as the burden of proof falls upon him who wants to change an established state of affairs. If that which is new prevails rationally (and not by violence) it is because of the fact that it better satisfies preexisting criteria or exigencies.

Reasons which bring about the modification of an old rule, or its replacement by a new one are not universally valid. They must, however, be admitted by those who need to be persuaded of the utility of the new legislation. In other words, as reliance cannot be put in the self-evidence of the rule, the statement of the motives must show its desirability in a given political context; the values and the norms which are actually admitted furnish the point of departure for the argument which should justify the introduction of new rule.

But the argumentation which forms the statement of the motives does not in any way constitute a deduction, and the conclusion which it reaches is in no way constraining. The reasons in favor of the rule are arguments of greater or lesser strength to which reasons in an adverse sense, themselves arguments of greater or lesser strength, can normally be opposed. Actually, the values, the norms, and the facts from which an agreement stems are extremely varied, and the one who argues is obliged to choose among them. This choice will put a certain group of facts, this or that value, such and such a norm in the foreground of consciousness by conferring on it a *presence* in the minds of the listeners. Certain of these given facts are going to become reformulated or reinterpreted in order to better illustrate the pertinence of the proposed measures and their suitability to the pursued goal. There will be an opportunity, should the occasion arise, to refute the objections and the criticisms of those who uphold other facts, other values, and other norms.

Thus in establishing, by new legislation, a system of old age pensions, there would be occasion not only to show the utility of that form of insurance against misery, but also that the resulting burden to the community can be assumed without requiring the sacrifice of any other service which the community would judge more important. One can see that, on all these questions, and more particularly when it is a matter of determining the total pensions, different opinions are equally justified and perhaps even equally reasonable. When it is a question of establishing norms of action, no single solution exists which in such matters could impose itself on all the members of the community as self-evident. For this reason, as no decision can be recognized as the only reasonable one and, nevertheless, a decision must be made which will become obligatory, it is indispensable to determine who will have the power to make an authorized decision, to determine how legislative power will be conferred.

But the promulgation of laws does not suffice to render their application incontestable and uniform. Laws can usually be interpreted and applied in several ways: To avoid disorder, therefore pursuant to certain procedures, it is indispensable to accord to certain persons the power to govern, administer, and judge.

Laws are more or less clear, and they accord to those who apply them a more or less extensive power of interpretation. There is an inversely proportional relationship between the clarity of the law and the power of interpretation accorded to those who must apply it. This power becomes all the greater as with the evolution of society, technical progress, and the changes of mores, the letter of the law becomes more and more opposed to its spirit, that is, to the purpose it is supposed to realize. Must one accord preeminence to a formalistic and analytical interpretation of the law, which is more favorable to juridical security? On the contrary, must one accord primacy to a teleo-logical and pragmatic interpretation of the law, which essentially would take into account consequences involving questions of equity and the common good? Both approaches have their partisans, and for this reason the authority of a judge is indispensable in order to put an end to otherwise interminable controversies. Again, on this point, juridical reasoning is opposed to purely formal reasoning; in taking into account the consequences, the judge, and especially the Supreme Court, use the power of interpretation which has been accorded to the judiciary to reinterpret the text of the law which it has been given to apply. The reasoning of the judge is dialectical and opposed to the analytical reasoning of mathematicians, which always goes in a single direction, from premises toward conclusions.

Authority, which is indispensable for the making of laws, governing and judging, is superfluous when it is a question of demonstrating a theorem of arithmetic or geometry. In fact, all those who have some knowledge of these matters are at least capable of checking the accuracy of a demonstra-tion and, once the proof is admitted, they bow before the conclusion. If a formal system is coherent, the negation of a demonstrated thesis is necessarily false. There is no question, in a formal, usable system, of demonstrating the thesis and the antithesis. On the contrary, one can in law plead pro and con, and two incompatible decisions can be equally reasonable. But in order that this affirmation be theoretically defensible, the idea of reason must not be linked to that of truth.[12] The dissociation of these two notions is, moreover, indispensable in order that the idea of a rational decision be meaningful. What is a question of decision cannot be a question of truth. One must yield to truth; there is no room for deciding. I do not decide that two plus two make four or that Paris is the capital of France. A rational decision is not simply a decision conforming to truth, but rather that decision which can be justified by the best reasons, at least inasmuch as justification is necessary.

If there were an objective criterion, expressible in quantitative terms — for example in terms of probability — of what in each case was the best reason, then a single judgment would be reasonable, namely, to conform one's be-havior to the quantitatively determined result. But if the best reasons cannot be determined outside of a world-view which, once elaborated, produces a philosophy, then the existence of a plurality of irreducible philosophies makes it impossible to admit that, in all circumstances, a single decision merits the qualification of reasonable.

It is when the subject matter escapes the qualification of true or false, because it does not depend upon a unitary science but upon a philosophical pluralism, that an attitude of tolerance is justified and that a dialogue, permitting the perspectives to be enlarged, is not only useful but even indispensable. Just as the judge, before making a decision, should hear two sides — *audiatur et altera pars* — the adoption of a philosophical position, at the risk of lacking rationality, should take into account the opposed points of view concerning the subject matter.

When it is a question of decision, several theses are equally defensible, and none imposes itself with evidence. Hence, from this point on, an authority is indispensable to render certain decisions obligatory. It is because the elaboration and the application of the norms usually bring about divergencies that it is indispensable to know who has the power of making laws and who is competent to judge and terminate conflicts. Thus the obligation, which law has taught us, to establish authorities in these matters, reveals the fact that one does not find oneself confronted by truths which impose themselves upon every reasonable being.

A formal system does not tolerate any external interference. Because it is closed, because the elements which constitute it are given once and for all, because its basic principles and rules of inference are beyond discussion, the intervention of a third party can add nothing new, unless aiming to replace the system by another. This is altogether different in the case of law, and it is also different in philosophy. The philosopher, like the judge, has an interest in hearing the opposing points of view before making a decision. In fact, his role is not simply to describe and explain the real, in the manner of the scientist who aims at objectivity, but he must take a position concerning the real. His ontology is not simply description of the real, but articulating the hierarchy of its manifestations.[13] Rationality is linked to values which he would want not only common but also universal, hoping that they would obtain the adherence of the universal audience, that is, the audience composed of all men both rational and competent.[14] But, never being sure of the universality of his norms and his values, the philosopher must always be ready to listen to the objections which could be proposed to him and to take them into account, if he cannot refute them. The dialogue should be open, for he can never consider the theses he advocates as being definitive. If in law the need to establish an order requires that certain authorities have the power of decision, it is not the same in philosophy. There does not exist, in philosophy, an authority capable of according to certain theses the status of a *res judicata*.[15]

174 CHAPTER SEVENTEEN

After having sought, for centuries, to model philosophy on the sciences, and having considered each of its particularities as a sign of inferiority, perhaps the moment has come to consider that philosophy has many traits in common with law. A confrontation with the latter would permit better understanding of the specificity of philosophy, a discipline which is elaborated under the aegis of reason, but a reason which is essentially practical, turned toward rational decision and action.

NOTES

* First published in *Natural Law Forum*, 1966, pp. 1–12.
[1] P. Foriers, 'Les Utopies et le Droit,' in *Les Utopies à la Renaissance*, Presses Universitaires de Bruxelles, Brussels, 1963, pp. 233–67.
[2] *Ibid.*, pp. 234–35.
[3] *Ibid.*, p. 239.
[4] Eméric Crucé, 'Le Nouveau Cynée ou Discours d'Etat représentant les occasions et moyens d'establir une paix générale, et la liberté du commerce par tout le monde,' 167 (1623), cited by Foriers, in *op. cit.*, p. 240.
[5] Blaise Pascal, *Pensées*, in *L'Oeuvre*, Bibliothèque de la Pléiade, Paris, 1950, no. 230.
[6] John Locke, *An Essay Concerning Human Understanding*, Routledge, London, 1894, p. 389.
[7] *The Babylonian Talmud*, Seder Moed 2, Erubin 13B, edited in the English translation by I. Epstein, The Soncino Press, London, 1935–1948; cf. my article 'Désaccord et rationalité des décisions,' *Archivio di Filosofia*, 1966, pp. 87–93. English trans. in *The New Rhetoric and the Humanities*, Reidel, Dordrecht, 1979, Chapter 10.
[8] Cf. Ch. Perelman, *Justice et Raison*, Presses Universitaires de Bruxelles, Brussels, 1963, pp. 246–37.
[9] See, for details, E. Cammaerts, *Albert of Belgium, Defender of Right*, Nicholson and Watson, London, 1935, pp. 312–25, 332–35, 364.
[10] Cf. Ch. Perelman, 'The Rule of Justice,' *The Idea of Justice and the Problem of Argument*, Routledge and Kegan Paul, London, 1963, pp. 79–87.
[11] Perelman, *Justice et Raison, op. cit.*, pp. 249–50.
[12] Cf. Perelman, 'Désaccord et rationalité des décisions,' *op. cit.*, pp. 88 and 92 in *The New Rhetoric and the Humanities*, pp. 111 and 115.
[13] Cf. in the present vol. Chapter 6, pp. 70–71.
[14] For the idea of universal audience (*l'auditoire universel*), cf. Ch. Perelman and L. Olbrechts-Tyteca, *The New Rhetoric*, sections 6–9.
[15] Perelman, *Justice et Raison, op. cit.*, p. 102.

INDEX OF NAMES

* *Italic* numbers indicate that the reference appears in the *Notes*.

INDEX OF SUBJECTS

177

SYNTHESE LIBRARY

Studies in Epistemology, Logic, Methodology,
and Philosophy of Science

Managing Editor:
JAAKKO HINTIKKA (Florida State University)

Editors:
DONALD DAVIDSON (University of Chicago)
GABRIEL NUCHELMANS (University of Leyden)
WESLEY C. SALMON (University of Arizona)

1. J. M. Bochénski, *A Precis of Mathematical Logic.* 1959.
2. P. L. Guiraud, *Problèmes et méthodes de la statistique linguistique.* 1960.
3. Hans Freudenthal (ed.), *The Concept and the Role of the Model in Mathematics and Natural and Social Sciences.* 1961.
4. Evert W. Beth, *Formal Methods. An Introduction to Symbolic Logic and the Study of Effective Operations in Arithmetic and Logic.* 1962.
5. B. H. Kazemier and D. Vuysje (eds.), *Logic and Language. Studies Dedicated to Professor Rudolf Carnap on the Occasion of His Seventieth Birthday.* 1962.
6. Marx W. Wartofsky (ed.), *Proceedings of the Boston Colloquium for the Philosophy of Science 1961-1962.* Boston Studies in the Philosophy of Science, Volume I. 1963.
7. A. A. Zinov'ev, *Philosophical Problems of Many-Valued Logic.* 1963.
8. Georges Gurvitch, *The Spectrum of Social Time.* 1964.
9. Paul Lorenzen, *Formal Logic.* 1965.
10. Robert S. Cohen and Marx W. Wartofsky (eds.), *In Honor of Philipp Frank.* Boston Studies in the Philosophy of Science, Volume II. 1965.
11. Evert W. Beth, *Mathematical Thought. An Introduction to the Philosophy of Mathematics.* 1965.
12. Evert W. Beth and Jean Piaget, *Mathematical Epistemology and Psychology.* 1966.
13. Guido Küng, *Ontology and the Logistic Analysis of Language. An Enquiry into the Contemporary Views on Universals.* 1967.
14. Robert S. Cohen and Marx W. Wartofsky (eds.), *Proceedings of the Boston Colloquium for the Philosophy of Science 1964-1966. In Memory of Norwood Russell Hanson.* Boston Studies in the Philosophy of Science, Volume III. 1967.
15. C. D. Broad, *Induction, Probability, and Causation. Selected Papers.* 1968.
16. Günther Patzig, *Aristotle's Theory of the Syllogism. A Logical-Philosophical Study of Book A of the Prior Analytics.* 1968.
17. Nicholas Rescher, *Topics in Philosophical Logic.* 1968.
18. Robert S. Cohen and Marx W. Wartofsky (eds.), *Proceedings of the Boston Colloquium for the Philosophy of Science 1966-1968.* Boston Studies in the Philosophy of Science, Volume IV. 1969.

19. Robert S. Cohen and Marx W. Wartofsky (eds.), *Proceedings of the Boston Colloquium for the Philosophy of Science 1966-1968*. Boston Studies in the Philosophy of Science, Volume V. 1969.
20. J. W. Davis, D. J. Hockney, and W. K. Wilson (eds.), *Philosophical Logic*. 1969.
21. D. Davidson and J. Hintikka (eds.), *Words and Objections. Essays on the Work of W. V. Quine*. 1969.
22. Patrick Suppes, *Studies in the Methodology and Foundations of Science. Selected Papers from 1911 to 1969*. 1969.
23. Jaakko Hintikka, *Models for Modalities. Selected Essays*. 1969.
24. Nicholas Rescher *et al.* (eds.), *Essays in Honor of Carl G. Hempel. A Tribute on the Occasion of His Sixty-Fifth Birthday*. 1969.
25. P. V. Tavanec (ed.), *Problems of the Logic of Scientific Knowledge*. 1969.
26. Marshall Swain (ed.), *Induction, Acceptance, and Rational Belief*. 1970.
27. Robert S. Cohen and Raymond J. Seeger (eds.), *Ernst Mach: Physicist and Philosopher*. Boston Studies in the Philosophy of Science, Volume VI. 1970.
28. Jaakko Hintikka and Patrick Suppes, *Information and Inference*. 1970.
29. Karel Lambert, *Philosophical Problems in Logic. Some Recent Developments*. 1970.
30. Rolf A. Eberle, *Nominalistic Systems*. 1970.
31. Paul Weingartner and Gerhard Zecha (eds.), *Induction, Physics, and Ethics*. 1970.
32. Evert W. Beth, *Aspects of Modern Logic*. 1970.
33. Risto Hilpinen (ed.), *Deontic Logic: Introductory and Systematic Readings*. 1971.
34. Jean-Louis Krivine, *Introduction to Axiomatic Set Theory*. 1971.
35. Joseph D. Sneed, *The Logical Sstructure of Mathematical Physics*. 1971.
36. Carl R. Kordig, *The Justification of Scientific Change*. 1971.
37. Milic Capek, *Bergson and Modern Physics*. Boston Studies in the Philosophy of Science, Volume VII. 1971.
38. Norwood Russell Hanson, *What I Do Not Believe, and Other Essays* (ed. by Stephen Toulmin and Harry Woolf). 1971.
39. Roger C. Buck and Robert S. Cohen (eds.), *PSA 1970. In Memory of Rudolf Carnap*. Boston Studies in the Philosophy of Science, Volume VIII. 1971.
40. Donald Davidson and Gilbert Harman (eds.), *Semantics of Natural Language*. 1972.
41. Yehoshua Bar-Hillel (ed.), *Pragmatics of Natural Languages*. 1971.
42. Sören Stenlund, *Combinators, λ-Terms and Proof Theory*. 1972.
43. Martin Strauss, *Modern Physics and Its Philosophy. Selected Papers in the Logic, History, and Philosophy of Science*. 1972.
44. Mario Bunge, *Method, Model and Matter*. 1973.
45. Mario Bunge, *Philosophy of Physics*. 1973.
46. A. A. Zinov'ev, *Foundations of the Logical Theory of Scientific Knowledge (Complex Logic)*. (Revised and enlarged English edition with an appendix by G. A. Smirnov, E. A. Sidorenka, A. M. Fedina, and L. A. Bobrova.) Boston Studies in the Philosophy of Science, Volume IX. 1973.
47. Ladislav Tondl, *Scientific Procedures*. Boston Studies in the Philosophy of Science, Volume X. 1973.
48. Norwood Russell Hanson, *Constellations and Conjectures* (ed. by Willard C. Humphreys, Jr.). 1973.

49. K. J. J. Hintikka, J. M. E. Moravcsik, and P. Suppes (eds.), *Approaches to Natural Language*. 1973.
50. Mario Bunge (ed.), *Exact Philosophy – Problems, Tools, and Goals*. 1973.
51. Radu J. Bogdan and Ilkka Niiniluoto (eds.), *Logic, Language, and Probability*. 1973.
52. Glenn Pearce and Patrick Maynard (eds.), *Conceptual Change*. 1973.
53. Ilkka Niiniluoto and Raimo Tuomela, *Theoretical Concepts and Hypothetico-Inductive Inference*. 1973.
54. Roland Fraissé, *Course of Mathematical Logic* – Volume 1: *Relation and Logical Formula*. 1973.
55. Adolf Grünbaum, *Philosophical Problems of Space and Time*. (Second, enlarged edition.) Boston Studies in the Philosophy of Science, Volume XII. 1973.
56. Patrick Suppes (ed.), *Space, Time, and Geometry*. 1973.
57. Hans Kelsen, *Essays in Legal and Moral Philosophy* (selected and introduced by Ota Weinberger). 1973.
58. R. J. Seeger and Robert S. Cohen (eds.), *Philosophical Foundations of Science*. Boston Studies in the Philosophy of Science, Volume XI. 1974.
59. Robert S. Cohen and Marx W. Wartofsky (eds.), *Logical and Epistemological Studies in Contemporary Physics*. Boston Studies in the Philosophy of Science, Volume XIII. 1973.
60. Robert S. Cohen and Marx W. Wartofsky (eds.), *Methodological and Historical Essays in the Natural and Social Sciences. Proceedings of the Boston Colloquium for the Philosophy of Science 1969-1972*. Boston Studies in the Philosophy of Science, Volume XIV. 1974.
61. Robert S. Cohen, J. J. Stachel, and Marx W. Wartofsky (eds.), *For Dirk Struik. Scientific, Historical and Political Essays in Honor of Dirk J. Struik*. Boston Studies in the Philosophy of Science, Volume XV. 1974.
62. Kazimierz Ajdukiewicz, *Pragmatic Logic* (transl. from the Polish by Olgierd Wojtasiewicz). 1974.
63. Sören Stenlund (ed.), *Logical Theory and Semantic Analysis. Essays Dedicated to Stig Kanger on His Fiftieth Birthday*. 1974.
64. Kenneth F. Schaffner and Robert S. Cohen (eds.), *Proceedings of the 1972 Biennial Meeting, Philosophy of Science Association*. Boston Studies in the Philosophy of Science, Volume XX. 1974.
65. Henry E. Kyburg, Jr., *The Logical Foundations of Statistical Inference*. 1974.
66. Marjorie Grene, *The Understanding of Nature. Essays in the Philosophy of Biology*. Boston Studies in the Philosophy of Science, Volume XXIII. 1974.
67. Jan M. Broekman, *Structuralism: Moscow, Prague, Paris*. 1974.
68. Norman Geschwind, *Selected Papers on Language and the Brain*. Boston Studies in the Philosophy of Science, Volume XVI. 1974.
69. Roland Fraissé, *Course of Mathematical Logic* – Volume 2: *Model Theory*. 1974.
70. Andrzej Grzegorczyk, *An Outline of Mathematical Logic. Fundamental Results and Notions Explained with All Details*. 1974.
71. Franz von Kutschera, *Philosophy of Language*. 1975.
72. Juha Manninen and Raimo Tuomela (eds.), *Essays on Explanation and Understanding. Studies in the Foundations of Humanities and Social Sciences*. 1976.

73. Jaakko Hintikka (ed.), *Rudolf Carnap, Logical Empiricist. Materials and Perspectives*. 1975.
74. Milic Capek (ed.), *The Concepts of Space and Time. Their Structure and Their Development*. Boston Studies in the Philosophy of Science, Volume XXII. 1976.
75. Jaakko Hintikka and Unto Remes, *The Method of Analysis. Its Geometrical Origin and Its General Significance*. Boston Studies in the Philosophy of Science, Volume XXV. 1974.
76. John Emery Murdoch and Edith Dudley Sylla, *The Cultural Context of Medieval Learning*. Boston Studies in the Philosophy of Science, Volume XXVI. 1975.
77. Stefan Amsterdamski, *Between Experience and Metaphysics. Philosophical Problems of the Evolution of Science*. Boston Studies in the Philosophy of Science, Volume XXXV. 1975.
78. Patrick Suppes (ed.), *Logic and Probability in Quantum Mechanics*. 1976.
79. Hermann von Helmholtz: *Epistemological Writings. The Paul Hertz/Moritz Schlick Centenary Edition of 1921 with Notes and Commentary by the Editors*. (Newly translated by Malcolm F. Lowe. Edited, with an Introduction and Bibliography, by Robert S. Cohen and Yehuda Elkana.) Boston Studies in the Philosophy of Science, Volume XXXVII. 1977.
80. Joseph Agassi, *Science in Flux*. Boston Studies in the Philosophy of Science, Volume XXVIII. 1975.
81. Sandra G. Harding (ed.), *Can Theories Be Refuted? Essays on the Duhem-Quine Thesis*. 1976.
82. Stefan Nowak, *Methodology of Sociological Research. General Problems*. 1977.
83. Jean Piaget, Jean-Blaise Grize, Alina Szeminska, and Vinh Bang, *Epistemology and Psychology of Functions*. 1977.
84. Marjorie Grene and Everett Mendelsohn (eds.), *Topics in the Philosophy of Biology*. Boston Studies in the Philosophy of Science, Volume XXVII. 1976.
85. E. Fischbein, *The Intuitive Sources of Probabilistic Thinking in Children*. 1975.
86. Ernest W. Adams, *The Logic of Conditionals. An Application of Probability to Deductive Logic*. 1975.
87. Marian Przelecki and Ryszard Wójcicki (eds.), *Twenty-Five Years of Logical Methodology in Poland*. 1977.
88. J. Topolski, *The Methodology of History*. 1976.
89. A. Kasher (ed.), *Language in Focus: Foundations, Methods and Systems. Essays Dedicated to Yehoshua Bar-Hillel*. Boston Studies in the Philosophy of Science, Volume XLIII. 1976.
90. Jaakko Hintikka, *The Intentions of Intentionality and Other New Models for Modalities*. 1975.
91. Wolfgang Stegmüller, *Collected Papers on Epistemology, Philosophy of Science and History of Philosophy*. 2 Volumes. 1977.
92. Dov M. Gabbay, *Investigations in Modal and Tense Logics with Applications to Problems in Philosophy and Linguistics*. 1976.
93. Radu J. Bogdan, *Local Induction*. 1976.
94. Stefan Nowak, *Understanding and Prediction. Essays in the Methodology of Social and Behavioral Theories*. 1976.
95. Peter Mittelstaedt, *Philosophical Problems of Modern Physics*. Boston Studies in the Philosophy of Science, Volume XVIII. 1976.

96. Gerald Holton and William Blanpied (eds.), *Science and Its Public: The Changing Relationship*. Boston Studies in the Philosophy of Science, Volume XXXIII. 1976.

97. Myles Brand and Douglas Walton (eds.), *Action Theory*. 1976.

98. Paul Gochet, *Outline of a Nominalist Theory of Proposition. An Essay in the Theory of Meaning*. 1980.

99. R. S. Cohen, P. K. Feyerabend, and M. W. Wartofsky (eds.), *Essays in Memory of Imre Lakatos*. Boston Studies in the Philosophy of Science, Volume XXXIX. 1976.

100. R. S. Cohen and J. J. Stachel (eds.), *Selected Papers of Léon Rosenfeld*. Boston Studies in the Philosophy of Science, Volume XXI. 1978.

101. R. S. Cohen, C. A. Hooker, A. C. Michalos, and J. W. van Evra (eds.), *PSA 1974: Proceedings of the 1974 Biennial Meeting of the Philosophy of Science Association*. Boston Studies in the Philosophy of Science, Volume XXXII. 1976.

102. Yehuda Fried and Joseph Agassi, *Paranoia: A Study in Diagnosis*. Boston Studies in the Philosophy of Science, Volume L. 1976.

103. Marian Przelecki, Klemens Szaniawski, and Ryszard Wójcicki (eds.), *Formal Methods in the Methodology of Empirical Sciences*. 1976.

104. John M. Vickers, *Belief and Probability*. 1976.

105. Kurt H. Wolff, *Surrender and Catch: Experience and Inquiry Today*. Boston Studies in the Philosophy of Science, Volume LI. 1976.

106. Karel Kosík, *Dialectics of the Concrete*. Boston Studies in the Philosophy of Science, Volume LII. 1976.

107. Nelson Goodman, *The Structure of Appearance*. (Third edition.) Boston Studies in the Philosophy of Science, Volume LIII. 1977.

108. Jerzy Giedymin (ed.), *Kazimierz Ajdukiewicz: The Scientific World-Perspective and Other Essays, 1931-1963*. 1978.

109. Robert L. Causey, *Unity of Science*. 1977.

110. Richard E. Grandy, *Advanced Logic for Applications*. 1977.

111. Robert P. McArthur, *Tense Logic*. 1976.

112. Lars Lindahl, *Position and Change. A Study in Law and Logic*. 1977.

113. Raimo Tuomela, *Dispositions*. 1978.

114 Herbert A. Simon, *Models of Discovery and Other Topics in the Methods of Science*. Boston Studies in the Philosophy of Science, Volume LIV. 1977.

115. Roger D. Rosenkrantz, *Inference, Method and Decision*. 1977.

116. Raimo Tuomela, *Human Action and Its Explanation. A Study on the Philosophical Foundations of Psychology*. 1977.

117. Morris Lazerowitz, *The Language of Philosophy. Freud and Wittgenstein*. Boston Studies in the Philosophy of Science, Volume LV. 1977.

118. Stanislaw Leśniewski, *Collected Works* (ed. by S. J. Surma, J. T. J. Srzednicki, and D. I. Barnett, with an annotated bibliography by V. Frederick Rickey). 1980. (Forthcoming.)

119. Jerzy Pelc, *Semiotics in Poland, 1894-1969*. 1978.

120. Ingmar Pörn, *Action Theory and Social Science. Some Formal Models*. 1977.

121. Joseph Margolis, *Persons and Minds. The Prospects of Nonreductive Materialism*. Boston Studies in the Philosophy of Science, Volume LVII. 1977.

122. Jaakko Hintikka, Ilkka Niiniluoto, and Esa Saarinen (eds.), *Essays on Mathematical and Philosophical Logic*. 1978.

123. Theo A. F. Kuipers, *Studies in Inductive Probability and Rational Expectation*. 1978.

124. Esa Saarinen, Risto Hilpinen, Ilkka Niiniluoto, and Merrill Provence Hintikka (eds.), *Essays in Honour of Jaakko Hintikka on the Occasion of His Fiftieth Birthday*. 1978.
125 Gerard Radnitzky and Gunnar Andersson (eds.), *Progress and Rationality in Science*. Boston Studies in the Philosophy of Science, Volume LVIII. 1978.
126. Peter Mittelstaedt, *Quantum Logic*. 1978.
127. Kenneth A. Bowen, *Model Theory for Modal Logic. Kripke Models for Modal Predicate Calculi*. 1978.
128. Howard Alexander Bursen, *Dismantling the Memory Machine. A Philosophical Investigation of Machine Theories of Memory*. 1978.
129. Marx W. Wartofsky, *Models: Representation and the Scientific Understanding*. Boston Studies in the Philosophy of Science, Volume XLVIII. 1979.
130. Don Ihde, *Technics and Praxis. A Philosophy of Technology*. Boston Studies in the Philosophy of Science, Volume XXIV. 1978.
131. Jerzy J. Wiatr (ed.), *Polish Essays in the Methodology of the Social Sciences*. Boston Studies in the Philosophy of Science, Volume XXIX. 1979.
132. Wesley C. Salmon (ed.), *Hans Reichenbach: Logical Empiricist*. 1979.
133. Peter Bieri, Rolf-P. Horstmann, and Lorenz Krüger (eds.), *Transcendental Arguments in Science. Essays in Epistemology*. 1979.
134. Mihailo Marković and Gajo Petrović (eds.), *Praxis. Yugoslav Essays in the Philosophy and Methodology of the Social Sciences*. Boston Studies in the Philosophy of Science, Volume XXXVI. 1979.
135. Ryszard Wójcicki, *Topics in the Formal Methodology of Empirical Sciences*. 1979.
136. Gerard Radnitzky and Gunnar Andersson (eds.), *The Structure and Development of Science*. Boston Studies in the Philosophy of Science, Volume LIX. 1979.
137. Judson Chambers Webb, *Mechanism, Mentalism, and Metamathematics. An Essay on Finitism*. 1980. (Forthcoming.)
138. D. F. Gustafson and B. L. Tapscott (eds.), *Body, Mind, and Method. Essays in Honor of Virgil C. Aldrich*. 1979.
139. Leszek Nowak, *The Structure of Idealization. Towards a Systematic Interpretation of the Marxian Idea of Science*. 1979.
140. Chaim Perelman, *The New Rhetoric and the Humanities. Essays on Rhetoric and Its Applications*. 1979.
141. Wlodzimierz Rabinowicz, *Universalizability. A Study in Morals and Metaphysics*. 1979.